PC LEARNING LABS TEACHES MICROSOFT ACCESS

PC LEARNING LABS TEACHES MICROSOFT ACCESS

LOGICAL OPERATIONS

Ziff-Davis Press
Emeryville, California

Curriculum Development	Logical Operations
Writer	Christopher J. Benz
Editor	Deborah Craig
Technical Reviewer	Mark Hall
Project Coordinator	Bill Cassel
Proofreader	Kayla Sussell
Logical Operations Production Coordinator	Tary Simizon
Cover Design	Ken Roberts
Cover Illustration	Carrie English
Book Design	Laura Lamar/MAX, San Francisco
Technical Illustration	Cherie Plumlee Computer Graphics & Illustration
Word Processing	Howard Blechman and Cat Haglund
Page Layout	Tony Jonick and Bruce Lundquist
Indexer	Valerie Robbins

This book was produced on a Macintosh IIfx, with the following applications: FrameMaker®, Microsoft® Word, MacLink® *Plus*, Aldus® FreeHand™, Adobe Photoshop™, and Collage Plus™.

Ziff-Davis Press
5903 Christie Avenue
Emeryville, CA 94608

ISBN 1-56276-122-6

Manufactured in the United States of America
10 9 8 7 6 5 4 3

CONTENTS AT A GLANCE

TABLE OF CONTENTS

Chapter 8: Enhanced Table Design 253

Chapter 11: Enhanced Report Design 355

INTRODUCTION

Welcome to *PC Learning Labs Teaches Microsoft Access,* a hands-on instruction book designed to help you attain a high level of Access fluency in as short a time as possible. And congratulations on choosing Access, a powerful and elegant program that will improve your data-management capabilities greatly.

We at PC Learning Labs believe this book to be a unique and welcome addition to the ranks of "how-to" computer publications. Our instructional approach stems directly from over a decade of successful teaching in a hands-on classroom environment. Throughout the book, theory is consistently mixed with practice; a topic is explained and then immediately drilled in a hands-on activity. These activities are designed to be done with the included Data Disk, which contains sample Access files.

When you're done working your way through this book, you will have a solid foundation of skills in five of Access' six primary database components (known in Access as *objects*):

- *Tables*   Objects that store information, or *data*

- *Forms*   Objects that help you enter, edit, and review stored data on-screen

- *Queries*   Objects that enable you to ask questions about stored data

- *Reports*   Objects that enable you to present stored data on paper

- *Macros*   Objects that enable you to automate Access

The sixth type of Access objects, *modules*, are used for advanced database programming, and are not covered in this book. (Throughout this Introduction, we have italicized terms with which you may not be familiar.

Don't worry; we'll explain all of them throughout the book. In the meantime, please bear with us.)

IMPORTANT NOTE

We strongly advise you to read through the rest of this Introduction before beginning Chapter 1. If, however, you are eager to dive in, first work through the section below, "Creating Your Work Directory," as it is crucial to every activity in the book.

WHO THIS BOOK IS FOR

This book was written with the beginner in mind. While experience with databases and personal computers is certainly helpful, little or none is required. You should know how to turn on your computer, monitor, and printer; how to use your keyboard; and how to move your mouse. Everything beyond that will be explained in the text.

HOW TO USE THIS BOOK

This book is designed to be used as a learning guide, a review tool, and a quick reference.

 AS A LEARNING GUIDE

Each chapter covers one broad topic or set of related topics. Chapters are arranged in order of increasing Access proficiency; skills you acquire in one chapter are used and elaborated on in subsequent chapters. For this reason, you should work through the chapters in strict sequence.

Each chapter is organized into explanatory topics and hands-on, step-by-step activities. Topics provide the theoretical overview you need to master Access; activities enable you to apply this understanding immediately to specific examples.

AS A REVIEW TOOL

Any method of instruction is only as effective as the time and effort you are willing to invest in it. For this reason, we encourage you to review the more challenging topics and activities presented in this book.

 AS A QUICK REFERENCE

General procedures (such as opening a database or printing a report) are presented as a series of bulleted steps; you can find these bullets (•) easily as you page through the book.

At the end of every chapter, you'll find a quick reference listing the mouse and keyboard actions needed to perform the techniques introduced in that chapter.

WHAT THIS BOOK CONTAINS

The contents of this book are divided into the following chapters:

Chapter 1   Touring Access

Chapter 2   Table Basics

Chapter 3   Finding and Editing Records

Chapter 4   Query Basics

Chapter 5   Form Basics

Chapter 6   Report Basics

Chapter 7   Enhanced Query Design

Chapter 8   Enhanced Table Design

Chapter 9   Enhanced Form Design

Chapter 10   Using Macros with Forms

Chapter 11   Enhanced Report Design

In addition, there are three appendices:

Appendix A   Installation

Appendix B   Tool Bar and Shortcut Key Reference

Appendix C   Creating a Database

To attain the greatest Access fluency, you should work through all 11 chapters and the appendices.

This book is designed to expose you in stages to various Access database objects. Chapter 1 provides an overview of tables, forms, queries, and reports. Chapters 2 through 6 show you how to create and work with each of these object types. In Chapters 7 through 11, you'll learn advanced techniques for enhancing the look and performance of objects you've already seen, and how to create and use macros.

The following features of this book are designed to facilitate your learning:

- Carefully sequenced topics that build on the knowledge you've acquired from previous topics

- Frequent hands-on activities, designed to sharpen your Access skills

- Numerous illustrations that show how your computer screen should look at key points during these activities

- The Data Disk, which contains all the files you will need to complete the activities

- A quick reference at the end of each chapter, listing in easy-to-read table form the mouse and keyboard actions needed to perform the techniques introduced in the chapter

WHAT YOU NEED

To run Access and complete this book, you need a computer, monitor, keyboard, and a pointing device such as a mouse. A printer is strongly recommended, but optional.

 ### A COMPUTER AND MONITOR

To install and run Access, you need an IBM or IBM-compatible personal computer that has an 80386sx, 80386, or higher processor, and that is capable of running Microsoft Windows version 3.0 or higher. To install Access and this book's Data Disk files, your computer's hard disk must have at least 14 megabytes of free storage space. To run Access, your computer must have at least 4 megabytes of random-access memory (although 6 megabytes or more is strongly recommended). Finally, you need an EGA or higher (VGA, SVGA, and so on) graphics card and computer monitor to display Windows and Access at their intended screen resolution.

Before starting Chapter 1, you must have DOS 3.1 or higher and Windows 3.0 or higher installed on your computer; if you don't, see your DOS and Windows documentation for instructions. Access must also be installed, preferably *freshly* installed. After completing the section below, "Creating Your Work Directory," see Appendix A for help on installing or reinstalling Access.

 ### A KEYBOARD

IBM-compatible computers come with various styles of keyboards; these keyboards function identically, but have different layouts. Figures I.1, I.2, and I.3 show the three main desktop-computer keyboard styles and their key arrangements. If you are using a portable computer, your keyboard may not exactly match any of these three keyboard styles, but should contain all of the keys necessary to use Access.

Figure I.1   **The IBM PC–style keyboard**

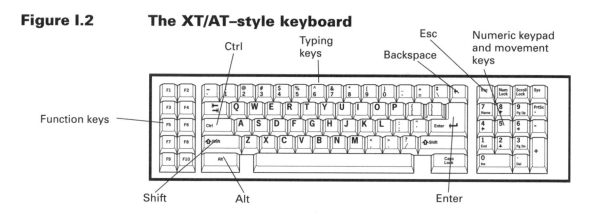

Figure I.2   **The XT/AT–style keyboard**

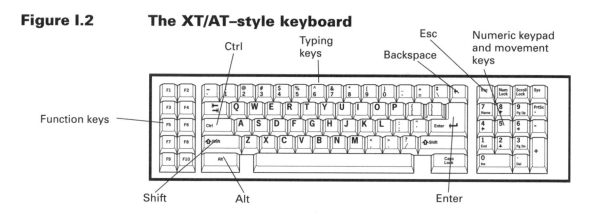

Figure I.3   **The PS/2–style Enhanced Keyboard**

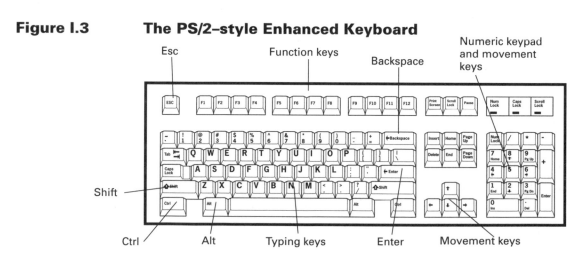

Access uses three main areas of the keyboard:

- The *function keys* (F1, F2, and so on) enable you to use many of Access' features. On the PC-, XT-, and AT-style keyboards, there are ten function keys at the left end of the keyboard; on the PS/2-style Enhanced Keyboard, there are 12 at the top of the keyboard.

- The *typing keys* are located in the main body of all the keyboards. These include letters, numbers, and punctuation marks, as well as the Shift, Ctrl, and Alt keys.

- The *numeric keypad* groups numbers (the same ones found across the top row of the typing keys) for convenient numeric data entry. The numeric keypad also contains the cursor movement keys: Up, Down, Left, and Right Arrows; Home; End; PgUp (Page Up); and PgDn (Page Down). For you to enter numeric data using the numeric keypad, Num Lock must be on. (Pressing the Num Lock key will toggle Num Lock on and off.) For you to use the cursor movement keys on the keypad, Num Lock must be off. To enter numeric data when Num Lock is off, use the number keys on the top row of the typing area.

The Enhanced Keyboard has an additional cursor movement keypad to the left of the numeric keypad. This enables you to use the numeric keypad for numeric data entry (keeping Num Lock on) and still be able to use the cursor movement keys.

 A MOUSE, TRACKBALL, OR OTHER POINTING DEVICE

You will need a mouse, trackball, or other pointing device to work through the activities in this book. Any Windows-compatible PC mouse, trackball, or other pointing device will do.

Throughout this book, we direct you to use a mouse, not a trackball or other pointing device. If you have a pointing device other than a mouse, simply use it to perform all the tasks that involve mouse techniques (dragging, clicking, and so on).

 A PRINTER

Although you aren't absolutely required to have a printer to work through the activities, we strongly recommend it. A PostScript-type laser printer is ideal, but a non-PostScript laser or dot-matrix one is acceptable.

To use your printer, you must first select it in Windows. If you already have printed successfully from Windows or any Windows program (for example, Windows Write or Windows Paintbrush), then your printer most likely will print from Access. If you have never printed from Windows or a Windows program, see your Windows documentation.

If you have no printer, select a PostScript printer in Windows anyway. In Chapter 1, you will learn how to view on your computer screen how a page will look when printed; this can only be accomplished by selecting a printer in Windows first.

CONVENTIONS USED IN THIS BOOK

The conventions used in this book are designed to help you learn Access easily and efficiently. Each chapter begins with a short introduction and ends with a summary that includes a quick-reference guide to the techniques introduced in the chapter. Main chapter topics (large, capitalized headings) and subtopics (headings preceded by a cube) explain Access features. Hands-on activities enable you to practice using Access' features. In these activities, menu choices, keystrokes, and anything you are asked to type are all presented in boldface. Here's an example from Chapter 2:

4. Click on **Close** to close the dialog box.

Activities follow a *cause-and-effect* approach. Most steps tell you what to do (cause) and then what will happen (effect). From the example above,

Cause   Click on **Close**.

Effect   The dialog box closes.

A plus sign (+) is used with the Shift, Ctrl, and Alt keys to denote a multiple-key keystroke. For example, Ctrl+F10 means, "Press and hold the Ctrl key, press the function key F10, and then release both."

To help you distinguish between steps presented for your general knowledge and steps you should carry out at your computer as you read, we have adopted the following system:

- A bulleted step, like this, is provided for your information and reference only.

1. A numbered step, like this, indicates one in a series of steps that you should carry out in sequence at your computer.

CREATING YOUR WORK DIRECTORY

In the course of this book, you will be working with several database and related files that you'll copy from this book's Data Disk to your hard drive. In order to keep these files together on your hard drive, you need to create a work *directory*. (A directory functions like a filing cabinet in which a group of related files is stored.)

 Follow these steps to create your work directory on your hard drive and copy the files on the Data Disk into that directory:

1. Turn on your computer; after a moment, your *operating environment* will load automatically. If you are in Windows, please go to step 2. If you are in DOS, please skip to step 4. If you are in a non-Windows, non-DOS operating environment (DOS Shell or GeoWorks, for example), exit to DOS, and then skip to step 4. (For help with exiting to DOS, see your operating environment's documentation.)

2. Within Windows, locate Program Manager, an on-screen window with "Program Manager" in its overhead title bar. (If Program Manager is running as an *icon*—a small picture with the words "Program Manager" beneath it—instead of as a window, use the mouse to move the on-screen mouse pointer to the icon. Then, double-click—

that is, press the left mouse button twice in rapid succession—to open the icon into a window.)

3. Move the mouse pointer to the word "File" in the upper-left corner of the Program Manager window. Click on **File** to open the File menu, and then click on **Exit Windows**. A *dialog box* entitled "Exit Windows" will appear in the middle of the screen. Click the mouse pointer once on the **OK** button within this dialog box to exit from Windows to DOS. Skip to step 8.

4. You may be prompted for the current date; if not, skip to step 6. If the date displayed is incorrect, type today's date. Use the format *mm-dd-yy* or *mm/dd/yy* (for example, 11-30-93 or 11/30/93).

5. Press **Enter** to send the command to your computer.

6. You may then be prompted for the current time; if not, skip to step 8. If the time displayed is incorrect, type the current time. Use the 24-hour format *hh:mm* (for example, 10:30 for 10:30 a.m. or 22:30 for 10:30 p.m.).

7. Press **Enter** to send the command to your computer to set your computer's internal clock.

8. The DOS prompt will appear on a line by itself:

```
C:\>
```

(Your DOS prompt may differ somewhat from this.)

9. Type **dir**, and then press **Enter**. The contents of the current directory are displayed, followed by a final line reporting the number of free bytes on your hard disk. If you have 1,000,000 or more bytes free, skip to step 10. If you have fewer than 1,000,000 bytes free, you may not be able to create your work directory and perform all the hands-on tasks in this book. Before you proceed, you'll have to delete enough files from your hard disk to bring the free-byte total up to 1,000,000. If you need help doing this, please refer to your

DOS documentation. Be sure to back up all important files before deleting them!

10. Remove the Data Disk from the back of this book and insert it, label up, into the appropriately sized disk drive. Then, if necessary, close the drive door or latch. Determine whether this is drive A or drive B. On a single floppy-disk system, the drive generally is designated as A. On a double floppy-disk system, the upper or left-hand drive is generally designated as A and the lower or right-hand drive as B.

11. Type **a:** if the Data Disk is in drive A, or type **b:** if the Data Disk is in drive B. Press **Enter** to change the current drive to the Data Disk drive.

12. Type **install c: acc-work** (be sure to leave a space between "install" and "c" and between "c:" and "acc-work"), and then press **Enter** to begin the installation. Your work directory will be called ACC-WORK. (If you wish to create your work directory on a hard disk that is not designated as drive C, substitute your hard-disk drive letter for the "c" in this command—for example, to install onto a drive-D hard disk, type *install d: acc-work.*)

13. If all is well, the message

```
Installation begun.
```

appears, followed by a message about copying files. When the procedure is complete, the message

```
Installation successful!
```

appears, followed by a line reporting the name of your work directory (for example, c:\acc-work).

If you get an error message indicating that the hard drive you specified does not exist, or that the directory name you specified already exists, repeat step 12, substituting a new hard-drive letter or work directory name as appropriate. For example, you might type *install d: acc-work* or *install c: mywork.* Your work directory name can be up to eight letters long. Do not use spaces, periods, or punctuation marks, and do not use the name *access,* as that name is normally used by the Access program itself. The activities in this book refer to your work directory as ACC-WORK. If you've chosen another name, please remember to mentally substitute it for the name ACC-WORK throughout the book.

14. If you have not yet installed the Access program, or if you need to re-install the program, go to Appendix A, "Installation," before you begin Chapter 1.

ABOUT THE ILLUSTRATIONS IN THIS BOOK

This book contains numerous illustrations, or figures, most picturing how your computer screen should look as you work through the activities.

When creating these figures, we ran Access under Windows 3.1 using a VGA monitor and a PostScript laser printer. If you run Access under a different version of Windows, use a different type of monitor, or select a non-PostScript laser printer, your screen may not *exactly* match the figures in this book. However, Access should still run as described in the text.

Also, Access often displays the current date on the screen. Most likely, your current date will not match the date we have used throughout this book: May 14, 1993. When comparing your screen to figures that display dates, note that your screen should display *your* current date.

BEFORE YOU START

The activities in each of the following chapters are designed to proceed sequentially. In many cases, you cannot perform an activity until you have performed one or more of the activities directly preceding it. For this reason, we recommend that you allot enough time to work through an entire chapter in each session.

You are now ready to begin. Good learning...and *bon voyage!*

CHAPTER 1: TOURING ACCESS

Orientation to
Access

Orientation to a
Table

Orientation to
Forms

Orientation to
Sorting and
Querying

Orientation to
Reports

Exiting Access

Welcome to Access and the world of electronic databases. Access provides you with a set of powerful tools for collecting, retrieving, and presenting data. In this first chapter, we'll take you on a whirlwind tour of Access; you'll start Access, open a database, explore some objects contained in that database (including tables, forms, queries, and reports), close the database, and exit Access.

When you're done working through this chapter, you will know how to:

- Start Access and open a database
- Open, navigate in, and close a table
- Open, navigate in, and close a form
- Sort records and run queries
- Preview and print a report
- Close a database and exit Access

As you work through this chapter, remember that we are just touring Access for now. In later chapters, we will explore the various components of the program in greater detail.

ORIENTATION TO ACCESS

A *database* is a collection of related information, or data. Paper-based databases that you already use may include a telephone book, a mailing list, or a set of personnel records.

Access is an electronic *database-management system* (or *DBMS*); its purpose is to help you collect, retrieve (or *extract*), and present data. For example, with a company-personnel database, you may want to collect data about new employees (name, address, telephone number, and so on), retrieve a list of employees according to their hire date, or print a list of employee telephone numbers.

Two advantages of electronic database-management systems over their paper-based counterparts are

- They can store very large amounts of data
- They enable you to quickly extract and rearrange that data

 INTRODUCTION TO DATABASE CONCEPTS

Before we start Access, let's examine a sample paper-based table of data.

Observe Figure 1.1:

- The *table* in the figure is a list of related data (names, addresses, and telephone extensions for all employees).

Figure 1.1   **A sample paper table of data**

```
Last        First       Adr                  City          St  Zip    Ext
----------  ----------  -------------------  ------------  --  -----  ---
Abel        Marie       127 Ford Avenue      Shackelford   TX  76430  339
Abot        Robert      99 Stonecreek Rd.    Trenton       NJ  08618  350
Beaton      Robert      391 State Street     West Seneca   NY  14224  323
Bell        William     66 Big Hill Rd.      Troy          NY  12182  340
Binder      Julia       10 Cory Drive        Trenton       NJ  08753  324
Binga       Sam         50 Dallas Street     Pasadena      CA  91106  348
Carter      Andrea      718 Prole Road       Rockville     SC  29204  360
Chase       Wilma       52 Pempleton Dr.     Albany        NY  12205  309
Conner      Bill        32 Ash Lane          Allentown     NJ  08501  328
DeMarco     Alice       34 Sable Ave.        Bentwood      IL  61820  332
Desoto      Frank       P.O. Box 7234        Trenton       NJ  07092  356
Easter      Ester       21 Stonecreek Rd.    Trenton       NJ  08620  390
Harper      Harry       82 East Avenue       Long Beach    CA  90745  395
Haslam      David       453 Lakeshore Dr.    Evans Mills   ND  58352  338
Henley      Albert      12 Divine Drive      San Pueblo    CO  80403  318
James       Ted         34 Fields Street     Fort Worth    TX  76116  300
Jones       Homer       466 Fairhaven St.    Los Alamos    MI  48104  337
Kyler       Dennis      273 Fireside Dr.     Great Neck    NY  11023  362
Martin      Jane        50 Smart Drive       Oceanside     CA  91762  349
McDonald    Ronald      8165 Main Street     Trenton       NJ  08690  303
Naylor      Ruth        532 Union Street     Nashville     TN  38109  334
Osowski     Dominick    23 Lakeside Ave.     S Granbury    TX  76048  368
Packer      Penny       9929 Clearview       Vienna        VA  22181  346
Sanders     Maria       12 East Avenue       Denton        TX  76201  310
Stira       Joe         200 Nester Street    Bath          NY  76708  315
Ward        Junior      7 Chamberlin St.     Massena       NC  28210  317
Zambito     Joseph      81 Pleasing Lane     Alhambra      CA  91801  311
```

- Each column contains a category of data (last name, first name, address, and so on). In a table, each category of data is called a *field*.

- Each row contains a unit of data on one person. In a table, a unit of data is called a *record*.

Now consider how, with this paper table, you would

- Sort the list by city

- List only three of the fields (columns)

- Search the list for a specific name

- List only those people who live in California

- Rearrange and print the data for a report

Any of these tasks would be time-consuming and tedious because you would need to retype some or all of the table and/or pore through every record. Your work would also be prone to errors—you might, for example, mistype a name or miss a record.

Observe Figure 1.2. This is a set of paper cards that lists the same data as in Figure 1.1, but in a different arrangement, known as a *forms*. (As you'll see later in this chapter, Access forms provide a way to view the same data in different arrangements.)

Figure 1.2   **Sample paper forms**

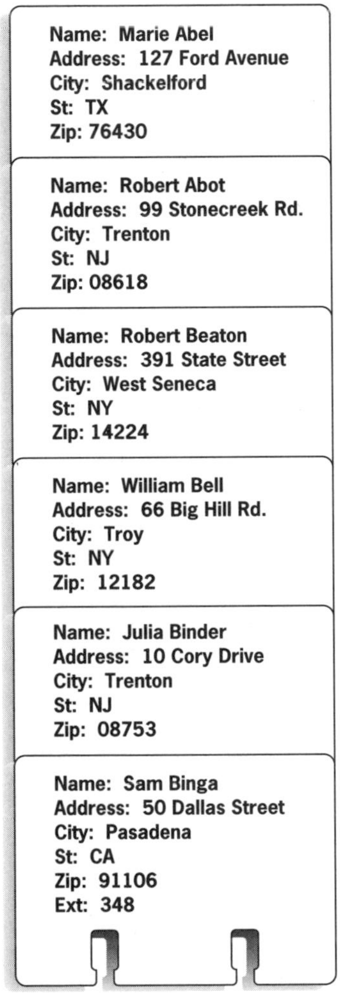

Name: Marie Abel
Address: 127 Ford Avenue
City: Shackelford
St: TX
Zip: 76430

Name: Robert Abot
Address: 99 Stonecreek Rd.
City: Trenton
St: NJ
Zip: 08618

Name: Robert Beaton
Address: 391 State Street
City: West Seneca
St: NY
Zip: 14224

Name: William Bell
Address: 66 Big Hill Rd.
City: Troy
St: NY
Zip: 12182

Name: Julia Binder
Address: 10 Cory Drive
City: Trenton
St: NJ
Zip: 08753

Name: Sam Binga
Address: 50 Dallas Street
City: Pasadena
St: CA
Zip: 91106
Ext: 348

Contrast Figure 1.1 with Figure 1.2. In Figure 1.2:

- There is one record on each card, rather than several records on a single page.

- The name of each field is placed on the left side of each card, rather than across the top of the page.

In Access, the view that enables you to see multiple records at one time is called *Datasheet view*; the view that enables you to view only one record at a time is called *Form view*.

Observe Figure 1.3. Each table contains different types of data (one on employees, another on customers, and so on). In Access, a group of related tables is called a *database*. The database also includes tools to work with the data, such as forms, reports, and queries. (We'll discuss these tools later in this chapter.)

Figure 1.3   **A sample paper database**

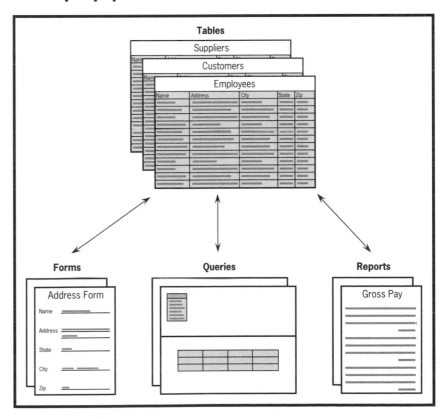

In short, tables are data containers; forms, reports, and queries are tools for using the data in those containers; and databases hold everything together.

 STARTING ACCESS

To start Access, you must copy the program, or *application,* from your hard disk into computer memory (sometimes called *RAM*). Access will remain in memory as long as you continue running it. When you exit Access, it will remove itself from memory, thus freeing space for other programs to use. (Note that computer memory is a temporary data-storage space. When you exit Access, the program is cleared from computer memory. However, Access remains installed on the hard drive, ready to copy again into memory.)

Because Access is a Windows application (that is, a program that is designed to run in the Microsoft Windows environment), you must start Windows before you can start Access.

If you did not complete the activity in the "Creating Your Work Directory" section of the Introduction, please do so now. Otherwise, you will not be able to perform the tasks in this book.

Follow these steps to start Access:

1. Turn on your computer; your operating environment will load automatically. If you are already in Windows, you may skip to step 7. If you are in DOS, you should continue with step 2. If you are in another operating environment (DOS Shell or Geo-Works, for example), exit to DOS and continue with step 2. For help with exiting to DOS, see your operating environment's reference manuals.

2. Next, you may be prompted for the current date; if not, skip to step 4. If the date is correct, skip to step 3. If the date is incorrect, type today's date. Use the format *mm-dd-yy* or *mm/dd/yy* (for example, 11-30-93 or 11/30/93).

3. Press the **Enter** key to send the command to the computer.

4. You may then be prompted for the current time; if not, skip to step 6. If the time is correct, skip to step 5. If the time is incorrect, type the current time. Use the 24-hour format *hh:mm* (for example, 10:30 for 10:30 a.m. or 22:30 for 10:30 p.m.).

5. Press **Enter** to set the computer's internal clock.

6. Type **win** and then press **Enter** to start Windows.

7. When Windows is loaded, look for a small on-screen picture (or *icon*) entitled Microsoft Access. If this icon looks like a small square containing six tiny pictures, continue with step 8. If the icon contains a key, continue with step 9.

8. Use your mouse to move the tip of the on-screen *mouse pointer* (it's shaped like a leftward-pointing arrow) to the Microsoft Access icon containing the six pictures. *Double-click* (press and release the **left mouse button** two times in rapid succession) on the icon to turn it into a window. (If you do not double-click rapidly enough, a list of commands may appear adjacent to the icon. If this happens, click once on Restore.)

9. Move the mouse pointer to the Microsoft Access icon containing a large key and double-click on the icon. The mouse pointer will change temporarily into an hourglass as Access loads, indicating that you need to wait for the computer.

10. Observe your screen. If it displays a large rectangle entitled Welcome to Microsoft Access, use the left mouse button to click inside the *check box* (a small, empty square) entitled Don't display this startup screen again. When the check box displays an X, click on **Close**. (The buttons in this rectangle enable you to start Access' Cue Cards system, which you'll learn about in Chapter 2.)

11. If the Microsoft Access window completely fills the screen, as in Figure 1.4, you are ready to work in Access. Otherwise, locate the upward-pointing triangle in the upper-right corner of the Microsoft Access window and use the left mouse button to click on it once. (Throughout the rest of this book, when we say click on something, we mean that you should point to the item with the tip of the mouse pointer, and then press and release the left mouse button. We will let you know when it is appropriate to use the right mouse button.) This should enlarge the window to fill the screen completely.

Figure 1.4   **The maximized Access application window upon startup**

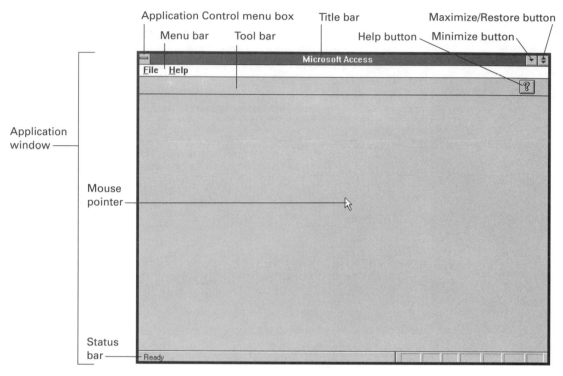

THE ACCESS APPLICATION WINDOW

Because Access is a Windows application, it is structured around a set of interactive *windows*—rectangular, on-screen boxes of varying sizes through which information is passed between the user (you) and the application (Access). These windows contain some common items.

Table 1.1 defines the elements of the Access application window upon startup. Figure 1.4 illustrates where each of these elements is located.

Let's take a closer look at some of these screen elements.

1. Click on the **Application Control menu box** to open the Application Control menu (Figure 1.5); do not double-click, as this would cause you to exit Access. Note the menu items: Restore, Move, Size, Minimize, and so on. Click on the **Application Control menu box** again to close the Application Control menu.

Table 1.1   **Access Application Window Elements**

Term	Definition
Application window	The window that contains all of the items relevant to Access; it provides an interface between the user and Access. When maximized, the application window fills your entire screen.
Application Control menu box	Located in the upper-left corner of the application window, it controls the size and position of the application window, and enables you to exit Access.
Title bar	Located across the top of the application window, it displays the name of the application (Microsoft Access); at times, it may display additional information.
Application Maximize/ Restore button	Located in the upper-right corner of the application window, it controls the size of the application window. (The Maximize/Restore button is actually two buttons: the Maximize button, which expands the window to full size, and the Restore button, which returns the window to its former size.)
Minimize button	Located to the left of the Maximize/Restore button, it shrinks the application window to an icon.
Menu bar	Located below the title bar, it lists the Access menu options. (In Figure 1.4, Access displays only the File and Help menu options. Access will display more menu options, however, as they become relevant to the task at hand.) You can open an Access menu by clicking on the menu option.
Tool bar	Located below the menu bar, it contains buttons that provide quick access to some of Access' most frequently used commands; the buttons available on the tool bar will change as you perform various tasks. (In Figure 1.4, Access is displaying only the Help button.)
Status bar	Located along the bottom of the application window, it displays information relevant to the task at hand.

Figure 1.5   **The Control menu**

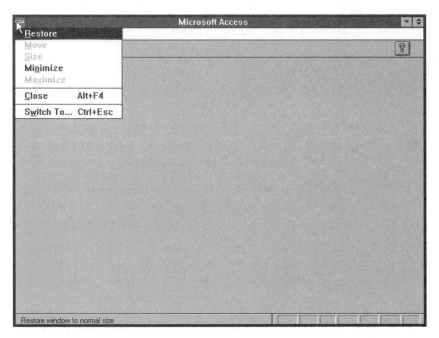

2. Click on the **Application Maximize/Restore button** (it currently contains upward- and downward-pointing triangles) to restore (shrink) the application window. Note that the button now contains only an upward-pointing triangle, indicating that its function is to maximize (rather than restore) the application window. Click on the button again to maximize the application window so that it once again fills the entire screen.

3. Click on **File** in the menu bar to open the File menu (see Figure 1.6). Note that some of the menu items are dimmed (Show Window and Run Macro), indicating that those items are not currently available. Note also that the status bar displays a short description of the highlighted (or *selected*) menu item; New Database. Click on **File** again to close the File menu.

4. Click on the **Help button** on the tool bar (it displays a question mark) to open the Microsoft Access Help window. Note the common elements between the Access application window and the Access Help window (both have Application Control menu boxes, Maximize/Restore and Minimize buttons, title bars, and menu bars).

Figure 1.6   **The File menu**

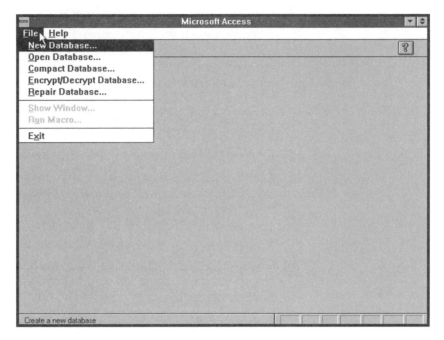

5. Double-click on the Help window's **Control menu box** to close the window. (Be sure not to double-click on Access' Application Control menu box.)

OPENING A DATABASE

When you first start Access, no databases are open. To work with data in an Access database, you must first open one. To open a database, you would follow these steps:

- Choose File, Open Database (that is, choose the Open Database command from the File menu) to open the Open Database dialog box. (A *dialog box* is a special window that helps you communicate with Access.)

- Within the dialog box, select the appropriate disk drive, directory (area of the disk drive), and database file name.

- Click on OK to open the Database window.

Let's open a database now:

1. Click on **File** to open the File menu.

2. Observe the Open Database menu item. It is followed by an ellipsis (...), which indicates that choosing this item will open a dialog box. (For the sake of simplicity, this book does not include ellipses when referring to menu commands or buttons containing ellipses. For example, in the next step, we ask you to click on Open Database, even though Open Database... is how the menu item actually appears on your screen.)

3. Click on **Open Database** to open the Open Database dialog box.

4. Observe that the dialog box is a smaller window within the application window. Click outside the dialog box, nothing happens. When you open a dialog box, you must complete all of your work inside the box and then close it before you can work elsewhere in the application window.

5. Observe the Drives drop-down list box (at the bottom of the dialog box). This box enables you to set the current disk drive. If the box does not display the letter of the disk drive onto which you installed the Access work files in the "Creating Your Work Directory" section of the Introduction, click on the **downward-pointing arrow** to the right of the box to display the list of available drives, and then click on the letter of the appropriate drive. (For the rest of this book, we will assume that both the Access program and your Access work files are located on drive C. If they are not, substitute your drive letter as necessary.)

6. Observe the Directories list box (in the center of the dialog box). The text under the word *Directories* indicates the current disk drive and directory. For example, if the line reads c:\access, the current drive is C (your hard disk) and the current directory is ACCESS (an area of the C drive where the Access program files are stored).

7. Observe the File Name list box (on the left side of the dialog box). It lists in alphabetical order any Access database files— files that end with .MDB—that are stored in the current directory. If you have just installed Access, you may see the three sample database files that install with the Access program: nwind.mdb, ordentry.mdb, and pim.mdb.

8. In the Directories list box, double-click on the open-folder icon labeled **c:**. The line under Directories should change to c:\ and a new set of folder icons should appear in the list box. You have

now moved up to the top-level directory of your C drive—the *root directory*. From the root directory, you can view all of your second-level directories. (For more information on directories, see your DOS or Windows documentation.)

9. In the Directories list box, locate and double-click on the closed-folder icon labeled **acc-work** to move into the directory containing your Access work files. The line under Directories should now read c:\acc-work. (If you named your directory something other than ACC-WORK when installing your Access work files, substitute that directory name as necessary.)

10. The File Name list box should now list the three database files that you installed in the "Creating Your Work Directory" section of the Introduction: company.mdb, employee.mdb and practice.mdb. Click on **employee.mdb**, the database file that we will be working with for the first half of this book. The name of the file, employee.mdb, should now be displayed in the box directly below File Name, indicating that it is the selected file. At this point, your screen should look like Figure 1.7.

Figure 1.7   **The Open Database dialog box**

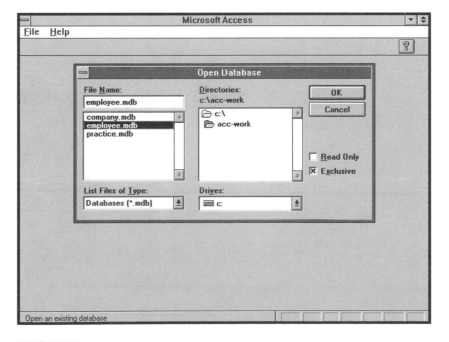

11. Click on **OK** to open the employee.mdb database file. After a moment, a window entitled Database: EMPLOYEE will appear, indicating that you have successfully opened the database file. This window is called the Database window.

 ORIENTATION TO THE DATABASE WINDOW AND THE MENU BAR

The *Database window* is a window that appears within the Access application window when you open a database. You can have only one database and Database window open at a time.

The Database window serves as a command center for the database, providing you with access to any *objects* within the database. (In Access, major items within a database—such as tables and forms—are called objects.)

Let's take a closer look at the Database window, whose major elements are pointed out in Figure 1.8.

Figure 1.8   **The maximized Database window**

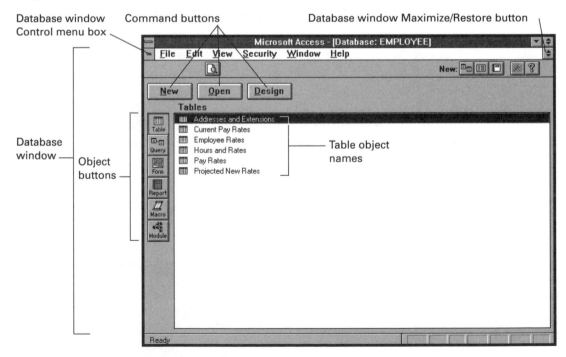

1. Like the Access application window, the Database window has a Control menu box, a title bar, a Minimize button, and a Maximize/Restore button. These elements enable you to control the size and position of the Database window.

2. Click on the Database window's **Maximize/Restore button** to maximize the Database window. The window now fits seamlessly within the application window, and the two windows now share a common title bar and Minimize button. Note that the Database window's Control menu box now sits directly below the Application Control menu box and the Database window's Maximize/Restore button sits directly below the Application Maximize/Restore button.

3. Observe that the window has New, Open, and Design *command buttons* across the top.

4. Notice that a series of *object buttons* are displayed in a vertical row on the left-hand side of the window. Objects that can comprise an Access database include tables, queries, forms, reports, macros, and modules.

5. Since the Table object button is selected, note that a list of table object names is displayed.

6. Click on the **Form object button** to display a list of form object names. Note that the icon next to each form object name matches the icon on the Form object button.

7. Click on the **Table object button** to return to the list of table object names.

Because a Database window is open, the number of menu options in the menu bar have increased. (Note also that some additional buttons are available on the tool bar.)

Let's explore some of the menus now:

1. The menu options are File, Edit, View, Security, Window, and Help.

2. Click on **File** to open the File menu. Because the Database window is open, some different menu items are available.

3. Click on **Edit** to open the Edit menu. Note that the File menu closes automatically when you open another menu.

4. Open the **View** menu. This menu offers an alternative to clicking on the object buttons in the Database window.

5. Open the **Help** menu. In addition to clicking on the Help button, you can open the Help window through this menu.

6. Click on **Help** again to close the Help menu.

 INTRODUCTION TO HELP

Like many Windows applications, Access provides an extensive on-line Help system. One way to access the Help system is through the Help menu.

To search for a specific subject in Help, you would follow these steps:

- Choose Help, Search to open Help's Search dialog box.
- Begin typing the name of the subject until the appropriate subject rises to the top of the subject list.
- Click on Show Topics to display a list of available topics.
- Select the appropriate topic, and then click on Go To to open the Help window on that topic.

Let's work with Access' Help system now to search for help on the Database window's tool bar:

1. Choose **Help, Search** to open the Help system's Search dialog box.

2. Type **t**. Notice how the list of topics below the text box scrolls to the subjects that begin with *t*.

3. Type **o**. The list of subjects now scrolls to the subjects that begin with *to*.

4. Type a second **o**. The selected subject is now tool bars.

5. Click on **Show Topics** to display a list of topics on tool bars at the bottom of the dialog box. Your screen should now look like Figure 1.9.

6. In the list of topics, observe that Database Tool Bars is already selected. Click on **Go To** to open the Help window on Database Tool Bars.

7. Maximize and then observe the Help window. A picture of the Database tool bar is displayed.

Figure 1.9   **Searching for Help**

8. Place the mouse pointer on one of the buttons on the picture of the Database tool bar until it changes to a hand with a single pointing finger. This pointer indicates that you can get more help by clicking on the button (see Figure 1.10).

9. With the single finger pointer, click on one of the buttons. A *glossary definition window* opens, displaying the name and a brief explanation of the button.

10. Click on the **glossary definition window** to close the window, and then double-click on the Help window's **Control menu box** to close the Help window.

ORIENTATION TO A TABLE

Tables are one type of object in an Access database, and serve as data storehouses. Tables are the only type of Access object that actually store data; the other objects—including forms and reports—serve only as tools to manipulate that data.

Figure 1.10   **Using Help**

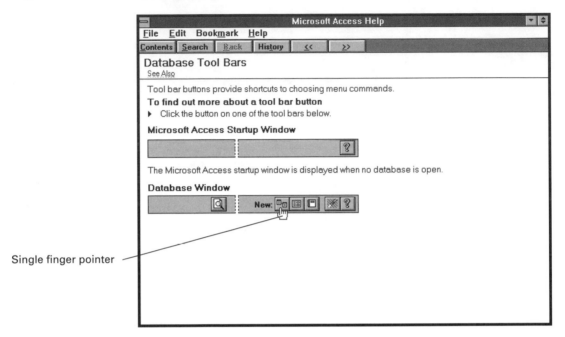

Single finger pointer

Tables store data in tabular form; that is, in a grid of rows and columns. Like the sample paper table we saw earlier, each field (column) of a table stores a certain category of data, while each record (row) stores one unit of data that spans those categories.

Because Access enables you to have multiple tables within a database, you can have separate tables for separate types of data. For example, you might have one table that stores data about your employees and another table that stores data about your customers.

 OPENING AND EXAMINING A TABLE

To view or edit information contained within a table, you can open the table.

Let's open a table in our database:

1. Observe the Database window. Table object names are listed alphabetically. The first table object name, Addresses and Extensions, is selected.

2. Click on **Open** to open the Addresses and Extensions table in its own *Table window*. Your screen should now look like Figure 1.11.

Figure 1.11   **The Addresses and Extensions table**

Vertical scroll bar — Vertical scroll box — Up scroll arrow

Last	First	Adr	City	St	Zip	Ext
Martin	Jane	50 Beach Drive	Oceanside	CA	91762	349
James	Ted	34 Fields Street	Fort Worth	TX	76116	300
Abel	Marie	127 Ford Avenue	Shackelford	TX	76430	339
Binder	Julia	10 Cory Drive	Trenton	NJ	08753	324
Binga	Sam	50 Dallas Street	Pasadena	CA	91106	348
Sanders	Maria	12 East Avenue	Denton	TX	76201	310
Harper	Harry	82 East Avenue	Long Beach	CA	90745	395
Conner	Bill	32 Ash Lane	Allentown	NJ	08501	328
Donaldson	Roger	8165 Main Street	Trenton	NJ	08618	303
Packer	Penny	9929 Clearview	Vienna	VA	22181	346
Abot	Robert	99 Stonecreek Rd.	Trenton	NJ	08618	350
Evans	Nancy	21 Stonecreek Rd.	Trenton	NJ	08618	390
Zambito	Joseph	81 Pleasing Lane	Alhambra	CA	91801	311
Osowski	Dominick	23 Lakeside Ave.	S Granbury	TX	76048	368
Chase	Wilma	52 Pempleton Dr.	Albany	NY	12205	309
DeMarco	Alice	34 Sable Ave.	Bentwood	IL	61820	332
Kyler	Dennis	273 Fireside Dr.	Great Neck	NY	11023	362
Desoto	Frank	P.O. Box 7234	Trenton	NJ	07092	356
Henley	Albert	12 Divine Drive	San Pueblo	CO	80403	318
Beaton	Robert	391 State Street	West Seneca	NY	14224	323
Stira	Joe	200 Nester Street	Bath	NY	14708	315
Jones	Homer	466 Fairhaven St.	Los Alamos	MI	48104	337
Bell	William	66 Big Hill Rd.	Troy	NY	12182	340
Haslam	David	453 Lakeshore Dr.	Evans Mills	ND	58352	338
Carter	Andrea	718 Prole Road	Rockville	SC	29204	360
Naylor	Ruth	532 Union Street	Nashville	TN	38109	334

Microsoft Access - [Table: Addresses and Extensions]

File Edit View Records Layout Window Help

Field: Last   New:

Record: 1

Datasheet View

Specific Record number box

Previous Record navigation button

First Record navigation button

Next Record navigation button   Last Record navigation button   Down scroll arrow

3. Observe the status bar. This is Datasheet view; that is, we are viewing the data contained in the table.

4. Observe the tool bar. Because a table is open, buttons relevant to working with tables are displayed.

5. Examine the table. Each column is a field; the *field names* are listed across the top.

6. Examine the rows. Each row is a record.

NAVIGATING IN A TABLE WITH THE MOUSE

Access provides a great number of ways to navigate through a table.

Let's look first at some ways to navigate using the mouse:

1. Move the mouse pointer over the City field for the third record (Marie Abel's record). Note that the pointer has changed from an arrow to an *I-beam*, indicating that the pointer is over an area where you can type text. Click once to place a flashing, vertical *insertion point* in the City field. (Access uses the insertion point to determine where to place text when you type on the keyboard.)

2. Examine the *vertical scroll bar* (located along the right-hand edge of the Table window). You can use this scroll bar to scroll up and down in the table. Click on the **down scroll arrow** (the downward-pointing arrow at the bottom of the scroll bar) to scroll down one record per click.

3. Examine the *vertical scroll box* (the small box located near the top of the scroll bar). Point to the **vertical scroll box**, press and hold the mouse button, and *drag* the box to the bottom of the scroll bar. Then release the mouse button. You can now view the very bottom of the table (a blank record).

4. Click on the **up scroll arrow** (the upward-pointing arrow located at the top of the scroll bar) to scroll up one record per click.

5. Drag the **vertical scroll box** to the top of the scroll bar to scroll to the top of the table.

6. Examine the Table window's *navigation buttons*, which are located in the lower-left corner of the Table window, directly above the status bar. They are, from left to right, the First Record navigation button, the Previous Record navigation button, the Next Record navigation button, and the Last Record navigation button. The Specific Record Number box lies in the center of the navigation buttons, to the right of the word *Record*, and indicates the current record number.

7. Click on the **Next Record navigation button** to move to the next record.

8. Click on the **Previous Record navigation button** to move to the previous record.

9. Click on the **Last Record navigation button** to move to the last record in the table.

10. Click on the **First Record navigation button** to move to the first record in the table.

11. Double-click on the **Specific Record Number box** to select the number 1. Type **9** and press **Enter** to move to the ninth record.

NAVIGATING IN A TABLE WITH THE KEYBOARD

You can also use the keyboard to navigate in a table.

Let's try some keyboard navigation:

1. First, use the mouse to place the insertion point in the City field for the first record in the table (Jane Martin's record).

2. Press the **Tab** key to move to the next field to the right, St.

3. Press **Shift+Tab** to move to the field to the left, City.

4. Press the **End** key to move to the last (rightmost) field in the current record, Ext.

5. Press the **Home** key to move to the first field in the current record, Last.

6. Press the **Down Arrow** key to move to the same field in the next record.

7. Press the **Up Arrow** key to move to the same field in the previous record.

8. Press **Ctrl+End** to move to the last field in the last record in the table.

9. Press **Ctrl+Home** to move to the first field in the first record in the table.

FINDING A RECORD IN A TABLE

As tables get larger and larger, it gets harder and harder to find a specific record. In the table we have open now, it wouldn't be too hard to locate Julia Binder's record manually because there are so few records in the table. However, imagine if you had to find her record in a table of 1,000 records.

Fortunately, Access provides the Edit, Find command to help you find records in tables of any size.

To find a specific record, you would follow these steps:

- Move to the field in which you want to search. For example, if you want to search for the record of someone whose last name is Smith, move to the last-name field.

- Choose Edit, Find to open the Find dialog box for that field.

- In the Find What text box, type the text for which you want to search (for example, Smith).

- Click on Find First to find the first record that contains, in the current field, the text you typed.

- If you have not found the correct record, click on Find Next to find the next occurrence and repeat as necessary until you do find the correct record.

- Once you find the record, click on Close to close the Find dialog box.

Let's find Andrea Carter's record in our table:

1. If necessary, move to the Last field.

2. Choose **Edit, Find** to open the Find in field: 'Last' dialog box. Note that the title of the dialog box reflects our current field.

3. In the Find What text box, type **Carter** (see Figure 1.12).

4. Click on **Find First** and examine the table. The last name **Carter** in Record 25 (Andrea Carter's record) is selected.

5. Click on **Close** to close the dialog box.

 CLOSING A TABLE

Once you are finished viewing or editing a table, you may want to close it in order to clear it from the screen and from your computer's memory. (When you clear the table from memory, the table—and the data within it—will still remain in storage on your hard disk.)

To close the table, double-click on the Table window's Control menu box.

Figure 1.12   **Finding a record**

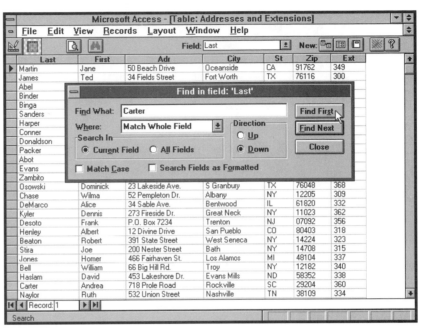

Let's close the table:

1. Locate the Table window's Control menu box. It's in the upper-left corner of the screen, directly below the Application Control menu box. (Do not double-click on the Application Control menu box, as this will close Access itself.)

2. Double-click on the **Control menu box**. The Table window closes, revealing the Database window that has been lying underneath all the time.

PRACTICE YOUR SKILLS

You've already learned a great deal about getting around in Access. The following activity enables you to apply this knowledge on your own. Please don't think of this activity as a test, but rather as an opportunity to hone your Access skills. It is only through practice that you'll internalize the techniques you've learned.

In this activity, you will open a table, navigate through the table, find a record, and close the table.

1. Open the Addresses and Extensions table.

2. Move to the last field in the last record in the table (Record 27).

3. Move to the first field in the last record in the table.

4. Move to Record 4 (Julia Binder's record).

5. Find David Haslam's record (Record 24).

6. Move to the first field in the first record in the table.

7. Close the Table window and return to the Database window.

ORIENTATION TO FORMS

Forms are Access objects that you can use to view and edit data that is stored in a table. Like the sample paper form we saw earlier, Access forms enable you to create a custom layout (that is, a layout other than rows and columns) for your data.

OPENING AND EXAMINING A SINGLE-COLUMN FORM

Access enables you to create and use forms in just about any layout. For simplicity's sake, however, we will start by looking at a single-column form based on the table you just closed, Addresses and Extensions.

Opening a form is quite similar to opening a table:

1. In the Database window, click on the **Form object button** to display the list of forms.

2. Select Address Data Entry, and then click on **Open** to open the Address Data Entry form. Your screen should now look like Figure 1.13.

3. Examine the Form window. One record from the Addresses and Extensions table is displayed.

4. Examine the *labels* that are displayed to the left of each field (Last, First, Adr, and so on).

Figure 1.13   **The Address Data Entry form**

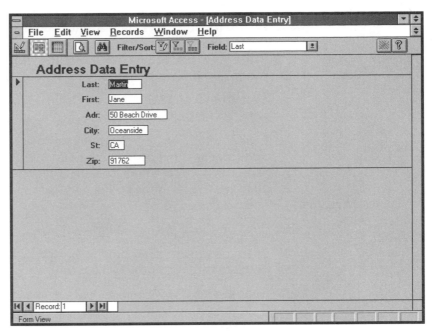

5. Examine the tool bar. Buttons appropriate to working with forms are displayed. (You will learn how to use these buttons in Chapter 5.)

6. At the bottom of the Form window, click on the **Next Record navigation button** to view the next record.

7. Click on the **Last Record navigation button** to move to the last record in the table, Record 27.

8. Click on the **First Record navigation button** to move to Record 1.

 FINDING A RECORD THROUGH A FORM

As with tables, you can use the Edit, Find command to find records through a form. To save keystrokes, you can access the Edit, Find command through the Find button on the tool bar.

1. Click on the label **First** to select Jane and make First the current field.

2. Observe the Specific Record Number box. The current record is Record 1.

3. On the tool bar, click on the **Find button** (the fifth button from the left, it displays a pair of binoculars) to open the Find in field: 'First' dialog box. Note that the last search value you used is entered in the Find What text box.

4. Type **Roger**, and then click on **Find First** to find the first record with the first name Roger.

5. Examine the Form window. Access has found the record, but you can't see that because the dialog box is in the way. However, the number in the Specific Record Number box has changed to 9, and the status bar displays the message *Search succeeded*.

6. Click on **Close** to close the dialog box.

7. Examine the Form window again. The value Roger is selected in the record for Roger Donaldson.

8. Choose **File, Close** to close the Form window and return to the Database window. (The File, Close command is an alternative to double-clicking on an object window's Control menu box.)

ORIENTATION TO SORTING AND QUERYING

As your database tables grow larger, you will need ways to control the order and amount of data that you see on the screen. Two ways that you can accomplish this are through sorting and querying.

 SORTING RECORDS

By default, records are stored in tables by order of entry. That is, the first record ever entered into a table is always Record 1, the second record entered is Record 2, and so on. However, when you are working with large tables, it may be easier to work with records if they are in a certain order. For example, you may want to sort invoices by invoice number or invoice date.

When working in a form, you can sort records by any single field, or by a combination of fields. For example, in a telephone book, entries are sorted by last name and then by first name, so that Mary Smith is listed after John Smith, but before John Smythe.

You define the sorting you want through a form's *Filter window*, a special window available by choosing Records, Edit Filter/Sort from a Form window.

Let's sort some records by last name:

1. In the Database window, double-click on **Internal Phone List** to open the Internal Phone List form. (Double-clicking on a form object name is an alternative to selecting the name and then clicking on Open.) Your screen should now look like Figure 1.14.

Figure 1.14   **The Internal Phone List form**

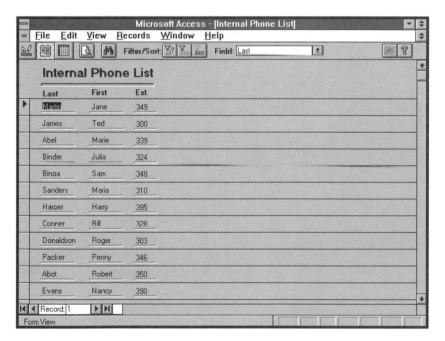

2. Examine the form. This form is also based on the Addresses and Extensions table. Instead of a single-column form, however, this is a tabular form that enables you to view more than one record at a time. Remember that forms are completely customizable and can be created with any layout.

3. Observe the order of the records. They are in data-entry (or *natural*) order.

4. Choose **Records, Edit Filter/Sort** to open the Filter window (see Figure 1.15).

5. Examine the Filter window, which is divided into two *panes*. Displayed on the left-hand side of the upper pane is the *field list* from the Addresses and Extensions table (you may not be able to read the entire table name). The lower pane contains a *filter grid*.

6. Examine the grid. Like a table, the grid consists of rows and columns. In a grid, each intersection of a row and column is called a *cell*.

7. Observe the first cell in the grid. It is a Field cell containing the insertion point and a drop-down list arrow.

8. Click on the **drop-down list arrow** to open a drop-down list of available field names.

Figure 1.15   The Filter window

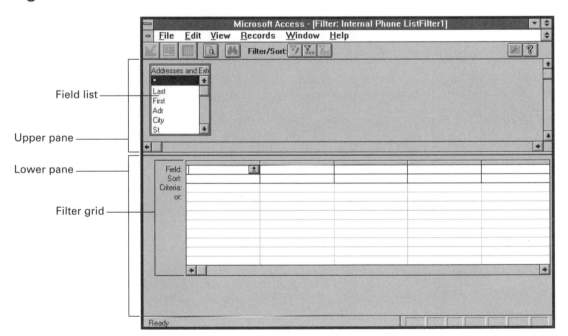

9. Since you want to sort by last name, select **Last** to place the field name in the cell.

10. Press **Down Arrow** to move the insertion point down to the Sort cell. Another drop-down list arrow will appear in the cell.

11. Click on the **drop-down list arrow** to open the drop-down list, and select **Ascending**. The last names will now be sorted in ascending order, from *A* to *Z*. (Descending order would sort them from *Z* to *A*.) Your Filter window should now look like Figure 1.16.

Figure 1.16   **Setting sort options in the Filter window**

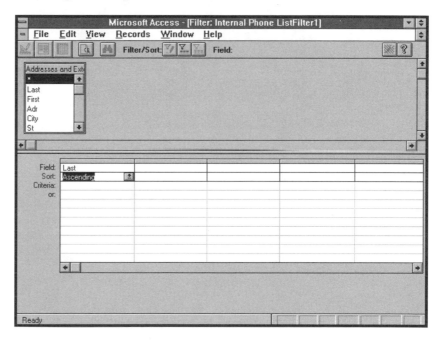

12. Choose **Records, Apply Filter/Sort** to close the Filter window and perform the sort.

13. Examine the form. Records are now displayed in ascending order by last name, as shown in Figure 1.17.

14. Close the Form window.

Figure 1.17   **The Internal Phone List form after sorting**

Microsoft Access - [Internal Phone List]						
File	**Edit**	**View**	**Records**	**Window**	**Help**	

Filter/Sort: ▾ ▾ ▦   Last

Internal Phone List

Last	First	Ext
Aba	Marie	339
Abot	Robert	350
Beaton	Robert	323
Bell	William	340
Binder	Julia	324
Binoa	Sam	348
Carter	Andrea	360
Chase	Wilma	309
Conner	Bill	328
DeMarco	Alice	332
Desoto	Frank	356
Donaldson	Roger	303

Record: 1

Form View   FLTR

RUNNING A QUERY

Queries are stored questions that you ask about data. Keep in mind that a query is a *question* about data, not the data that *answers* that question. Because of this, you get up-to-date information every time you run a query.

For example, you might run a query to see a list of the people in your company who make more than $10 per hour. A month later, you could run the same query and get a new list because some peoples' salaries have since increased. If you had stored the answer to the query, your list would be out of date. However, since you stored the question instead, this is not a problem.

Running a query is similar to using a form's Filter window, but queries offer greater flexibility. In addition, queries are saved as database objects; Filter windows need to be set up manually each time you use them.

Let's run a query that asks the Addresses and Extensions table for a list of the people who live in California.

1. First, open the Addresses and Extensions table. (In the Database window, click on the **Table object button** and then double-click on the table name.)

2. Examine the table. The records are in data-entry order and list everyone regardless of their state.

3. Close the Table window. (Double-click on the Table window's **Control menu box** or choose **File, Close.**)

4. In the Database window, click on the **Query object button** to view the list of query object names.

5. Double-click on **CA Addresses** to run the CA Addresses query.

6. Examine the Query window and compare it to Figure 1.18. The employees are listed in alphabetical order by last name, and only employees who live in California are listed.

7. Close the Query window. (Double-click on the Query window's **Control menu box**, or choose **File, Close.**)

Figure 1.18   **The result of the CA Addresses query**

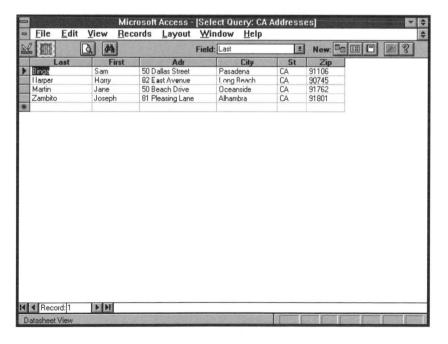

ORIENTATION TO REPORTS

Reports are the last database object that we will explore in this chapter. Although you can print from tables, forms, and queries, reports provide the best way to present your data as a printed document.

Some examples of reports are telephone lists, mailing labels, invoices, and sales summaries. Reports can be based on tables or queries and can include summary information. For example, on an invoice, you may want to include such summary information as the number of items purchased and the total cost of those items.

 PREVIEWING A BASIC REPORT

When you *preview* a report you can see on the screen how a report will look when printed. Because previewing is a WYSIWYG ("what-you-see-is-what-you-get") tool, what you see on the screen will closely match what you get when you print on paper.

Previewing reports, especially when you are working with and creating new reports, can save you both time and paper.

Let's preview a basic report that is based on the Pay Rates table:

1. First, open the Pay Rates table.

2. Examine the table. It includes data on employees' hours and pay rates.

3. Close the Table window.

4. In the Database window, click on the **Report object button** to display the list of report object names.

5. Select **Employee Hours and Rates**, and then click on **Preview** to preview the report. (The mouse pointer may change to an hourglass while Access generates the report.) Except for the report's date, which will vary, your report should look like the one in Figure 1.19.

6. Observe the tool bar. It displays Print, Setup, Zoom, Cancel, and Help buttons.

7. Click on **Zoom** to view the full page.

8. Click on **Zoom** again to return to a close-up view.

Figure 1.19   **Previewing the Employee Hours and Rates report**

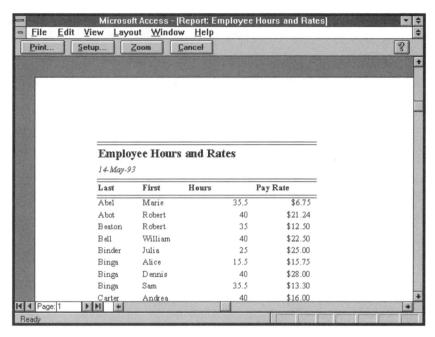

9. Use the **vertical** and **horizontal scroll bars** to scroll through the report. The report has a title, displays the current date, and lists employees alphabetically with their hours and pay rates.

10. Scroll to the bottom of the report to view the summary information: grand totals for hours and pay rates.

11. Click on **Cancel** to close the Report window.

PREVIEWING A REPORT WITH GROUPS AND TOTALS

Reports also enable you to group your data, and to total each group of data separately. For example, if you are creating a gross-pay report, you may want to group employees by department and then calculate each department's total gross pay.

Let's preview a report that does just that:

1. In the Database window, double-click on **Dept Gross Pay** to preview the report. (Double-clicking on a report object name is an alternative to selecting the name and then clicking on Preview.) Then compare your screen to Figure 1.20.

Figure 1.20   **Previewing the Dept Gross Pay report**

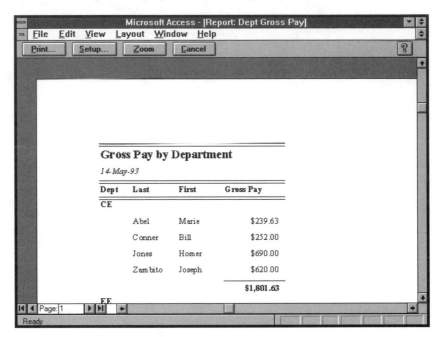

2. Use the **vertical scroll bar** to scroll down through the first page of the report. Note that the records are grouped alphabetically by department, and that gross pay is totaled for each department.

3. Click on the **Last Page navigation button** and then scroll up, if necessary, to view the grand total at the end of the report. (When previewing a report, Access displays *page navigation buttons* rather than record navigation buttons.) This number sums the totals from each department.

 PRINTING A REPORT

Once you are satisfied with how a report looks on the screen, you can print it to your printer directly from the Report window. Access prints entire reports by default. You can, however, choose to print only certain pages of a report.

Let's print the entire report that you have on the screen:

1. On the tool bar, click on **Print** to open the Print dialog box, which is shown in Figure 1.21.

2. Examine this dialog box. Because the current printer is the default printer set in Windows, your dialog box may differ from the one shown in Figure 1.21. The print range of All is already selected.

3. Click on **OK** to print the report. (Or, if you do not have a printer, click on Cancel to close the dialog box without printing.)

4. If your printer fails to print, refer to your printer and your Windows documentation for information on setting up your printer.

5. When the report has printed, close the Report window (click on **Cancel**), and compare your printout to Figures 1.22 and 1.23.

Figure 1.21 **A sample Print dialog box**

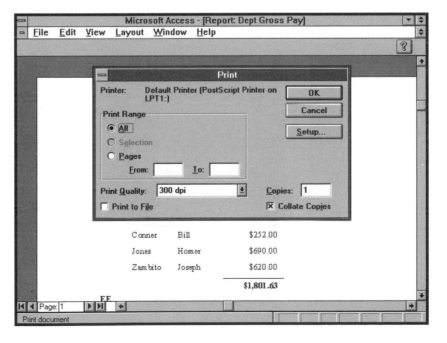

Figure 1.22   **Page 1 of the printed Dept Gross Pay report**

Gross Pay by Department
14-May-93

Dept	Last	First	Gross Pay
CE			
	Abel	Marie	$239.63
	Conner	Bill	$252.00
	Jones	Homer	$690.00
	Zambito	Joseph	$620.00
			$1,801.63
EE			
	Binga	Alice	$244.13
	Carter	Andrea	$640.00
	Donaldson	Roger	$480.00
	Evans	Nancy	$600.00
	Martin	Jane	$680.00
	Stira	Joe	$525.00
			$3,169.13
ES			
	DeMarco	Alice	$226.95
	Harper	Harry	$400.00
	Henley	Albert	$430.00
	Sanders	Maria	$501.50
	Ward	John	$212.50
			$1,770.95
MK			
	Abot	Robert	$849.60
	Bell	William	$900.00
	Binder	Julia	$625.00
	Binga	Dennis	$1,120.00
	James	Ted	$898.70
	Naylor	Ruth	$1,080.00
	Osowski	Dominick	$880.00

1

Figure 1.23 **Page 2 of the printed Dept Gross Pay report**

Dept	Last	First	Gross Pay
	Packer	Penny	$840.00
	Stira	Barbara	$1,040.00
			$8,233.30
MS			
	Desoto	Frank	$640.00
			$640.00
SS			
	Beaton	Robert	$437.50
	Binga	Sam	$472.15
	Chase	Wilma	$620.00
	Haslam	David	$540.00
	Packer	Opal	$350.00
			$2,419.65
		Grand Total :	18034.65

2

EXITING ACCESS

Your final step of every Access session is to exit Access. *Never* just turn off your computer while Access, Windows, or any program is open and running, as this could result in the loss of data.

To exit Access, you can use the File, Exit command (or, you can double-click on the Application Control menu box). Access will automatically close any open objects and databases before closing its own application window.

Let's exit Access now:

1. Choose **File, Exit**. The Database window will close first, followed by the Access application window, leaving you back in Windows.

SUMMARY

In this chapter, you learned how to start and exit Access, how to open a database, and about some key database objects: tables, forms, queries, and reports. Congratulations! You're on your way to mastering Access.

Here's a quick reference guide to the Access features introduced in this chapter:

Desired Result	How to Do It
Start Access	Start Windows, and then double-click on the **Microsoft Access program-item icon** in the Microsoft Access program group
Maximize/Restore a window	Click on the window's **Maximize/Restore button**
Minimize a window	Click on the window's **Minimize button**
Choose a menu item	Click on the menu option in the menu bar to display the drop-down menu, and then click on the menu item
Open the Help window	Click on the **Help button** in the tool bar; or, choose **Help, Contents**
Close a window	Double-click on the window's **Control menu box**

Desired Result	How to Do It
Open a database	Choose **File, Open Database**, select the appropriate drive and directory, select the database file name, and then click on **OK**
View lists of database object names	In the Database window, click on the appropriate object button
Search for Help	Choose **Help, Search**, type the name of a subject to search for until it rises to the top of the subject list, click on **Show Topics**, select the appropriate topic from the topic list, and then click on **Go To**
Open a table	In the Database window, click on the **Table object button**, select the table object name, and then click on **Open**; or, click on the **Table object button** and double-click on the table object name
Place the insertion point in a field	Click on the field
Scroll down one record in a table	Click on the **down scroll arrow**
Scroll up one record in a table	Click on the **up scroll arrow**
Scroll to the bottom of a table	Drag the **vertical scroll box** to the bottom of the vertical scroll bar
Scroll to the top of a table	Drag the **vertical scroll box** to the top of the vertical scroll bar
Move to the next record in a table	Click on the **Next Record navigation button**; or, press **Down Arrow**
Move to the previous record in a table	Click on the **Previous Record navigation button**; or, press **Up Arrow**
Move to the last record in a table	Click on the **Last Record navigation button**
Move to the first record in a table	Click on the **First Record navigation button**

Desired Result	How to Do It
Move to a specific record in a table	Double-click on the **Specific Record Number box**, type the desired record number, and then press **Enter**
Move to the next field in a record	Press **Tab**
Move to the previous field in a record	Press **Shift+Tab**
Move to the last field in a record	Press **End**
Move to the first field in a record	Press **Home**
Move to the last field in the last record in a table	Press **Ctrl+End**
Move to the first field in the first record in a table	Press **Ctrl+Home**
Find a record	Move to the field in which you want to search, choose **Edit, Find** (or click on the Find button in the tool bar), type the text you want to find, click on **Find First** (or **Find Next**), and then click on **Close**
Close a table	Double-click on the Table window's **Control menu box**; or, choose **File, Close**
Open a form	In the Database window, click on the **Form object button**, select the form object name, and then click on **Open**; or, click on the **Form object button** and double-click on the form object name
Move to the next record in a form	Click on the **Next Record navigation button**
Move to the last record in a form	Click on the **Last Record navigation button**

Desired Result	How to Do It
Move to the first record in a form	Click on the **First Record navigation button**
Close a form	Double-click on the Form window's **Control menu box**; or, choose **File, Close**
Sort records in a form	Choose **Records, Edit Filter/Sort**; in the filter grid, select the fields you want to sort on and the sort order (Ascending or Descending); then choose **Records, Apply Filter/Sort**
Run a query	In the Database window, click on the **Query object button**, select the query object name, and then click on **Open**; or, click on the **Query object button** and double-click on the query object name
Close a query	Double-click on the Query window's **Control menu box**; or, choose **File, Close**
Preview a report	In the Database window, click on the **Report object button**, select the report object name, and then click on **Preview**; or, click on the **Report object button** and double-click on the report object name
Zoom in and out on a previewed report	Click on **Zoom**
Close a previewed report	Click on **Cancel**
Print a report	Preview a report, click on **Print**, and then click on **OK**
Close a database and exit Access	Choose **File, Exit**; or, double-click on the **Application Control menu box**

A NOTE ON HOW TO PROCEED

If you wish to stop here, please feel free to do so. If you want to press onward, please proceed directly to the next chapter. Remember to allot enough time to work through an entire chapter at one sitting.

CHAPTER 2: TABLE BASICS

Examining a Table
and Its Design

Designing and
Creating a Table

Adding Records to
a Table

Modifying a Table
Design

In Chapter 1, you got a passing glance at some of the major elements of an Access database: objects (including tables, forms, queries, and reports). In this chapter, you will take a closer look at Access' cornerstone objects: tables.

When you're done working through this chapter, you will know how to:

- Design a table
- Create, save, and modify a table design
- Use Cue Cards to help you design a table
- Create and modify fields
- Set a primary key
- Add and save records
- Modify the Datasheet-view layout
- Preview and print a table

EXAMINING A TABLE AND ITS DESIGN

You learned in Chapter 1 that tables are the only type of database object that actually store data. There is more to a table, however, than its *contents*; there is also its *design*.

A table design is like the design of a house: It determines how the table (house) will look, and what kind of data (possessions) will belong inside it.

The design of a table includes

- The assignment of field names
- The order in which fields will appear in the table
- The type of data each field will contain
- *Field properties* (which can determine, among other things, a field's size, appearance, and behavior)
- Optionally, field descriptions

An Access table can contain up to 255 fields.

You can view and modify the design of a table through the table's *Design view*.

To switch to the Design view of an open table, choose View, Table Design, or click on the leftmost button on the tool bar, the Design View button.

If you are not currently running Access with the EMPLOYEE Database window open, please follow the steps outlined in Chapter 1 under "Starting Access" and "Opening a Database" to start the program and open the EMPLOYEE database.

To become more familiar with table design before you create your own table, first take a brief look at an existing table and its design:

1. If they aren't already maximized, maximize the application window and the Database window (click on each window's **Maximize/Restore** button until the windows completely fill the screen).

2. Open the Hours and Rates table (see Figure 2.1). (In the Database window, display the list of table object names, and then double-click on **Hours and Rates**.)

3. Examine the table's fields. They are ID, Last, First, Hired, Dept, Hours, Pay Rate, and Health.

Figure 2.1   **The Hours and Rates table in Datasheet view**

ID	Last	First	Hired	Dept	Hours	Pay Rate	Health
0001	James	Ted	4/1/87	MK	38	$23.65	Yes
0002	Harper	Harry	4/19/88	ES	40	$10.00	Yes
0003	Packer	Penny	1/15/81	MK	35	$24.00	Yes
0004	Binder	Julia	2/17/89	MK	25	$25.00	Yes
0005	Sanders	Maria	8/17/90	ES	29.5	$17.00	Yes
0006	Evans	Nancy	5/20/86	EE	40	$15.00	No
0007	Martin	Jane	6/7/83	EE	40	$17.00	Yes
0008	Binga	Alice	9/1/85	EE	15.5	$15.75	Yes
0009	Conner	Bill	3/8/91	CE	40	$6.30	Yes
0010	Osowski	Dominick	7/18/90	MK	40	$22.00	Yes
0011	Binga	Sam	7/5/80	SS	35.5	$13.30	No
0012	Abel	Marie	11/25/82	CE	35.5	$6.75	Yes
0013	Abot	Robert	9/18/84	MK	40	$21.24	No
0014	Zambito	Joseph	7/9/80	CE	40	$15.50	Yes
0015	Donaldson	Roger	4/8/92	EE	40	$12.00	No
0016	Chase	Wilma	8/17/84	SS	40	$15.50	No
0017	DeMarco	Alice	8/7/92	ES	25.5	$8.90	Yes
0018	Desoto	Frank	9/18/84	MS	40	$16.00	No
0019	Henley	Albert	10/13/90	ES	40	$10.75	No
0020	Binga	Dennis	5/12/84	MK	40	$28.00	Yes
0021	Stira	Joe	2/22/89	EE	37.5	$14.00	Yes
0022	Jones	Homer	4/13/90	CE	40	$17.25	Yes
0023	Packer	Opal	3/31/85	SS	25	$14.00	No
0024	Haslam	David	5/13/87	SS	40	$13.50	Yes
0025	Stira	Barbara	11/1/86	MK	40	$26.00	Yes
0026	Naylor	Ruth	9/1/83	MK	40	$27.00	Yes

4. Examine the records. Values in the ID field have leading zeros. Values in the Hired field display in the *mm/dd/yy* format. Values in the Hours field display decimals only when necessary. Values in the Pay Rate field display dollar signs and two decimal places. Values in the Health field are either Yes or No.

5. Choose **View, Table Design** to switch to the table's Design view, and then compare your screen to Figure 2.2.

Figure 2.2   **The Hours and Rates table in Design view**

6. Observe the Table window. It is split into two panes. The upper pane contains a *design grid*. The lower pane displays field properties.

7. Observe the design grid. Each row defines one of the table's fields. Within each row are cells to specify a field name, data type, and field description. To the left of each field name is a *field selector*.

8. Observe the ID row. ID is defined with the Text data type.

9. Click on the **field selector** to the left of ID to select that row.

10. Examine the *Field Properties pane*. It displays properties for the ID field: The Field Size property is set to 4, and the Indexed property is set to Yes (No Duplicates). You will learn more about the elements of a Table window's Design view later in this chapter when you create your own table.

11. Close the Table window. (Double-click on its **Control menu box**.)

DESIGNING AND CREATING A TABLE

The keys to a well-designed database are well-designed tables. Conversely, poorly designed tables make for poorly designed databases.

Before you start creating a table in Access, carefully consider the type of information you will need to store and retrieve. Then, plan your table design around those needs.

When you're planning a table, you should follow these steps:

- Examine the data you want to include; then determine the fields (categories) of data you need and what data types they should be. (Table 2.1 describes the data types available in Access.) If you use paper forms to collect data, they are an excellent tool for determining fields and data types.

- Decide if the data is closely related and should be in one table or if it can be split into multiple tables. For example, you might divide your data into one table for employee information and a second table for supplier information.

- Anticipate what questions you will need to ask about the data and how you will want to sort and group the data.

- Identify the types of reports you will need to produce from your data. Look at any existing reports if they are available.

For each field in a table, you will need to specify a unique field name. In Microsoft Access, field names can be up to 64 characters long and can include any combination of letters (upper- and lowercase), numbers, spaces, and special characters with the following exceptions:

- Leading spaces
- Periods (.)
- Exclamation points (!)
- Square brackets ([])
- Control characters (ASCII values 0 through 32)

Table 2.1   **Data Types**

Data Type	Use for
Text	Text, numbers on which you will not do calculations, and numbers that need to contain leading zeros. Examples include names, telephone numbers, zip codes, and product-identification codes. You can define text fields to contain up to 255 characters; the default field size is 50 characters.
Yes/No	Values that are restricted to only one of two logical values: Yes or No, True or False, On or Off.
Date/Time	Dates and times that you can use for date arithmetic.
Number	Numerical data on which you will perform calculations, excepting calculations on money. Number fields can store numbers with up to ten digits of precision.
Currency	Values representing money. Currency fields can store numbers with up to 15 digits to the left of the decimal point and up to 4 digits to the right. By default, currency-field values display dollar signs ($) and thousands separators.
Counter	Automatically sequential numbers, such as invoice or check numbers, beginning with 1.
Memo	Lengthy text and numbers, such as comments or explanations. Memo fields can each store up to 32,000 characters.
OLE Object	Object Linking and Embedding (OLE) objects created in another application and linked to Access using Windows' OLE protocol. (See your Windows documentation for an overview of OLE.)

DESIGNING THE TABLE

Let's now plan the design of your first table, an employee-information table. First, examine Figure 2.3. It is a paper data-collection form upon which we will base our table. Now consider these table-design questions and answers:

Figure 2.3   **A sample paper data-collection form**

> # Employee Information Form
>
> Employee ID: _____   Date Hired: _____
>
> Name (Last, First): _____
>
> Hours/Week: _____   Rate/Hour:_____
>
> Gross Pay: _____
>
> Health Insurance: ___ Yes   ___ No

- Should an employee's name be one field, as it is on the form, or two, one for first name and one for last name? We will make it two fields so that we can sort employee records by first *or* last name.

- Should the ID field be a text field or a number field? Because our ID numbers include leading zeros and we will never need to use them in calculations, we will make ID a text field.

- What data type should we use for the hired dates? Date/Time would be ideal because we could later use these dates in *date arithmetic*—for example, to find all employees hired before a certain date.

- What data type should we use for hours? Because we'll use this field in calculations, we'll use the Number data type.

- Should we also create a number field for the hourly rate? Because the hourly rate is a currency value, we'll do best by using the Currency data type.

- Should we include a field for gross pay? It's not necessary because we can always calculate gross pay by multiplying hours worked by hourly rate. To increase accuracy and efficiency in your tables, never include a field that you can calculate from other fields.

- Should the health-insurance field be two fields (as on the form) or one? If we use the Yes/No data type, we can use just one field.

- Now examine Figure 2.4. It is a report that displays selected information on members of the Marketing Department. What additional information do we need in our table to create this report? We need a field that identifies each employee's department.

Figure 2.4   **A sample report**

Marketing Department - Wages

Dept	Last	First	Gross Pay
MK			
	Abot	Robert	$849.60
	Bell	William	$900.00
	Binder	Julia	$625.00
	Binga	Dennis	$1,120.00
	James	Ted	$898.70
	Naylor	Ruth	$1,080.00
	Osowski	Dominick	$880.00
	Packer	Penny	$840.00
	Stira	Barbara	$1,040.00
			$8,233.30

CREATING THE TABLE

Once you have determined your needs for a table, you can create a new table by following these steps:

- In the Database window, display the table object names; then click on New. This will open an empty Table window in Design view.

- For each field you need in your table, enter a field name and select the appropriate data type in the Table window's design grid. If you wish, also specify for each field a description and field properties.

- Decide whether you want to set a *primary key* and, if so, on what field or fields. (We will discuss primary keys later in this chapter.)

- Choose File, Save As.

- In the Save As dialog box, type a name for the new table, and then click on OK.

Let's start creating our employee table now:

1. In the Database window, click on **New** to open a new Table window in Design view.

2. Examine the Table window, and then compare it to Figure 2.5. Because this is a new table, the design grid is empty and Access does not display any field properties. Note that the insertion point is in the Field Name cell of the first row, ready for you to add the table's first field name.

Figure 2.5   **The Design view of a new table**

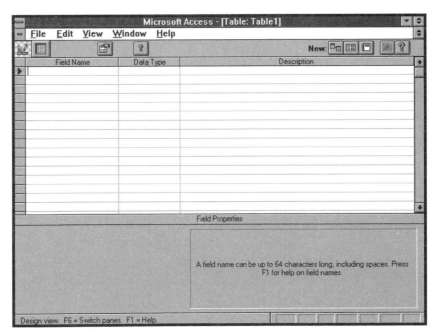

CREATING A TEXT FIELD

As you saw in Table 2.1, you should use text fields for numbers that need to contain leading zeros.

So, now create your first field, ID, as a text field:

1. In the Field Name cell of the first row of the design grid, type **ID**; then press **Tab** to move to the Data Type column.

2. Observe the Data Type column. Access has already selected the default data type of Text, so you do not need to select it yourself. Note that Access now displays field properties applicable to text fields at the bottom of the Table window, and has filled in default values for the Field Size and Indexed properties. (You will learn more about the Indexed property later in this chapter under "Setting a Primary Key.")

3. Observe the status bar. It indicates that you can use the F6 function key to switch to the Field Properties pane.

4. Press **F6** to move to the Field Properties pane and select the default value of 50 in the Field Size property box. (Alternatively, you can double-click on the box.)

5. Because the ID numbers will be only four digits long, type **4** to replace the default value. Your screen should now look like Figure 2.6.

 USING CUE CARDS

When you are designing a table in Access, you may need some help in, for example, choosing an appropriate data type. For this reason, a feature called *Cue Cards* is interwoven with Access' Help system. Cue Cards walk you step by step through common tasks like creating a table. You can access Cue Cards by choosing Help, Cue Cards.

Now create your last-name field, Ln, and try out Cue Cards in the process.

1. Place the insertion point in the Field Name cell of the second row (place the I-beam in the cell, and then click the mouse button).

Figure 2.6   **The table design after defining the ID field**

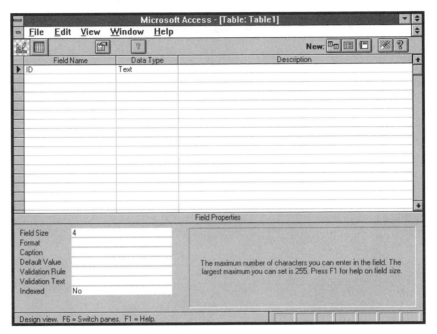

2. Type **Ln**; then press **Tab** to move to the Data Type column (later you'll change this field name so that it's more descriptive).

3. In the Data Type column, click on the **drop-down list arrow** to open the drop-down list of data types. If you hadn't already learned about Access' data types, this could be an intimidating list from which to choose. Click on the **drop-down list arrow** to close the list.

4. Choose **Help, Cue Cards** to open the Help window for Cue Cards. Note that Cue Cards can provide help for a number of tasks, from building a database to "I'm Not Sure."

5. Click on the button to the left of **Build a Database with Tables** to open the Cue Cards window on that subject.

6. Click on the button to the left of **Choose a data type**; then click on the button to the left of **Read tips for choosing a data type** to see explanations of the available data types (see Figure 2.7). Text seems to be the right choice for Ln after all.

Figure 2.7   **Using Cue Cards to decide on a data type**

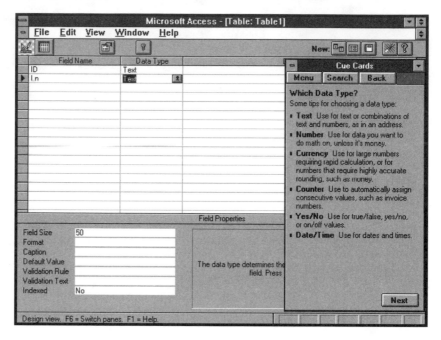

7. Press **F6** to move the selection to the Field Size box. Note how the Cue Cards window remains on the screen. Unlike the Help window, you can keep the Cue Cards window open and displayed while you work elsewhere in Access.

8. In the Field Size text box, type **15** to allow up to 15 characters for employees' last names.

9. Close the Cue Cards window to exit Cue Cards. (Double-click on the window's **Control menu box**.)

PRACTICE YOUR SKILLS

1. Add a third field, **Dept**, to the table.

2. Define Dept as a text field.

3. Change the field size to **2**.

4. Compare your screen to Figure 2.8.

Figure 2.8 **The table design after adding the Dept field**

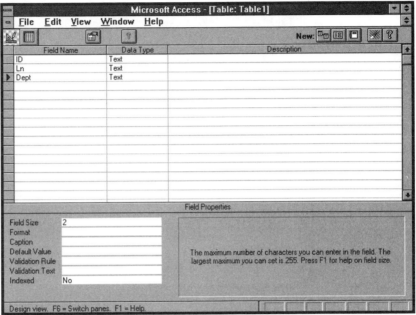

 CREATING A YES/NO FIELD

As we saw earlier, a single field with the Yes/No data type would be ideal for the health-insurance field because employees either do or don't have health insurance.

Let's create a yes/no field for health insurance:

1. Place the insertion point in the Field Name cell of the next blank grid row.

2. Type **Health**, and then press **Tab**.

3. In the Data Type column, select **Yes/No** from the drop-down list.

4. Observe the list of field properties. Fewer field properties are applicable to yes/no fields than to text fields. Access sets the Format property by default to Yes/No (yes/no fields can also display True and False or On and Off). Your screen should now match the one shown in Figure 2.9.

Figure 2.9   **The table design after defining the Health field**

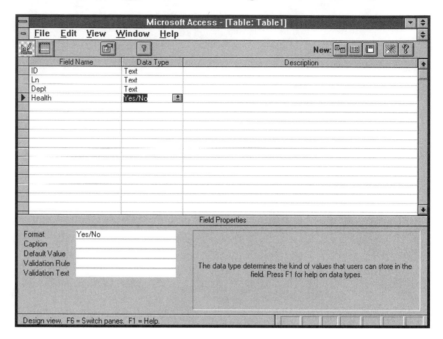

 CREATING A DATE FIELD

The Date/Time data type is the clear choice for our hired-date field. The Date/Time data type, however, is not only ideal because it can *store* dates and times, but because you can use values in date/time fields to perform date arithmetic. Among other things, you can use date arithmetic to sort records by date and to calculate the average number of days it takes between accepting and shipping an order.

With a hired-date field in your employee table, you'll be able to generate a seniority list or schedule annual performance appraisals and raises.

Let's create that field now:

1. Place the insertion point in the Field Name cell of the next blank grid row.

2. Type **Hd** (hired date); then press **Tab**.

3. In the Data Type cell, select **Date/Time** from the drop-down list; then compare your screen to Figure 2.10.

Figure 2.10   **The table design after defining the Hd field**

```
 ─                    Microsoft Access - [Table: Table1]              ▼ ▲
 ─   File   Edit   View   Window   Help                                 ▲
 ◪ ▦          ☞              ▼                       New: ▫▫ ▦ ▣  ✖ ▮
         Field Name              Data Type                  Description        ▲
      ID                   Text                                             ▒
      Ln                   Text
      Dept                 Text
      Health               Yes/No
 ▶    Hd                   Date/Time    ▼
                                                                           ▼
                              Field Properties
      Format
      Caption
      Default Value
      Validation Rule                    The data type determines the kind of values that users can store in the
      Validation Text                            field. Press F1 for help on data types.
      Indexed       No

 Design view.  F6 = Switch panes.  F1 = Help.
```

CREATING A NUMBER FIELD

Because you will want to use your hours-worked field in calculations, you'll use the Number data type. Also, because someone else
using this table may be unsure whether the value in the hours-
worked field is hours per week or hours per month, actual hours
worked or normal hours, you'll add a description that will display in
the status bar whenever someone works in that field.

Now create your hours-worked field:

1. Place the insertion point in the Field Name cell of the next
   blank grid row.

2. Type **Hours**, and then press **Tab**.

3. In the Data Type column, select **Number** from the drop-down
   list, and then press **Tab** to move to the Description column.

4. In the Description column, type **Normal weekly hours**.

5. Observe all the default values Access has set for the Hours field: The Field Size is set to Double, the most flexible and accurate number-field size; Decimal Places is set to Auto, so decimal places will only be displayed when necessary; Default Value is set to 0, so if no other value is entered for this field in a record, Access will assign a value of 0; and Indexed is set to No (see Figure 2.11).

Figure 2.11   **The table design after defining the Hours field**

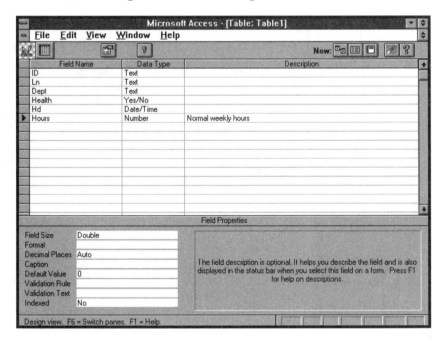

 CREATING A CURRENCY FIELD

You'll be using your hourly-rate field for calculations, but because it will store currency values, you'll assign it the Currency data type.

Let's create a currency field named Pay Rate:

1. Place the insertion point in the Field Name cell of the next blank grid row.

2. Type **Pay Rate**; then press **Tab**.

3. In the Data Type column, select **Currency** from the drop-down list.

4. Observe the default values Access sets for currency fields: Auto for Decimal Places, 0 for Default Value, No for Indexed (see Figure 2.12).

Figure 2.12　　**The table design after defining the Pay Rate field**

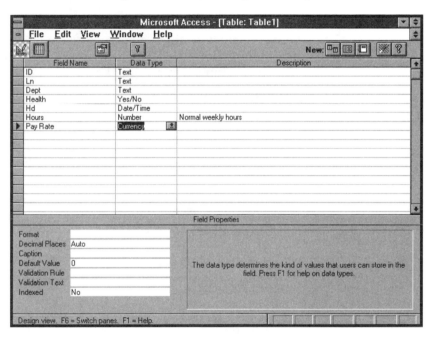

 SETTING A PRIMARY KEY

A *primary key* is any field or combination of fields in a table that uniquely identifies each table record. You could use a product part number as a primary-key field, for example.

When you set a primary key, Access will

• Automatically sort the table records by the values in the primary key.

- Not permit you to enter records that contain duplicate values in the primary key. For example, no two employees can have the same ID number if the ID field is set as the primary key.

- Use the primary key as a main *index* to speed data retrieval from large tables. In this way, Access uses a primary key as you would use the index in the back of this book: Instead of you (Access) searching through the entire book (table) for a certain word (record), you (Access) can use the index (primary key) to find the word (record) very quickly.

Primary keys also enable you to define default relationships between tables so that you can more easily use multiple tables together. You will learn more about table relationships in Chapter 8, "Enhanced Table Design."

Although Access does not require you to set a primary key for a table, it strongly encourages you to do so. In fact, if you try to save the design of a new or modified table and have not set a primary key, Access offers to create a specialized primary-key field for you. You will learn how to instruct Access to create a specialized primary-key field in Chapter 8.

To set a primary key in the Design view of a table, select the appropriate field or fields, and then choose Edit, Set Primary Key (or click on the fourth button from the left on the tool bar, the *Primary Key button*).

Because our employee ID numbers will always be unique, let's set the ID field as the primary key:

1. Place the insertion point in the design grid row for ID (the first row).

2. Choose **Edit, Set Primary Key** to set ID as the primary key.

3. Note that a key indicator now appears on the field selector to the left of ID, as it does in Figure 2.13. This indicates that you have successfully set ID as the primary key.

4. Observe the Indexed property box. When you set ID as the primary key, Access automatically changed the property from No to Yes (No Duplicates). This property prevents anyone entering data into this table from entering a duplicate ID number. Without this precaution, Access might lose its ability to uniquely identify records.

Figure 2.13   **The table design after setting a primary key**

Primary Key button ⎯

Key indicator ⎯

```
┌──────────────────────────────────────────────────────────────────────────┐
│ ═                    Microsoft Access - [Table: Table1]            ▾ ⬍    │
│ ═   File   Edit   View   Window   Help                                ⬍    │
│ ▦ ▦              ▦          ▦                    New: ▦ ▦ ▦   ▨ ?         │
│         Field Name        Data Type              Description            ▲  │
│ ▸▸ ID                  Text                                               │
│    Ln                  Text                                               │
│    Dept                Text                                               │
│    Health              Yes/No                                            │
│    Hd                  Date/Time                                         │
│    Hours               Number        Normal weekly hours                │
│    Pay Rate            Currency                                          │
│                                                                          │
│                                                                       ▼  │
│                               Field Properties                           │
│   Field Size     4                                                       │
│   Format                                                                 │
│   Caption                                                                │
│   Default Value             A field name can be up to 64 characters long,│
│   Validation Rule           including spaces. Press F1 for help on field │
│   Validation Text           names.                                       │
│   Indexed        Yes (No Duplicates)                                     │
│                                                                          │
│ Design view.  F6 = Switch panes.  F1 = Help.                            │
└──────────────────────────────────────────────────────────────────────────┘
```

SAVING THE TABLE DESIGN

Once you have created and defined your fields, and have set a primary key, you are ready to save your table design. *Saving* is the process of taking information stored in computer memory (a temporary storage area) and copying it to a more permanent storage area, such as your hard disk. By saving, you protect your work against such computer problems as loss of power. For example, if you save your table design and then accidentally shut off the computer, computer memory will be completely cleared. However, when you reload Access and your database file back into memory from your hard disk, your table design will be available. If you hadn't saved your table design, it would have been lost.

To save a table design, you would follow these steps:

- From the table's Design view, choose File, Save As to open the Save As dialog box. (You should use the File, Save As command for objects that have not yet been named or that you wish to rename. You'll use the File, Save command later when you modify and then save already named objects.)

- Type a name for the table. Table names can be up to 64 characters long and must follow the same naming conventions as
field names (see "Designing and Creating a Table" earlier in
this chapter).

- Click on OK.

Because you're done designing the table for now, save the design:

1. Choose **File, Save As** to open the Save As dialog box.

2. Observe the dialog box. By default, Access suggests that you
name the table Table1.

3. Type **My Rates and Hours** to replace the existing text and give
the table a more descriptive name, as shown in Figure 2.14. (In
this book, any time you create a new object you'll begin its
name with "My" so that you can distinguish it from the supplied objects.)

4. Click on **OK** to close the dialog box.

5. Observe the title bar. It now displays your new table name.

Figure 2.14   **Saving the table design**

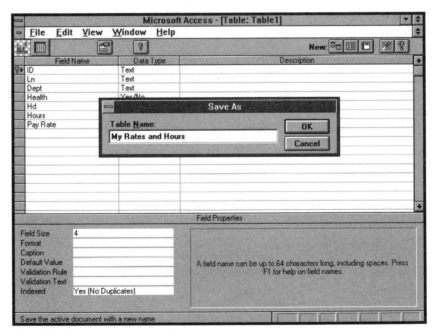

ADDING RECORDS TO A TABLE

Once you have finished designing your table, you are ready to begin adding records to it. Using the house analogy, a new table is like a new house: empty and ready to be filled.

You cannot add records, however, in a table's Design view; you must first switch to Datasheet view either by choosing View, Datasheet or by clicking on the second button from the left on the tool bar, the *Datasheet View button*.

When you first switch to Datasheet view for a new table, you'll find only a row of the table's field names across the top of the table and a blank record underneath. If any of your fields have default values (such as the Hours and Pay Rate fields), Access will have entered those default values in the otherwise blank row. Access tables always contain such a blank record at the bottom to enable you to add more records; because a new table contains no data, the blank row is also the only row.

Once you are in Datasheet view, you can begin to add records just by typing in the blank record. As you begin to enter data in the first record, Access will automatically add a second, blank record so that the table always has a blank record. To move from field to field, you can press either Tab or Enter to move to the next field.

When you are finished with a record, press Tab or Enter in the record's last (rightmost) field to automatically save the record (that is, copy the record from computer memory to the hard disk) and move to the first field in the second record. (This book just instructs you to use the Tab key to advance to the next field. If you prefer to use the Enter key instead, please do so.) If, for some reason, you want to save data in a record without actually leaving the record, choose File, Save Record.

As you enter data in Datasheet view, you can get information about a record by observing the record's *record selector*, the button located to the left of the record's leftmost field.

Different indicators on record selectors have different meanings:

- A rightward-pointing triangle indicates that the record is the current record and contains the *focus*. (The focus, in a table or any Access object, is synonymous with the current location of the insertion point or selection.)

- A pencil indicator indicates that the current record has been edited but not yet saved.

- An asterisk indicates that the record is the last (blank) row in the table. (When the last record has the focus, however, its record selector displays a rightward-pointing triangle rather than an asterisk.)

- A slashed circle indicates that the record is *locked*. (See your Access documentation for more information on locked records.)

ADDING AND SAVING RECORDS

Now switch your table to Datasheet view and see what happens when you add some records:

1. Choose **View, Datasheet** to switch to the table's Datasheet view.

2. Examine the table, and then compare it to Figure 2.15. The table displays the fields you created in Design view, and contains only one blank record. Click on the **right scroll arrow** at the bottom of the screen to view the right edge of the table.

3. Examine the blank record. Access has entered default values of 0 and $0.00, respectively, in the Hours and Pay Rate fields; the rightward-pointing triangle on the record selector indicates that this is the current record.

4. Click on the **left scroll arrow** to return to the left side of the table, and then verify that the insertion point is in the ID field.

5. Type **0020** to enter the value in the ID field. Note that when you begin typing in this record, Access automatically adds a blank record beneath it (see Figure 2.16).

6. Examine the two record selectors. The current record selector now displays a pencil indicator, indicating that you have made changes to the record that have not yet been saved. The second record selector displays an asterisk to indicate that it is the last record in the table.

7. Press **Tab** to move to the Ln field, and then type **Carney**.

8. Press **Tab** to move to the Dept field, and then type **MS** (the two-letter code for the Marketing Support Department).

Figure 2.15 **The empty My Rates and Hours table in Datasheet view**

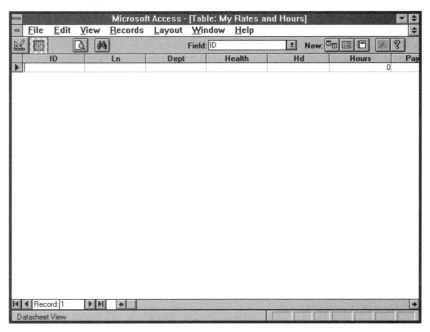

Figure 2.16 **Adding data to the table**

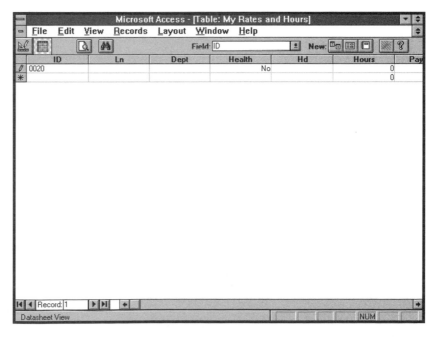

9. Press **Tab** to move to the Health field; then type **yes** to replace the default value of No and indicate that the employee is covered by health insurance.

10. Press **Tab** to move to the Hd field. Note that when you left the Health field, Access automatically changed the *yes* you typed to *Yes*. For consistency, Access will sometimes adjust the case and/or punctuation of your data.

11. Type **2-20-90** to enter the date of hire, and then press **Tab** to move to the Hours field. Note that Access automatically adjusted the date in the Hd field to 2/20/90.

12. Observe the status bar. When you are in the Hours field, the status bar displays the field description you entered in Design view: *Normal weekly hours*.

13. Type **32.5** to enter the normal weekly hours, and then press **Tab**. Note how Access automatically scrolls to the right as you enter the Pay Rate field.

14. Type **15** to enter the hourly pay rate. Even though this is a dollar amount, you do not need to type a dollar sign before the value; because this is a currency field, Access takes care of that for you automatically.

15. Press **Tab** once more to move to the first field of the next record. Access automatically scrolls back to the left side of the table and saves the current record.

16. Examine the two record selectors, and then compare your screen to Figure 2.17. The first selector is blank, indicating that the record is no longer current and has been saved. The second selector displays a rightward-pointing triangle to indicate that this is the current record.

PRACTICE YOUR SKILLS

1. Enter the following values into the table:

ID:	Ln:	Dept:	Health:	Hd:	Hours:	Pay Rate:
0021	Schneider	MK	Yes	2/25/86	40	12
0022	Rudniki	EE	No	11/15/90	40	20.75
0023	Carney	MK	Yes	10/4/91	32.5	21.5

Figure 2.17   **The table after completing and saving the first record**

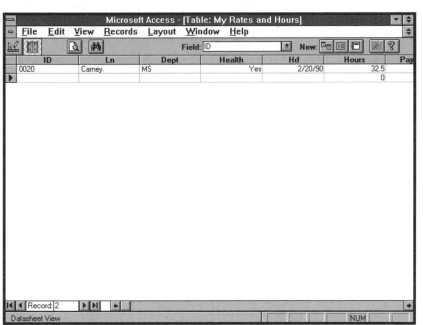

2. Move the focus off the last record to save it.

3. Compare your screen to Figure 2.18.

MODIFYING A TABLE DESIGN

Even with the best planning, you may find that you need to modify your table design. Through a table's Design view, you can add, rename, delete, move, and/or redefine the data type and properties of any field. Once you have completed the modifications to the table design, choose File, Save to save those changes.

While you can and should modify the design of a table to increase the table's usefulness, you should consider these important cautions:

• For safety's sake, we recommend that you make a backup copy of a table (or of the entire database) before modifying a table design.

• If you delete a field, Access will also delete any data it contains.

Figure 2.18   **The table after adding and saving three more records**

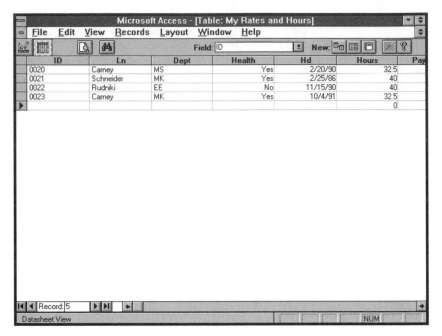

- When you delete or rename a field in the table design, you must also delete it from or rename it in related objects. Until you do, any queries in which the field appears will not work, and forms and reports containing the field will display error messages.

- If you reduce a field to a smaller size or type, Access may truncate (cut off) data that will not fit in the smaller field.

- If you change a field's data type, Access will attempt to convert your existing data, which may create unexpected results. (See your Access documentation for information on the possibilities and pitfalls of data conversion.)

IDENTIFYING IMPROVEMENTS TO THE TABLE

As you can see, you will save time and effort in the long run if you learn to fine-tune your table designs as soon as possible. However, some design problems will not be apparent until you have entered at least some data, or have tried to create other objects based on your table. And, of course, there are *always* changes.

Take a look at your new table and identify some possible improvements:

1. Observe the Ln field. You could change the field name to Last to be more descriptive. Also, it looks as if you'll need to add a first-name field to distinguish employees with the same last name, such as Carney.

2. Observe the Hd field. You could change the field name to Hired to be more descriptive.

3. Observe the Health field. Due to a new company policy that gives health insurance to *all* employees, you no longer need this field.

 CHANGING FIELD NAMES

Once in Design view, you can edit field names like any other text in Access: You can modify the existing field name, or delete it altogether and replace it with a new field name.

1. Click on the **Design View button** (the leftmost button on the tool bar) to view the design of the My Rates and Hours table.

2. In the Field Name column, double-click on **Ln** to select the field name.

3. Type **Last** to replace Ln.

4. In the Field Name column, place the insertion point directly after the *H* in Hd.

5. Type **ire** to change the field name to Hired, and then compare your screen to Figure 2.19.

 INSERTING AND DELETING FIELDS

You can always add a field to the end of a table design, but to add a field within the table, you need to create a new field row to make room. To insert a new row between existing field rows, select the field that is positioned where you want to add the new row and then choose Edit, Insert Row, or press the Insert key. Access will insert a blank row and move the remaining fields down one row. Then, you can create a new field as you would at the end of the table design.

Figure 2.19   **The table design after changing two field names**

Design View
button

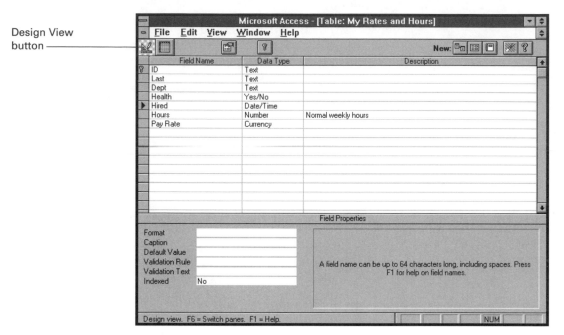

To delete a field instead, select the field and choose Edit, Delete Row, or press the Delete key. When you do, Access will display a dialog box that:

- Reminds you that by deleting a field, you also delete any data contained within that field

- Asks you to confirm the deletion

Click on OK to confirm the deletion, or Cancel to not delete.

Let's add a first-name field and delete the Health field:

1. Click on the **field selector** for Dept to select where to insert a new row for the first-name field: directly below the Last field. This not only makes Dept the current field, but selects the entire field as well.

2. Choose **Edit, Insert Row** (or press the Insert key) to insert a new, blank row above the selected row (see Figure 2.20).

Figure 2.20 **The table design after inserting a new field row**

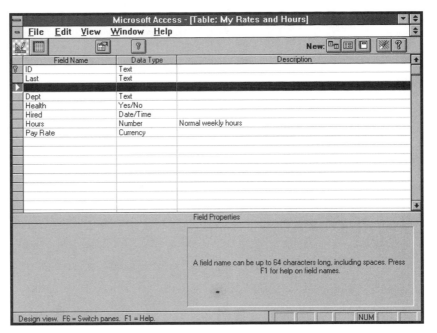

3. Place the insertion point in the Field Name column of the new row, and then type **First** to name the field.

4. Press **Tab** to move to the Data Type column. Accept the default data type, Text.

5. Change the field size from the default of 50 to **15**. (You can use F6 to switch to the Field Properties pane, or just double-click on 50. Then type 15.)

6. Select the Health field row (use the field selector), and then choose **Edit, Delete Row** (or press the Delete key).

7. Observe the dialog box. Access is asking you to confirm the deletion of the Health field.

8. Click on **OK** to delete the Health field and the data that it contains, and then compare your screen to Figure 2.21.

Figure 2.21   **The table design after inserting and deleting fields**

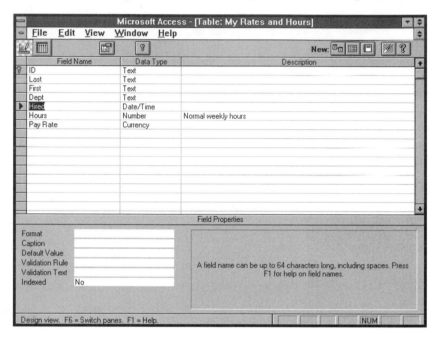

 MOVING A FIELD

By default, fields appear across a table in Datasheet view in the same order that they are listed down the left side of the Table window in Design view. To change the order of fields, you can select and then drag a field to a new location. As you drag, Access displays a dark line to indicate where it will place the field when you release the mouse button.

Because it might be easier to enter employee names if the First field precedes the Last field, let's move the First field:

1. Observe the table design. The First field appears after the Last field.

2. Place the mouse pointer over the field selector for First until the pointer changes to a rightward-pointing arrow; then click on the field selector to select the field.

3. Now, place the mouse pointer over the field selector until the pointer changes to a leftward-pointing arrow; then press and

hold down the mouse button and drag the pointer upward. As you drag, a dark line appears above the Last field (see Figure 2.22). When it does, release the mouse button.

Figure 2.22   **Moving the First field**

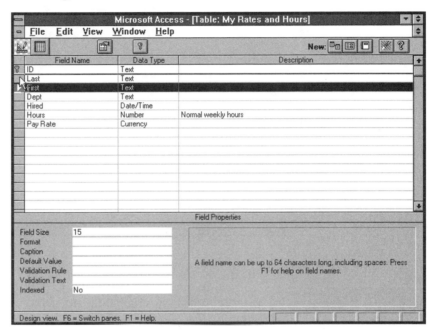

4. Observe the table design again. First now appears before Last.

5. Choose **File, Save** to save all the changes you have made to the table design. (Because the table is already named, you do not have to use the File, Save As command.)

 VIEWING THE MODIFIED TABLE AND ADDING VALUES

Now that you've finished modifying the table design, take a look at the table.

1. Click on the **Datasheet View button** (the second button from the left on the tool bar) to change to Datasheet view (see Figure 2.23).

Figure 2.23   **The modified table in Datasheet view**

Datasheet View
button

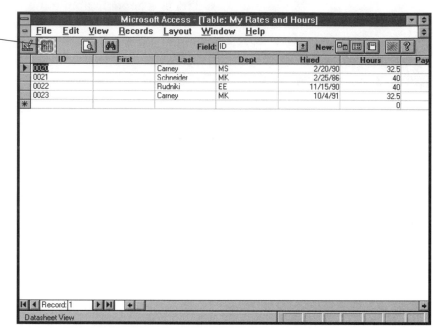

2. Examine the modified table. (You will need to use the horizontal scroll bar to view the entire table.) The First field is now part of the table, the last-name field is now named Last, the hired-date field in now named Hired, and there is no longer a Health field.

PRACTICE YOUR SKILLS

1. Using Figure 2.24 as a guide, add the following names to the First field. To move from one record to the next within the First field, remember to press **Down Arrow**.

ID:	First:
0020	**Joan**
0021	**Lillian**
0022	**Emilka**
0023	**Harry**

2. Move the focus off the last record to save it.

Figure 2.24   **The table after adding values to the first field**

ID	First	Last	Dept	Hired	Hours	Pay
0020	Joan	Carney	MS	2/20/90	32.5	
0021	Lillian	Schneider	MK	2/25/86	40	
0022	Emilka	Rudniki	EE	11/15/90	40	
0023	Harry	Carney	MK	10/4/91	32.5	
					0	

Microsoft Access - [Table: My Rates and Hours]

File Edit View Records Layout Window Help

Field: First   New:

Record: 5

Datasheet View

MODIFYING THE DATASHEET-VIEW LAYOUT

In Datasheet view, the widths of field columns are determined by default. If these default widths are inconvenient—for example, if they don't allow you to view the entire width of a field or of a table at one time—you can change each column width to suit your needs.

To narrow a column, place the mouse pointer on the right edge of the column's field selector until the pointer changes to a cross with a horizontal, two-headed arrow. (In Datasheet view, field selectors run across the top of the table and bear field names.) Then, drag the column boundary to the left until it is the desired width. To widen a column instead, drag to the right. When you narrow or widen a column, the entire table width decreases or increases by the same amount.

Changes made to the *Datasheet-view layout* do not affect a table's design or any of the field properties; they only affect the appearance of the table in Datasheet view.

To make permanent changes to the layout of Datasheet view, choose File, Save Layout after you have made your modifications.

Now reduce the width of some columns in your table so that you can view the entire table width without scrolling:

1. Place the mouse pointer on the right edge of the field selector labeled ID (at the top of the column). When you are positioned correctly, the mouse pointer will change to a cross with a horizontal two-headed arrow.

2. Now press the mouse button, drag the line to the left until it touches the *D* in ID, and then release the mouse button. The ID field column should now be about half its original width.

3. Narrow the Dept field to about half its original width.

4. Observe the table, and then compare it to Figure 2.25. You can now view the entire width of the table at once.

5. Choose **File, Save Layout** to save the new Datasheet-view layout.

Figure 2.25   **The table after changing the Datasheet-view layout**

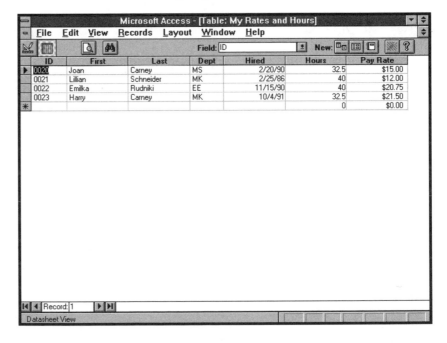

ID	First	Last	Dept	Hired	Hours	Pay Rate
0020	Joan	Carney	MS	2/20/90	32.5	$15.00
0021	Lillian	Schneider	MK	2/25/86	40	$12.00
0022	Emilka	Rudniki	EE	11/15/90	40	$20.75
0023	Harry	Carney	MK	10/4/91	32.5	$21.50
					0	$0.00

6. Close the table; then reopen and observe the My Rates and Hours table. Your layout changes remain in effect.

PREVIEWING THE TABLE

You learned in Chapter 1 that reports are the best way to present your data in print. However, if you just want a quick-and-dirty printout of a table or form, for example, Access can accommodate you.

As with reports, you can preview tables before you print them in order to make sure that what you want is what you are going to get.

Now preview and print your table:

1. Choose **File, Print Preview** (or, click on the third button from the left on the tool bar, the *Print Preview button*) to preview the printed table.

2. Observe the Table window. It now displays a full-page view of the table as it would print (see Figure 2.26).

Figure 2.26 **Previewing the table**

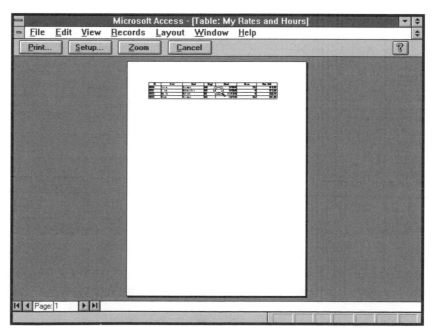

3. Place the mouse pointer over the table until it changes to a magnifying-glass icon; then click the **left mouse button** to view the page close up. (This technique is an alternative to clicking on the **Zoom** button.)

4. Use the **scroll bars** as necessary to view the table as it would print. Note that the printed table will include field names and grid lines, and will use the custom column widths you set in Datasheet view.

5. After verifying that your printer is on and properly connected, click on **Print** to open the Print dialog box, and then click on **OK** to print the table. (Or, if you'd prefer not to print, skip to step 6.)

6. Once you are done printing, click on **Cancel** in the Table window to return to Datasheet view. Then close the Table window and compare your printout to Figure 2.27.

SUMMARY

In this chapter, you developed a firm foundation for creating and working with tables. You now know how to design and create a table, use Cue Cards for help, create and modify fields, set a primary key, save a table design, add and save records, change the Datasheet-view layout, and preview and print a table.

Here's a quick reference guide to the Access features introduced in this chapter:

Desired Result	How to Do It
Switch to a table's Design view	From the Table window, choose **View, Table Design**; or, click on the **Design View button** on the tool bar
Select a field	Click on the field's field selector
Create a table	In the Database window, display table object names, and then click on **New**
Create a field	In the table's design grid, type a field name in the Field Name column, and then select a data type in the Data Type column; optionally, also type a description and set field properties

Figure 2.27   **The printed table**

ID	First	Last	Dept	Hired	Hours	Pay Rate
0020	Joan	Carney	MS	2/20/90	32.5	$15.00
0021	Lillian	Schneider	MK	2/25/86	40	$12.00
0022	Emilka	Rudniki	EE	11/15/90	40	$20.75
0023	Harry	Carney	MK	10/4/91	32.5	$21.50

Desired Result	How to Do It
Set field properties	In the table's design grid, press **F6** (or use the mouse) to move to the Field Properties pane; then type or select the desired properties
Access Cue Cards	Choose **Help, Cue Cards**
Set a primary key	Select the row or rows to include in the primary key; then choose **Edit, Set Primary Key** or click on the **Primary Key button** on the tool bar
Save a new table design	From the table's Design view, choose **File, Save As**, type a table name, and then click on **OK**
Save a modified table design	From the table's Design view, choose **File, Save**
Switch to a table's Datasheet view	From the table's Design view, choose **View, Datasheet** or click on the **Datasheet View button** on the tool bar
Scroll horizontally	Use the **horizontal scroll bar**
Add a record to a table	Place the insertion point in the last, blank table record, and then enter data in each field
Save an edited record	Move the focus off the record or choose **File, Save Record**
Change a field name	In the table's Design view, edit or replace the field name
Insert a field	In the table's Design view, select the field row at the position you want to insert a field, choose **Edit, Insert Row** or press the **Insert** key, and then use the resulting blank field row to define the field
Delete a field	In the table's Design view, select the field row; then choose **Edit, Delete Row** or press the **Delete** key

Desired Result	How to Do It
Move a field	In the table's Design view, click on the field selector to select the field row; then use the field selector to drag the field up or down to the desired position
Change a column width in Datasheet view	Place the mouse pointer on the right edge of the column's field selector until it changes into a cross with a horizontal, two-headed arrow. Then drag to the left (to narrow the column) or to the right (to widen the column)
Save changes to the Datasheet-view layout	Choose **File, Save Layout**
Preview a table	From the table's Datasheet view, select **File, Print Preview** or click on the **Print Preview button** on the tool bar
Print a table	Preview the table, click on **Print**, and then click on **OK**

In the next chapter, you'll learn how find and edit records in a table, and how to undo mistakes you might make while editing. With these skills, you'll be able to work quickly, efficiently, and confidently in tables of any size.

IF YOU'RE STOPPING HERE

If you need to break off here, please exit Access (for help, see "Exiting Access" in Chapter 1). If you want to proceed directly to the next chapter, please do so now.

CHAPTER 3: FINDING AND EDITING RECORDS

Finding Records

Editing Records

In Chapter 2, you learned how to design, create, add records to, preview, and print tables. In this chapter, you will learn how to work efficiently with tables once they contain many records. First, you'll learn more about the Edit, Find command to enhance the record-finding skills you developed in Chapter 1. Then you'll learn a number of techniques for editing records once you have found them, including how to undo your edits.

When you're done working through this chapter, you will know how to:

- Find records by searching through a specific field
- Find records by searching through all fields in a table
- Select records
- Delete records
- Undo and redo edits
- Copy values
- Copy records

FINDING RECORDS

Data management frequently involves finding and then editing specific records. As you learned in Chapter 1, Access' Find dialog box enables you to search for a record by specifying a value contained in one of the record's fields.

This chapter covers some of the options available in the Find dialog box that can help you to find records most efficiently.

 FINDING RECORDS WITH EDIT, FIND

As a review, you'll first find a record in the same way you did in Chapter 1. This time, however, you're going to see also that searches, by default, are not case sensitive. In other words, Access ignores whether values are in upper- or lowercase. For example, if you are searching for the name Smith, you can specify smith or SMITH and still find Smith.

If you do want a search to be case sensitive, you can check Match Case in the Find dialog box.

If you do not have both the Access application and EMPLOYEE Database windows opened and maximized, please open and maximize them now.

Now find your first record:

1. Open and examine the Projected New Rates table. It is similar to the table you created in Chapter 2.

2. Press **Tab** twice to move to and select the Last field.

3. Choose **Edit, Find** to open the Find in field: 'Last' dialog box; then observe the dialog box's title. Because Last is the current field and by default the Search In Current Field option is selected, Access will search only through the Last field (see Figure 3.1).

Figure 3.1   **The Find in field: 'Last' dialog box**

Find button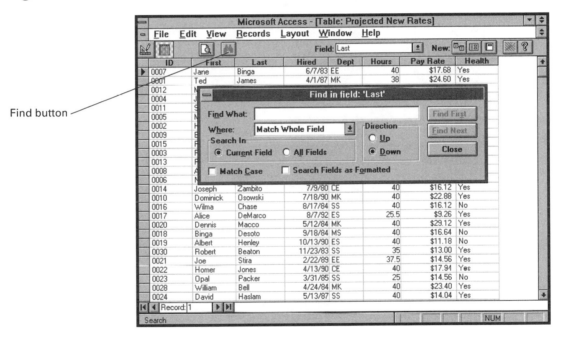

4. Observe the Match Case check box. By default, Match Case is not checked, so your search will not be case sensitive.

5. In the Find What text box, type **evans**, and then click on **Find First** to find the first occurrence of Evans. (Regardless of where the focus is—that is, the location in the table of the insertion point or selection—Access will always start searching from the first record in a table when you click on Find First.)

6. Observe the screen. Access has found and selected Evans, but the dialog box is most likely blocking the way. Note, however, that the status bar displays the message *Search succeeded*.

Also, you can see by the Specific Record Number box (in the lower-left corner of the Table window) that the current record has changed to Record 13. (Notice that record numbers do not necessarily match employee ID numbers.)

7. Move the dialog box out of the way by clicking and dragging on its title bar. (In Windows, you can use this technique to move any window that has a title bar.) As you move your mouse, your screen should look like Figure 3.2, with an outline indicating where the dialog box will move to when you release the mouse button.

8. Release the mouse button. You can now see that Access has selected Evans in Nancy Evans' record.

9. Click on **Close** to close the dialog box.

Figure 3.2   **Moving the dialog box**

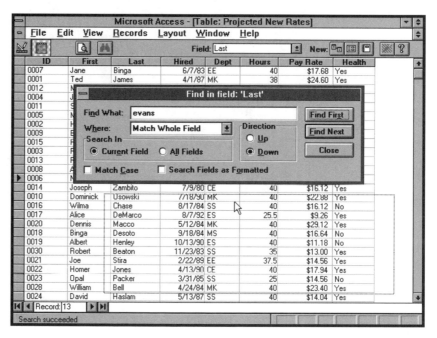

FINDING RECORDS WITH THE FIND BUTTON

You've already learned that you can open Access' Find dialog box by choosing Edit, Find. However, you can also use the *Find button*, the fourth button from the left on the tool bar; it displays a pair of binoculars.

Let's find a record using the Find button:

1. Verify that the focus is still in the Last field; then click on the **Find button** to open the Find in field: 'Last' dialog box. Note that Access places the find value you last used, evans, in the Find What text box.

2. Type **carter** to replace evans, and then click on **Find First**.

3. Click on **Close** to close the Find dialog box, and then observe the table. Access has selected Carter in Andrea Carter's record.

 USING FIND TO SEARCH ALL FIELDS

So far, you have searched for values only in the current field because, by default, Access selects the Search In Current Field option in the Find dialog box.

However, if you do not know what field holds the value for which you are searching, or if you know that the value is not in the current field, you can instead select the Search In All Fields option. Then Access will search every field in the table.

The chief disadvantage of using the Search In All Fields option, particularly in large tables, is that it can take Access significantly longer to perform searches. This is because Access has to sift through more data.

1. Press **Ctrl+Home** to move to the first field in the first record in the table.

2. Click on the **Find button** (or choose Edit, Find) to open the Find in field: 'ID' dialog box.

3. Type **binga** to replace carter. Then click on **Find First** to find the first occurrence of Binga.

4. Observe the screen. Access opens a dialog box to inform you that it found no match (even though a number of records contain the value Binga).

5. Click on **OK** to close the dialog box.

6. Observe the Find in field: 'ID' dialog box. The search was performed only in the ID field because ID is the current field and the Search In Current Field option is selected.

7. Select **Search In All Fields**; then observe the dialog box's title. It has changed from Find in field: 'ID' to Find to show that Access will now search through every field (see Figure 3.3).

Figure 3.3   **The Find dialog box**

8. Click on **Find First**, and then observe the table. The current record is now Jane Binga's record.

9. Click on **Find First** again. The focus does not move because when you click on Find First, Access always starts searching at the top of the table.

10. Click on **Find Next**; then observe the table. Access has found the *next* record containing Binga: Sam Binga's record. (Note that when you use Find Next, Access searches in the direction specified in the Find dialog box: either Up or Down. By default, the direction is Down.)

11. Click on **Find Next** three more times. Access finds Alice Binga's record, then Binga Desoto's record, and then displays a dialog box informing you that there are no more occurrences of Binga and asking if you want to search from the top of the table again.

12. Click on **No** to close the dialog box and stop searching.

13. Close the Find dialog box.

PRACTICE YOUR SKILLS

1. Find Barbara Stira's record (Record 27).

2. Close the Find dialog box.

EDITING RECORDS

In Chapter 2, you learned how to add records, a relatively straight-forward process.

When it comes to editing records, however, Access provides great flexibility so that you can use the editing techniques that are most appropriate for your situation. Ideally, you will find and use editing techniques that are easy to remember, easy to use, and, above all, save you time and typing.

 SELECTING AND DELETING VALUES AND RECORDS

In Chapter 2, you learned that you can select a single word by double-clicking on it. You've also seen a number of times, especially in dialog boxes, that you can usually delete and replace selected text just by typing over the text.

Now, you're going to learn a wider variety of ways to select and delete in Access, from fields to entire tables.

Let's start small and work our way up. Some ways you can select fields include

- Dragging over them

- Moving the mouse pointer to the left edge of a field until it changes to a rightward-pointing arrow, and then clicking once

- Placing the focus in an adjacent field, and then pressing Tab (to select the field to the right) or Shift+Tab (to select the field to the left)

- Placing the insertion point within the field and pressing F2 (F2 toggles between a selection and an insertion point)

- Placing the focus anywhere in the record, and then selecting the field name from the *Field drop-down list box* on the tool bar

You can select an entire record by:

- Clicking on the record selector (on the left end of the record)

- Placing the focus in the record, and then choosing Edit, Select Record

You can select multiple, *contiguous* records (that is, records that are all right next to each other) by:

- Clicking on the record selector of the first record in the group, and then dragging down to the last record

You can select multiple, *noncontiguous* records (that is, records that are not all next to one another) by:

- Holding down Ctrl while you click on each record's record selector

Finally, you can select all records in a table by:

- Clicking on the selector in the upper-left corner of the table, at the intersection of the record and field selectors

- Choosing Edit, Select All Records

Don't let these long lists of choices intimidate you. From each list, just pick one or two selection methods that suit you best. We'll use a sampling as we go through this chapter.

Once you've selected a field or record, you can delete it by choosing Edit, Delete or pressing the Delete key.

Let's find Bill Conner's record, select it, and then delete it.

1. Open and observe the Find dialog box. Note that Search In All Fields is still selected.

2. In the Find What text box, type **conner**, and then click on **Find First**.

3. Close the dialog box, and then observe the table. Access has found Bill Conner's record (Record 8).

4. Choose **Edit, Select Record** (or use any other record-selection technique) to select the entire record (see Figure 3.4).

5. Choose **Edit, Delete** (or press the Delete key).

6. Observe the dialog box that opens. For safety's sake, Access is asking you to confirm the deletion because once deleted, this record will be irretrievable.

7. Click on **OK** to delete the record.

Figure 3.4   **A selected record**

ID	First	Last	Hired	Dept	Hours	Pay Rate	Health
0007	Jane	Binga	6/7/83	EE	40	$17.68	Yes
0001	Ted	James	4/1/87	MK	38	$24.60	Yes
0012	Marie	Abel	11/25/82	CE	35.5	$7.02	Yes
0004	Julia	Binder	2/17/89	MK	25	$26.00	Yes
0011	Sam	Binga	7/5/80	SS	35.5	$13.83	No
0005	Maria	Sanders	8/17/90	ES	29.5	$17.68	Yes
0002	Harry	Harper	4/19/88	ES	40	$10.40	Yes
0009	Bill	Conner	3/8/91	CE	40	$6.55	Yes
0015	Roger	Donaldson	4/8/92	EE	40	$12.48	No
0003	Penny	Packer	1/15/81	MK	35	$24.96	Yes
0013	Robert	Abot	9/18/84	MK	40	$22.09	No
0008	Alice	Binga	9/1/85	EE	15.5	$16.38	Yes
0006	Nancy	Evans	5/20/86	EE	40	$15.60	No
0014	Joseph	Zambito	7/9/80	CE	40	$16.12	Yes
0010	Dominick	Osowski	7/18/90	MK	40	$22.88	Yes
0016	Wilma	Chase	8/17/84	SS	40	$16.12	No
0017	Alice	DeMarco	8/7/92	ES	25.5	$9.26	Yes
0020	Dennis	Macco	5/12/84	MK	40	$29.12	Yes
0018	Binga	Desoto	9/18/84	MS	40	$16.64	No
0019	Albert	Henley	10/13/90	ES	40	$11.18	No
0030	Robert	Beaton	11/23/83	SS	35	$13.00	Yes
0021	Joe	Stira	2/22/89	EE	37.5	$14.56	Yes
0022	Homer	Jones	4/13/90	CE	40	$17.94	Yes
0023	Opal	Packer	3/31/85	SS	25	$14.56	No
0028	William	Bell	4/24/84	MK	40	$23.40	Yes
0024	David	Haslam	5/13/87	SS	40	$14.04	Yes

UNDOING EDITS WITHIN A FIELD

As you edit records, there may be times when you want to reverse, or *undo*, a change that you've just made.

If you haven't yet left the field you are editing, you can undo your change by using any one of the following methods:

* Choosing Edit, Undo Typing

* Choosing Edit, Undo Current Field

* Pressing Esc

* Clicking on the Undo button, the second button from the right on the tool bar; it displays an erasing pencil

Note that these options are only available while you remain within the field you just changed. Should you move out of that field, but still remain within the same record, you can undo every change you've made to every field in that record by choosing Edit, Undo Current Record.

If you use Edit, Undo Typing or the Undo button to reverse a change, you can *redo* your edit (that is, undo your undo operation), by choosing Edit, Redo (u) Typing or clicking on the Undo button again.

Let's undo and redo some edits:

1. Find Maria Sanders' record.

2. Close the Find dialog box.

3. If necessary, select **Sanders**. Then type **Kossowski** to replace Sanders.

4. Choose **Edit, Undo Typing**; then observe the field. Access has changed Kossowski back to the original value, Sanders (see Figure 3.5).

5. Choose **Edit, Redo (u) Typing** to return the value to Kossowski.

6. Click on the **Undo button** to return the value to Sanders.

7. Click on the **Undo button** again to return the value to Kossowski.

Figure 3.5   **Undoing and redoing an edit**

Undo button

ID	First	Last	Hired	Dept	Hours	Pay Rate	Health
0007	Jane	Binga	6/7/83	EE	40	$17.68	Yes
0001	Ted	James	4/1/87	MK	38	$24.60	Yes
0012	Marie	Abel	11/25/82	CE	35.5	$7.02	Yes
0004	Julia	Binder	2/17/89	MK	25	$26.00	Yes
0011	Sam	Binga	7/5/80	SS	35.5	$13.83	No
0005	Maria	Sanders	8/17/90	ES	29.5	$17.60	Yes
0002	Harry	Harper	4/19/88	ES	40	$10.40	Yes
0015	Roger	Donaldson	4/8/92	EE	40	$12.48	No
0003	Penny	Packer	1/15/81	MK	35	$24.96	Yes
0013	Robert	Abot	9/18/84	MK	40	$22.09	No
0008	Alice	Binga	9/1/85	EE	15.5	$16.38	Yes
0006	Nancy	Evans	5/20/86	EE	40	$15.60	No
0014	Joseph	Zambito	7/9/80	CE	40	$16.12	Yes
0010	Dominick	Osowski	7/18/90	MK	40	$22.88	Yes
0016	Wilma	Chase	8/17/84	SS	40	$16.12	No
0017	Alice	DeMarco	8/7/92	ES	25.5	$9.26	Yes
0020	Dennis	Macco	5/12/84	MK	40	$29.12	Yes
0018	Binga	Desoto	9/18/84	MS	40	$16.64	No
0019	Albert	Henley	10/13/90	ES	40	$11.18	No
0030	Robert	Beaton	11/23/83	SS	35	$13.00	Yes
0021	Joe	Stira	2/22/89	ES	37.5	$14.56	Yes
0022	Homer	Jones	4/13/90	CE	40	$17.94	Yes
0023	Opal	Packer	3/31/85	SS	25	$14.56	No
0028	William	Bell	4/24/84	MK	40	$23.40	Yes
0024	David	Haslam	5/13/87	SS	40	$14.04	Yes
0025	Barbara	Stira	11/1/86	MK	40	$27.04	Yes

Microsoft Access - [Table: Projected New Rates]

File   Edit   View   Records   Layout   Window   Help

Field: Last   New:

Record: 6

Datasheet View

UNDOING EDITS TO A SAVED RECORD

The undo and redo options you just learned about are only available while you remain within the field or record you just changed.

Once you have saved a record (by moving the focus off that record or by choosing File, Save Record), the only way you can undo the changes you have just made is by choosing Edit, Undo Current Record. (By now, you may have noticed that the first command on the Edit menu changes to fit the situation. If you just typed some characters, the choice is Edit, Undo Typing; if you just chose Edit, Undo Typing, the choice is Edit, Redo (u) Typing; if you just saved a record, the choice is Edit, Undo Saved Record.)

A note of caution: All forms of the Edit, Undo command are available only until you perform another action that can be undone. That is, Edit, Undo commands can reverse only your previous action. For example, once you begin editing another record, you will no longer be able to undo the previous record changes. For safety's sake, only use Edit, Undo commands when you need them, and use them right away. If you start depending on the commands regularly, you will very likely find yourself in trouble.

Let's change Maria Kossowski's first name to Marianne, and then try out the Edit, Undo Saved Record command:

1. Press **Shift+Tab** to select Maria in the First field.

2. Click on **Edit** to open the Edit menu; then observe the first two menu choices. Because you moved from the field you just changed, the Undo Typing and Undo Current Field options are no longer available.

3. Click on **Edit** again to close the menu.

4. Press **F2** to change the selection in the First field to an insertion point at the end of the field.

5. Type **nne** to change Maria to Marianne.

6. Press **Down Arrow** to move the focus off the record, thereby saving the record.

7. Choose **Edit, Undo Saved Record**; then observe the record. Access has restored both the first and last names.

PRACTICE YOUR SKILLS

1. Change Maria's last name back to **Kossowski**.

2. Save the record.

3. Compare your screen to Figure 3.6.

Figure 3.6 **The table after changing the last name and saving the record**

ID	First	Last	Hired	Dept	Hours	Pay Rate	Health
0007	Jane	Binga	6/7/83	EE	40	$17.68	Yes
0001	Ted	James	4/1/87	MK	38	$24.60	Yes
0012	Marie	Abel	11/25/82	CE	35.5	$7.02	Yes
0004	Julia	Binder	2/17/89	MK	25	$26.00	Yes
0011	Sam	Binga	7/5/80	SS	35.5	$13.83	No
0005	Maria	Kossowski	8/17/90	ES	29.5	$17.68	Yes
0002	Harry	Harper	4/19/88	ES	40	$10.40	Yes
0015	Roger	Donaldson	4/8/92	EE	40	$12.48	No
0003	Penny	Packer	1/15/81	MK	35	$24.96	Yes
0013	Robert	Abot	9/18/84	MK	40	$22.09	No
0008	Alice	Binga	9/1/85	EE	15.5	$16.38	Yes
0006	Nancy	Evans	5/20/86	EE	40	$15.60	No
0014	Joseph	Zambito	7/9/80	CE	40	$16.12	Yes
0010	Dominick	Osowski	7/18/90	MK	40	$22.88	Yes
0016	Wilma	Chase	8/17/84	SS	40	$16.12	No
0017	Alice	DeMarco	8/7/92	ES	25.5	$9.26	Yes
0020	Dennis	Macco	5/12/84	MK	40	$29.12	Yes
0018	Binga	Desoto	9/18/84	MS	40	$16.64	No
0019	Albert	Henley	10/13/90	ES	40	$11.18	No
0030	Robert	Beaton	11/23/83	SS	35	$13.00	Yes
0021	Joe	Stira	2/22/89	EE	37.5	$14.56	Yes
0022	Homer	Jones	4/13/90	CE	40	$17.94	Yes
0023	Upal	Packer	3/31/85	SS	25	$14.56	No
0028	William	Bell	4/24/84	MK	40	$23.40	Yes
0024	David	Haslam	5/13/87	SS	40	$14.04	Yes
0025	Barbara	Stira	11/1/86	MK	40	$27.04	Yes

COPYING VALUES

As you add records to a table, you may find that you often repeat values from record to record. For example, in an employee-information table, several employees may have been hired on the same date, may work in the same department, or may work the same number of hours.

When this happens, you can save yourself some time and typing, plus increase your data accuracy, by copying values from other records.

If the same field in the previous record contains the value you need, you can copy that value down to the next record by moving the focus into the field of the lower record, and then pressing Ctrl+".

To copy a value from a record that is *not* directly above the record you are adding, you would follow these steps:

- Select the value.
- Choose Edit, Copy.
- Move to the field where you want to paste the value.
- Choose Edit, Paste.

Let's add a record, filling in some fields by copying values:

1. Click on the **Last Record navigation button**; then click on the **Next Record navigation button** to move to the blank record at the end of the table.

2. If necessary, press **Home** to move to the ID field.

3. In the ID field, type **0031**; then press **Tab**.

4. In the First field, type your first name, and then press **Tab**.

5. In the Last field, type your last name, and then press **Tab**.

6. In the Hired field, type today's date, and then press **Tab**.

7. Observe the Dept field of the record above your record. Your department code will be the same as John Ward's: ES.

8. In the Dept field for your record, press **Ctrl+"**; then observe your record. Access has copied the value from the field above into the current record.

9. Press **Tab** to move to the Hours field; then press **Ctrl+"** to copy 25 from John Ward's record into the current record (see Figure 3.7).

10. Press **Tab** to move to the Pay Rate field; then observe John Ward's pay rate. John Ward makes $8.84 per hour. However, your pay rate will match that of William Bell (Record 24).

11. Select the value in William Bell's Pay Rate field, **$23.40** (see Figure 3.8).

12. Choose **Edit, Copy**.

13. Now, place the insertion point back in the Pay Rate field for your record.

Figure 3.7   **Copying values from the previous record**

ID	First	Last	Hired	Dept	Hours	Pay Rate	Health
0011	Sam	Binga	7/5/80	SS	35.5	$13.83	No
0005	Maria	Kossowski	8/17/90	ES	29.5	$17.68	Yes
0002	Harry	Harper	4/19/88	ES	40	$10.40	Yes
0015	Roger	Donaldson	4/8/92	EE	40	$12.48	No
0003	Penny	Packer	1/15/81	MK	35	$24.96	Yes
0013	Robert	Abot	9/18/84	MK	40	$22.09	No
0008	Alice	Binga	9/1/85	EE	15.5	$16.38	Yes
0006	Nancy	Evans	5/20/86	EE	40	$15.60	No
0014	Joseph	Zambito	7/9/80	CE	40	$16.12	Yes
0010	Dominick	Osowski	7/18/90	MK	40	$22.88	Yes
0016	Wilma	Chase	8/17/84	SS	40	$16.12	No
0017	Alice	DeMarco	8/7/92	ES	25.5	$9.26	Yes
0020	Dennis	Macco	5/12/84	MK	40	$29.12	Yes
0018	Binga	Desoto	9/18/84	MS	40	$16.64	No
0019	Albert	Henley	10/13/90	ES	40	$11.18	No
0030	Robert	Beaton	11/23/83	SS	35	$13.00	No
0021	Joe	Stira	2/22/89	EE	37.5	$14.56	Yes
0022	Homer	Jones	4/13/90	CE	40	$17.94	Yes
0023	Opal	Packer	3/31/85	SS	25	$14.56	No
0028	William	Bell	4/24/84	MK	40	$23.40	Yes
0024	David	Haslam	5/13/87	SS	40	$14.04	Yes
0025	Barbara	Stira	11/1/86	MK	40	$27.04	Yes
0029	Andrea	Carter	8/23/84	EE	40	$16.64	Yes
0026	Ruth	Naylor	9/1/83	MK	40	$28.08	Yes
0027	John	Ward	4/24/92	ES	25	$8.84	No
0031	Christopher	Benz	5/14/93	ES	25		

Record: 30

Datasheet View

Figure 3.8   **Selecting a nonadjacent value for copying**

ID	First	Last	Hired	Dept	Hours	Pay Rate	Health
0011	Sam	Binga	7/5/80	SS	35.5	$13.83	No
0005	Maria	Kossowski	8/17/90	ES	29.5	$17.68	Yes
0002	Harry	Harper	4/19/88	ES	40	$10.40	No
0015	Roger	Donaldson	4/8/92	EE	40	$12.48	No
0003	Penny	Packer	1/15/81	MK	35	$24.96	Yes
0013	Robert	Abot	9/18/84	MK	40	$22.09	No
0008	Alice	Binga	9/1/85	EE	15.5	$16.38	Yes
0006	Nancy	Evans	5/20/86	EE	40	$15.60	No
0014	Joseph	Zambito	7/9/80	CE	40	$16.12	Yes
0010	Dominick	Osowski	7/18/90	MK	40	$22.88	Yes
0016	Wilma	Chase	8/17/84	SS	40	$16.12	No
0017	Alice	DeMarco	8/7/92	ES	25.5	$9.26	Yes
0020	Dennis	Macco	5/12/84	MK	40	$29.12	Yes
0018	Binga	Desoto	9/18/84	MS	40	$16.64	No
0019	Albert	Henley	10/13/90	ES	40	$11.18	No
0030	Robert	Beaton	11/23/83	SS	35	$13.00	Yes
0021	Joe	Stira	2/22/89	EE	37.5	$14.56	Yes
0022	Homer	Jones	4/13/90	CE	40	$17.94	Yes
0023	Opal	Packer	3/31/85	SS	25	$14.56	No
0028	William	Bell	4/24/84	MK	40	$23.40	Yes
0024	David	Haslam	5/13/87	SS	40	$14.04	Yes
0025	Barbara	Stira	11/1/86	MK	40	$27.04	Yes
0029	Andrea	Carter	8/23/84	EE	40	$16.64	Yes
0026	Ruth	Naylor	9/1/83	MK	40	$28.08	Yes
0027	John	Ward	4/24/92	ES	25	$8.84	No
0031	Christopher	Benz	5/14/93	ES	25		

Record: 24

Datasheet View

14. Choose **Edit, Paste**; then press **Tab**.

15. Observe your record. The Pay Rate field now displays $23.40.

16. In the Health field, press **Ctrl+"** to copy the value No from the previous record; then press **Tab** to save your record and move to the new blank record.

 COPYING A RECORD

If most of the values in a new record match those of an existing record, you may prefer to make a copy of the entire existing record, and then make changes as necessary. For example, if two employees were hired on the same day for the same job, the only differences in their records might be their names and addresses.

To copy an entire record to the blank record at the end of the table, you would follow these steps:

- Select the record you wish to copy.
- Choose Edit, Copy.
- Choose Edit, Paste Append.

You can also copy an entire record to a record that is not at the end of a table. To do this, you would follow these steps:

- Select the record you wish to copy.
- Choose Edit, Copy.
- Select the record you wish to copy to.
- Choose Edit, Paste.

Although this second method is more flexible, it does have two disadvantages: It requires more steps, and it completely overwrites any values in the record to which you copy.

Let's try both methods now:

1. Select Opal Packer's record (Record 23). This is the record you will copy.

2. Choose **Edit, Copy**.

3. Select William Bell's record (Record 24); then choose **Edit, Paste**.

4. Observe Record 24. The values from Opal Packer's record have completely overwritten the original values (see Figure 3.9).

Figure 3.9   **The table after pasting one record's values over another**

ID	First	Last	Hired	Dept	Hours	Pay Rate	Health
0005	Maria	Kossowski	8/17/90	ES	29.5	$17.68	Yes
0002	Harry	Harper	4/19/88	ES	40	$10.40	Yes
0015	Roger	Donaldson	4/8/92	EE	40	$12.48	No
0003	Penny	Packer	1/15/81	MK	35	$24.96	Yes
0013	Robert	Abot	9/18/84	MK	40	$22.09	No
0008	Alice	Binga	9/1/85	EE	15.5	$16.38	Yes
0006	Nancy	Evans	5/20/86	EE	40	$15.60	No
0014	Joseph	Zambito	7/9/80	CE	40	$16.12	Yes
0010	Dominick	Osowski	7/18/90	MK	40	$22.88	Yes
0016	Wilma	Chase	8/17/84	SS	40	$16.12	No
0017	Alice	DeMarco	8/7/92	ES	25.5	$9.26	Yes
0020	Dennis	Macco	5/12/84	MK	40	$29.12	Yes
0018	Binga	Desoto	9/18/84	MS	40	$16.64	No
0019	Albert	Henley	10/13/90	ES	40	$11.18	No
0030	Robert	Beaton	11/23/83	SS	35	$13.00	Yes
0021	Joe	Stira	2/22/89	EE	37.5	$14.56	Yes
0022	Homer	Jones	4/13/90	CE	40	$17.94	Yes
0023	Opal	Packer	3/31/85	SS	25	$14.56	No
0023	Opal	Packer	3/31/85	SS	25	$14.56	No
0024	David	Haslam	5/13/87	SS	40	$14.04	Yes
0025	Barbara	Stira	11/1/86	MK	40	$27.04	Yes
0029	Andrea	Carter	8/23/84	EE	40	$16.64	Yes
0026	Ruth	Naylor	9/1/83	MK	40	$28.08	Yes
0027	John	Ward	4/24/92	ES	25	$8.84	No
0031	Christopher	Benz	5/14/93	ES	25	$23.40	No

Record: 24

Datasheet View

5. Choose **Edit, Undo Current Record** to restore the original values to Record 24.

6. Now, choose **Edit, Paste Append**; then observe the end of the table. Access has pasted the values into a new record at the end of the table (see Figure 3.10).

PRACTICE YOUR SKILLS

1. In the new record, change the ID field to **0042**.

2. Change the First field to **Robert**.

3. Change the Hired field to today's date.

4. Change the Pay Rate field to **$11.00**.

5. Save the record.

6. Compare your record to Figure 3.11.

7. Close the Table window.

8. Close the Database window.

Figure 3.10   **The table after pasting the record at the end of the table**

ID	First	Last	Hired	Dept	Hours	Pay Rate	Health
0005	Maria	Kossowski	8/17/90	ES	29.5	$17.68	Yes
0002	Harry	Harper	4/19/88	ES	40	$10.40	Yes
0015	Roger	Donaldson	4/8/92	EE	40	$12.48	No
0003	Penny	Packer	1/15/81	MK	35	$24.96	Yes
0013	Robert	Abot	9/18/84	MK	40	$22.09	No
0008	Alice	Binga	9/1/85	EE	15.5	$16.38	Yes
0006	Nancy	Evans	5/20/86	EE	40	$15.60	No
0014	Joseph	Zambito	7/9/80	CE	40	$16.12	Yes
0010	Dominick	Osowski	7/18/90	MK	40	$22.88	Yes
0016	Wilma	Chase	8/17/84	SS	40	$16.12	No
0017	Alice	DeMarco	8/7/92	ES	25.5	$9.26	Yes
0020	Dennis	Macco	5/12/84	MK	40	$29.12	Yes
0018	Binga	Desoto	9/18/84	MS	40	$16.64	No
0019	Albert	Henley	10/13/90	ES	40	$11.18	No
0030	Robert	Beaton	11/23/83	SS	35	$13.00	Yes
0021	Joe	Stira	2/22/89	EE	37.5	$14.56	Yes
0022	Homer	Jones	4/13/90	CE	40	$17.94	Yes
0023	Opal	Packer	3/31/85	SS	25	$14.56	No
0028	William	Bell	4/24/84	MK	40	$23.40	Yes
0024	David	Haslam	5/13/87	SS	40	$14.04	Yes
0025	Barbara	Stira	11/1/86	MK	40	$27.04	Yes
0029	Andrea	Carter	8/23/84	EE	40	$16.64	Yes
0026	Ruth	Naylor	9/1/83	MK	40	$28.08	Yes
0027	John	Ward	4/24/92	ES	25	$8.84	No
0031	Christopher	Benz	5/14/93	ES	25	$23.40	No
0028	Opal	Packer	3/31/85	SS	25	$14.56	No

Record: 31

Figure 3.11   **The table after editing and saving the pasted record**

ID	First	Last	Hired	Dept	Hours	Pay Rate	Health
0005	Maria	Kossowski	8/17/90	ES	29.5	$17.68	Yes
0002	Harry	Harper	4/19/88	ES	40	$10.40	Yes
0015	Roger	Donaldson	4/8/92	EE	40	$12.48	No
0003	Penny	Packer	1/15/81	MK	35	$24.96	Yes
0013	Robert	Abot	9/18/84	MK	40	$22.09	No
0008	Alice	Binga	9/1/85	EE	15.5	$16.38	Yes
0006	Nancy	Evans	5/20/86	EE	40	$15.60	No
0014	Joseph	Zambito	7/9/80	CE	40	$16.12	Yes
0010	Dominick	Osowski	7/18/90	MK	40	$22.88	Yes
0016	Wilma	Chase	8/17/84	SS	40	$16.12	No
0017	Alice	DeMarco	8/7/92	ES	25.5	$9.26	Yes
0020	Dennis	Macco	5/12/84	MK	40	$29.12	Yes
0018	Binga	Desoto	9/18/84	MS	40	$16.64	No
0019	Albert	Henley	10/13/90	ES	40	$11.18	No
0030	Robert	Beaton	11/23/83	SS	35	$13.00	Yes
0021	Joe	Stira	2/22/89	EE	37.5	$14.56	Yes
0022	Homer	Jones	4/13/90	CE	40	$17.94	Yes
0023	Opal	Packer	3/31/85	SS	25	$14.56	No
0028	William	Bell	4/24/84	MK	40	$23.40	Yes
0024	David	Haslam	5/13/87	SS	40	$14.04	Yes
0025	Barbara	Stira	11/1/86	MK	40	$27.04	Yes
0029	Andrea	Carter	8/23/84	EE	40	$16.64	Yes
0026	Ruth	Naylor	9/1/83	MK	40	$28.08	Yes
0027	John	Ward	4/24/92	ES	25	$8.84	No
0031	Christopher	Benz	5/14/93	ES	25	$23.40	No
0042	Robert	Packer	5/14/93	SS	25	$11.00	No

Record: 31

PRACTICE YOUR SKILLS

In Chapters 1 through 3, you learned how to open and create tables, and how to add, find, and edit records. The following two activities give you an opportunity to apply these techniques.

After each activity step, a chapter reference (in parentheses) informs you where we introduced the relevant technique for that step.

Follow these steps to produce the table shown in Figure 3.12:

1. Open the **practice.mdb** database file; then maximize the Database window (Chapter 1).

2. Create a new table with the following fields (Chapter 2):

Field Name:	Data Type:	Field Size:
ID #	**Text**	**6**
Equipment	**Text**	**25**
Serial #	**Text**	**15**
Purchase Date	**Date/Time**	
Service	**Yes/No**	
Purchase Price	**Currency**	

3. Set the ID # field as the primary key; then save the table as **My Inventory** (Chapter 2).

4. Switch to Datasheet view, and then enter and save the following records (Chapter 2):

ID #:	Equipment:	Serial #:	Purchase Date:	Service:	Purchase Price:
CE1023	**80286 PC**	**5251-874**	**11/3/91**	**Yes**	**$899.00**
CE1275	**Dot-matrix printer**	**PO63458**	**10/14/89**	**No**	**$369.00**
MK0236	**Laptop PC**	**5123-354**	**2/1/92**	**No**	**$2,149.00**
MS1645	**Fax machine**	**TO/444**	**5/1/92**	**Yes**	**$795.00**

Figure 3.12 **The completed My Inventory table**

Inventory #	Equipment	Serial #	Purchase Price	Purchase Date	Service
CE1023	80286 PC	5251-874	$899.00	11/3/91	Yes
CE1275	Dot-matrix printer	PO63458	$369.00	10/14/89	No
MK0236	Laptop PC	5123-354	$2,149.00	2/1/92	Yes
MS1645	Fax Machine	8JK475	$795.00	5/1/92	Yes

5. Return to Design view and change the ID # field name to **Inventory #** (Chapter 2).

6. Move the Purchase Price field to between the Serial # and Purchase Date fields (Chapter 2).

7. Save the modified table design (Chapter 2).

8. Switch to Datasheet view and, in the record for the Laptop PC, change the Service field to **Yes** (Chapter 3).

9. In the record for the Fax machine, change the Serial # field to **8JK475** (Chapter 3).

10. Preview and print the table; then compare your printout to Figure 3.12 (Chapter 2).

11. Close the Table window (Chapter 1).

Follow these steps to produce the table shown in Figure 3.13:

1. Open the **Parking** table (Chapter 1).

2. Add a new record with the following data (Chapter 2):

Id:	Last	First	Park Lot	Park Rate
EN90	(*your last name*)	(*your first name*)	**NE**	**$65.50**

3. Find Eugene Davis' record and then copy it to the end of the table (Chapter 3).

4. In the new record, change the ID field to **EN91** (Chapter 3).

5. Change the First field to **Peter** (Chapter 3).

6. Find the record for the employee with the ID EN39; then change the Last field to **Cook** (Chapter 3).

7. Save the record; then undo the change you just made (Chapter 3).

Figure 3.13   **The completed Parking table**

ID	Last	First	Park Lot	Park Rate
EN01	James	Ted	SW	$50.00
EN03	Harper	Hanna	NW	$65.00
EN04	Packer	Penny	NW	$55.00
EN05	Binder	Julia		
EN07	Sanders	Maria		
EN08	Easter	Connie	NW	$62.00
EN10	Martin	Jane	SE	$55.50
EN11	Binga	Allison	SW	$55.75
EN12	Conner	Bill		
EN13	Osowski	Dominick	NE	$65.00
EN14	Binga	Sam	NW	$60.00
EN15	Abel	Murray	NE	$62.00
EN16	Abot	Robert	NW	$65.00
EN17	Zambito	Joseph	NE	$67.75
EN18	McDonald	Peter	NE	$60.00
EN19	Chase	Wilma	SE	$52.00
EN20	DeMarco	Arlene	SW	$55.00
EN23	Desoto	Frank	NE	$67.75
EN24	Henley	Albert	SE	$52.50
EN26	Kyler	Dennis		
EN27	Zangari	Nick	NE	$67.75
EN30	Jones	Hugh	SE	$55.00
EN32	Vetch	Randall	SW	$50.00
EN34	Horn	Jason	SE	$52.50
EN36	Castile	Abraham	NW	$60.50
EN38	Wilson	Judy	NW	$65.50
EN39	Ellis-Cook	Naja	SE	$50.00
EN40	Ward	Rodney	SW	$50.00
EN41	Abel	Gary	NE	$60.00
EN50	Cline	Darren	SW	$52.50
EN53	Bell	William	NE	$60.00
EN56	Maoni	Brad	NW	$67.75
EN57	Carter	Ben	NW	$65.00
EN62	Beaton	Robert	NW	$67.75
EN66	McCarthy	Kathryn	SE	$52.75
EN69	Petty	Suzanna	SE	$57.75
EN71	Beasley	Ken	NW	$65.50
EN72	Weinstein	Andrew	NE	$67.75
EN73	Berry	Sharon	SW	$55.00
EN74	Hartle	Susan	SW	$55.00
EN76	Smith	Patricia	SW	$52.50
EN77	Clark	Thomas	NW	$62.50
EN78	Russell	Larry	NE	$60.00
EN79	Pierce	Edward	SE	$57.50
EN80	Nelson	Luke	SE	$57.50
EN81	Davis	Eugene	NE	$60.00
EN83	Warfield	Cristin	NE	$62.50
EN85	Cassada	Bruce	NW	$65.50
EN86	Murray	Nancy	NW	$62.75
EN87	Gardner	Gayle	SW	$57.75
EN90	Benz	Christopher	NE	$65.50
EN91	Davis	Peter	NE	$60.00

8. Change the Last field to **Ellis-Cook**, and then save the record (Chapter 3).

9. Find Luke Nelson's record; then copy the values SE and $57.50 from the previous record into the Park Lot and Park Rate fields (Chapter 3).

10. Find and then delete David Stevens' record (Chapter 3).

11. Preview and print the table; then compare your printout to Figure 3.13 (Chapter 2).

12. Close the Table window; then close the Database window (Chapter 1).

SUMMARY

In this chapter, you learned how to search for records, select and delete records, undo and redo edits, copy values, and copy records.

Here's a quick reference guide to the Access features introduced in this chapter:

Desired Result	How to Do It
Search for a value in a specific field	Move to the field in which you want to search, choose **Edit, Find** (or, click on the **Find Button**), type a search value in the Find What text box, select **Search In Current Field**, and then click on **Find First** to find the first occurrence of the value (or, click on **Find Next** to find the next occurrence of the value)
Search for a value in all fields	Choose **Edit, Find** (or, click on the **Find Button**), type a search value in the Find What text box, select **Search In All Fields**, and then click on **Find First** to find the first occurrence of the value (or, click on **Find Next** to find the next occurrence of the value)

Desired Result	How to Do It
Select a field	Drag over the field; or, move the mouse pointer to the left edge until it changes to a rightward-pointing arrow, and then click once; or, place the focus in an adjacent field, and then press **Tab** to select the field to the right (or press **Shift+Tab** to select the field to the left); or, place the insertion point within the field and press **F2**; or, place the focus anywhere within the record, and then select the field name from the **Field drop-down list box** on the tool bar
Select a record	Click on the **record selector**; or, place the focus in the record, and then choose **Edit, Select Record**
Select multiple, contiguous records	Click on the first record's **record selector**; then drag down
Select multiple, noncontiguous records	Hold down **Ctrl** while you click on each record's **record selector**
Select all records	Click on the **selector** in the upper-left corner of the table; or, choose **Edit, Select All Records**
Undo a field edit	Choose **Edit, Undo Typing**; choose **Edit, Undo Current Field**; press **Esc**; or, click on the **Undo button**
Redo an edit	Choose **Edit, Redo (u) Typing**; or, click on the **Undo button**
Undo all edits to an unsaved record	Choose **Edit, Undo Current Record**
Undo all edits to a saved record	Choose **Edit, Undo Saved Record**

Desired Result	How to Do It
Copy a value down from the previous record	Place the focus in the appropriate field in the second record; then press **Ctrl+"**
Copy a value from a non-adjacent record	Select the value to be copied, choose **Edit, Copy,** place the focus in the field to which you are copying, and then choose **Edit, Paste**
Copy a record	Select the record to be copied, choose **Edit, Copy,** select the record to which you are copying, and then choose **Edit, Paste**
Copy a record to the end of a table	Select the record to be copied, choose **Edit, Copy,** and then choose **Edit, Paste Append**

In the next chapter, you'll learn how to run, create, and save queries; how to sort records in queries; how to set criteria in queries; and how to perform calculations in queries.

IF YOU'RE STOPPING HERE

If you need to break off here, please exit Access (for help, see "Exiting Access" in Chapter 1). If you want to proceed directly to the next chapter, please do so now.

CHAPTER 4: QUERY BASICS

Specifying Fields
and Sorting
Records

Setting Criteria in
a Query

Performing
Calculations in
Queries

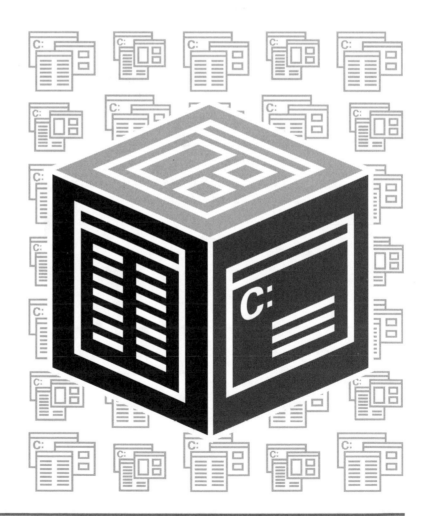

In Chapters 2 and 3, you learned how to create tables, add data to tables, and find and edit that data. In this chapter, you will take a closer look at using queries to control and ask questions about that data. Queries help you work efficiently with large amounts of data by enabling you to use the same data in many different ways to suit many different tasks. For example, from the same employee-information table, you can use one query to review employee pay rates, a second query to update home addresses, and a third query to calculate each department's weekly salary expenses.

When you are done working through this chapter, you will know how to

- Use select queries and dynasets
- View a query's design
- Create, design, and save queries
- Control the number of visible fields
- Sort records in a query
- Set criteria
- Edit values in a dynaset
- Perform calculations in queries

SPECIFYING FIELDS AND SORTING RECORDS

Because of the often huge amounts of data stored in tables, two primary uses of queries are to limit the number of visible fields and to sort records in the most useful order. (In Chapter 1, you learned how to sort records through a form's Filter window. As you'll see, however, queries provide a more powerful and convenient way to sort records without a filter.)

For example, if you need to review data about employee work hours, you can make the task easier by:

- Only viewing employee names and work hours, rather than wading through data such as home addresses, pay rates, health-insurance status, and so on
- Sorting the data in a useful order, such as alphabetically by employee last name or numerically by number of hours worked

Access calls these types of queries—queries that you use to select and view records—*select queries*. Unlike *action queries*, which can change data, select queries never change data; they only rearrange your view of it. Throughout this chapter, we'll be working solely with select queries. You'll learn more about other types of queries in Chapter 7.

RUNNING A SELECT QUERY

As a review of Chapter 1, you're going to examine an employee-information table, Hours and Rates, and then run a select query, MK Staff and Rates, that is based on that table.

Access calls the result of running a query a *dynaset*: a dynamic subset of the table's fields and records that answers the query. One reason that dynasets are dynamic is that they change as the data in your tables change. Remember from Chapter 1 that a query is a stored question, *not* the answer to, or dynaset of, that question. This arrangement enables dynasets to be dynamic by always reflecting the most current data.

If you do not have both the Access application and the Employee Database windows open and maximized, please open and maximize them now.

Let's run a select query:

1. Open and examine the Hours and Rates table. The table contains ID, Last, First, Hired, Dept, Hours, Pay Rate, and Health fields (see Figure 4.1).

Figure 4.1   **The Hours and Rates table**

ID	Last	First	Hired	Dept	Hours	Pay Rate	Health
0001	James	Ted	4/1/87	MK	38	$23.65	Yes
0002	Harper	Harry	4/19/88	ES	40	$10.00	Yes
0003	Packer	Penny	1/15/81	MK	35	$24.00	Yes
0004	Binder	Julia	2/17/89	MK	25	$25.00	Yes
0005	Sanders	Maria	8/17/90	ES	29.5	$17.00	Yes
0006	Evans	Nancy	5/20/86	EE	40	$15.00	No
0007	Martin	Jane	6/7/83	EE	40	$17.00	Yes
0008	Binga	Alice	9/1/85	EE	15.5	$15.75	Yes
0009	Conner	Bill	3/8/91	CE	40	$6.30	Yes
0010	Osowski	Dominick	7/18/90	MK	40	$22.00	Yes
0011	Binga	Sam	7/5/80	SS	35.5	$13.30	No
0012	Abel	Marie	11/25/82	CE	35.5	$6.75	Yes
0013	Abot	Robert	9/18/84	MK	40	$21.24	No
0014	Zambito	Joseph	7/9/80	CE	40	$15.50	Yes
0015	Donaldson	Roger	4/8/92	EE	40	$12.00	No
0016	Chase	Wilma	8/17/84	SS	40	$15.50	No
0017	DeMarco	Alice	8/7/92	ES	25.5	$8.90	Yes
0018	Desoto	Frank	9/18/84	MS	40	$16.00	No
0019	Henley	Albert	10/13/90	ES	40	$10.75	No
0020	Binga	Dennis	5/12/84	MK	40	$28.00	Yes
0021	Stira	Joe	2/22/89	EE	37.5	$14.00	Yes
0022	Jones	Homer	4/13/90	CE	40	$17.25	Yes
0023	Packer	Opal	3/31/85	SS	25	$14.00	No
0024	Haslam	David	5/13/87	SS	40	$13.50	Yes
0025	Stira	Barbara	11/1/86	MK	40	$26.00	Yes
0026	Naylor	Ruth	9/1/83	MK	40	$27.00	Yes

Microsoft Access - [Table: Hours and Rates]

File   Edit   View   Records   Layout   Window   Help

Field: ID   New:

Record: 1

Datasheet View

2. Close the Table window.

3. In the Database window, click on the **Query object button** to display the list of query object names.

4. Double-click on **MK Staff and Rates** to run the query.

5. Observe the Query window. It contains a dynaset that displays the Marketing department employees' department code (MK), last name, first name, and pay rate (see Figure 4.2).

6. Compare the dynaset to the Hours and Rates table shown in Figure 4.1. The dynaset displays only some of the fields and records from this table.

Figure 4.2   **The MK Staff and Rates query's dynaset**

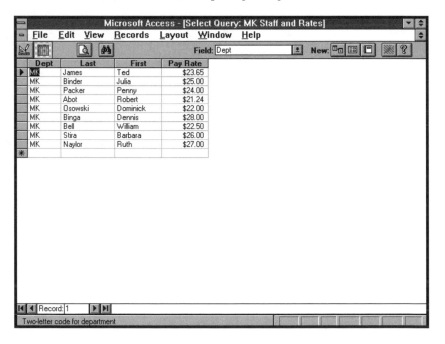

 EXAMINING THE QUERY DESIGN

Like Table windows, Query windows have two views: Design view and Datasheet view. Datasheet view (the only view of the Query window you've seen so far) displays a query's dynaset; Design view displays the query's design.

To switch a Query window from Datasheet view to Design view, choose View, Query Design or click on the leftmost button on the tool bar, the Design View button, which displays graphic design tools. (You can also open a Query window in Design view from the Database window by selecting the query object name, and then clicking on Design.)

In Design view, Access divides the Query window into two panes. (Notice that a Query window in Design view looks very similar to the Form window's Filter window you saw in Chapter 1.) The upper pane contains the field list or lists of the tables or queries upon which the query is based. (We'll look at queries based on multiple tables in Chapter 7.) The lower pane contains a *QBE* (*Query-by-Example*) *grid* that provides columns for specifying fields in the query, and rows for specifying:

- The order in which the query should sort records

- Whether the query should show fields in its dynaset

- Criteria to determine what records the query should include in its dynaset

Let's look at the design of the MK Staff and Rates query:

1. Choose **View, Query Design** to switch to the Query window's Design view (see Figure 4.3).

2. Observe the upper pane of the Query window. Because this query is based on the Hours and Rates table, the upper pane displays that table's field list.

3. Observe the lower pane. It contains a QBE grid.

4. Observe the Dept column in the QBE grid. The Criteria cell is set to "MK."

5. Compare the QBE grid to Figure 4.2. Note that for each column in the grid with a field name, there is a corresponding column in the dynaset, and the order of columns in the QBE grid determines the order of columns in the dynaset. Also, because of the criterion set in the QBE grid's Dept column, Access displays only MK Department employees in the dynaset.

6. Close the Query window.

Figure 4.3   **The MK Staff and Rates query design**

Field list

QBE grid

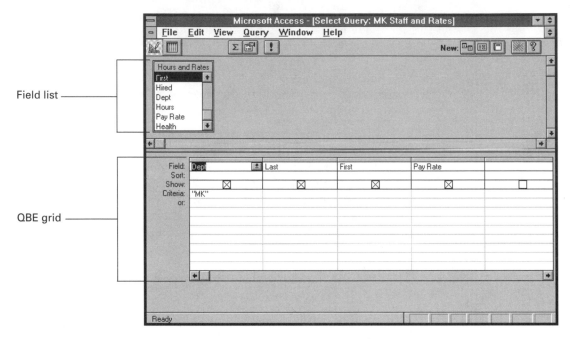

CREATING A QUERY AND SELECTING A TABLE

In addition to running existing queries, you can create your own query by opening a new, blank Query window, or by modifying an existing query and saving it with a new name.

You'll start by creating a new query from scratch. By default, Access sets all new queries as select queries. (You'll learn how to modify the query type in Chapter 7.)

To create a new query from the Database window, display the list of query object names, and then click on New. Access will open a new, blank Query window in Design view, and will then open an Add Table dialog box from which you can select the tables or queries upon which to base your query.

In this chapter, you'll create queries based upon single tables. In Chapter 7, you'll learn how to create queries based on other queries and on multiple tables. To create a single-table query from this point, select the desired table name, click on Add to add the table's field list to the upper pane of the Query window, and then click on Close to close the Add Table dialog box.

Let's create a new query now:

1. With query object names displayed in the Database window, click on **New** to open a new Query window in Design view.

2. Observe the Add Table dialog box. This dialog box enables you to select the tables and/or queries upon which to base your new query.

3. Select **Hours and Rates**; then click on **Add** to base your query on the Hours and Rates table.

4. Click on **Close** to close the Add Table dialog box.

5. Observe the Query window. The upper pane displays the field list of the Hours and Rates table; the QBE grid in the lower pane is empty, because you've created the query from scratch (see Figure 4.4).

Figure 4.4   **The new Query window**

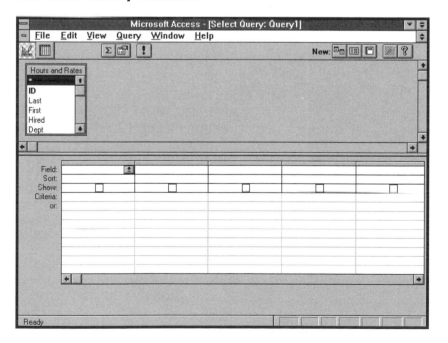

6. Open and examine the Query menu. Access has checked the Select option by default, making your new query a select query.

7. Close the **Query** menu.

 SPECIFYING FIELDS

You can use queries to limit the number of fields that you view by specifying in the QBE grid's Field row only the names of the fields you want to see. By adding fields to the QBE grid, you are asking Access: What are the values in just these fields?

Two ways to specify a field name in a Field cell are

- Place the insertion point in the Field cell, click on the resulting drop-down list arrow, and then select the desired field name from the list that opens.

- Select the field name from the table's field list in the upper pane, and then drag the field name to the Field cell.

Once you place a field name in a Field cell, Access automatically checks the check box in the Show row so that the field will display in the dynaset. If you do not wish to have a field displayed in the dynaset, uncheck the Show box. (You'll see some reasons for unchecking the Show box in Chapter 7.)

Let's build a query now by specifying some fields:

1. In the leftmost Field cell of the QBE grid, click on the **drop-down list arrow** to display a list of field names from the Hours and Rates table (see Figure 4.5); then select **Dept**. (This drop-down list contains the same field names as the field list in the upper pane.)

2. Observe the Dept column. Access has automatically checked the check box in the Show row (the third row) so that when the query is run, it will display the Dept field in its dynaset.

3. In the Hours and Rates field list in the upper pane, select **Last**; then start to drag the field name to the second Field cell of the QBE grid.

4. As you drag, notice that the mouse pointer changes alternately to a *field icon* (which appears as a small rectangle) and to a slashed circle. The field icon displays when the pointer is over the field list or the QBE grid, indicating an appropriate area to place the field name; the slashed circle displays when the pointer is over an area in which you cannot place the field name.

Figure 4.5   **Selecting a field name from a Field cell's drop-down list box**

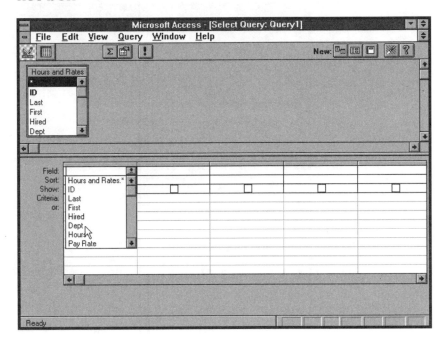

5. When the field icon displays in the second Field cell of the QBE grid, release the mouse button to add the Last field to the grid. Notice that Access has again checked the Show box for you.

PRACTICE YOUR SKILLS

1. Add the First and Pay Rate fields, respectively, to the third and fourth Field cells of the QBE grid (you may need to scroll through the field list to find the Pay Rate field name).

2. Compare your screen to the one shown in Figure 4.6.

RUNNING THE QUERY AND OBSERVING THE DYNASET

While you are designing a select query, you can view the query's dynaset by switching from Design view to Datasheet view, thereby running the query.

Figure 4.6   **The query design after adding four fields**

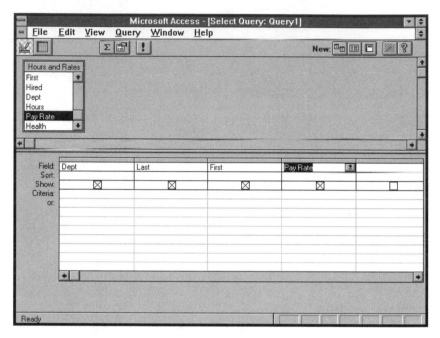

To run a select query and switch to Datasheet view, choose Query, Run, or click on the second button from the left on the tool bar, the Datasheet View button, which displays a miniature grid. Once in Datasheet view, Access will display a dynaset that answers your query by showing you the values in the fields you specified.

Let's run our query now:

1. Choose **Query, Run** to run the query and switch to Datasheet view.

2. Observe the dynaset. It displays only the four fields you specified in Design view, and in the order you specified them: Dept, Last, First, and Pay Rate (see Figure 4.7).

SORTING RECORDS IN A QUERY

By default, Access displays records in a dynaset in the order they have in the query's underlying tables and/or queries. You can sort your data, however, to make it easier to review and edit.

Figure 4.7   **The query's dynaset**

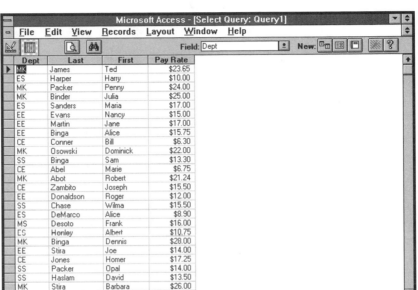

You can sort dynaset records in alphabetical, numerical, or chronological order by selecting options in the QBE grid's *Sort row* before running the query.

Selecting a sort option in a query's QBE grid is much like selecting a sort option in a Form window's Filter window (as you did in Chapter 1). Place the insertion point in the Sort cell of the field by which you want to sort records. (For example, if you want to sort by last name, place the insertion point in the Sort cell for the last-name field.) Then click on the cell's resulting drop-down list arrow. Finally, select the desired sort option, either Ascending or Descending.

You may also want to sort on multiple levels. For example, you may want to sort first by last name and then by first name, as in a telephone book. To instruct Access to perform such multiple-level sorts, select sort options for multiple fields. Access will sort records by the leftmost sort field first, and will then work its way rightward through the other sort fields. For example, if in your QBE grid the last-name field is leftmost, followed by the first-name field, and you set a sort option for both fields, Access will sort the records in the resulting dynaset first by last name, then by first name. Thus, Access would sort John Smith after Mary Quinn, and before Mary Smith.

In a query, you can sort on up to ten fields at one time.

Let's specify a two-level sort for our query, sorting first by last name, then by first name:

1. Compare your dynaset and the dynaset pictured in Figure 4.7 to the Hours and Rates table pictured in Figure 4.1. The records in the dynaset are in the same order as they are in the table.

2. Click on the **Design View button** to return to Design view (or choose **View, Query Design.**)

3. In the QBE grid's Last column (that is, the column containing the field name Last), click in the **Sort cell** (in the second row) to display the cell's drop-down list arrow.

4. Click on the **drop-down list arrow,** and then select **Ascending** to instruct the query to sort records in ascending order by last name (see Figure 4.8).

Figure 4.8 **Selecting a sort option**

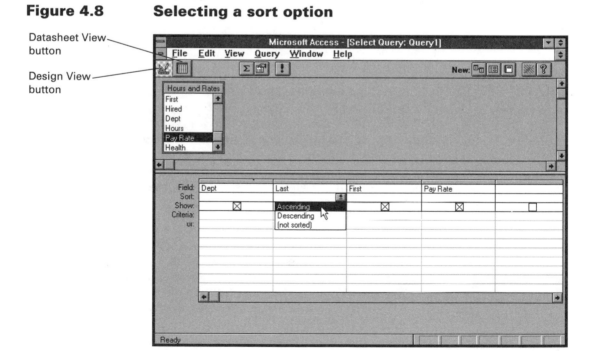

Datasheet View button

Design View button

5. In the First field's Sort cell (that is, the Sort cell of the column containing the field name First), select **Ascending** from the drop-down list box to specify a second-level sort by first name (that is, a sort *after* the last-name sort).

6. Click on the **Datasheet View button** to run the query (or choose **Query, Run**).

7. Observe the dynaset. Access has now sorted the records by last name, and then by first name (see Figure 4.9). Note particularly the Bingas, who are sorted together, and then alphabetically by first name (Alice, Dennis, Sam).

Figure 4.9 **The sorted dynaset**

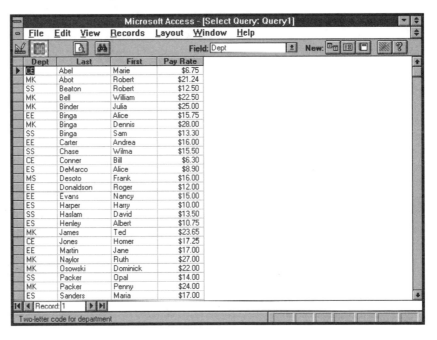

SAVING AND NAMING THE QUERY

As mentioned, one of the advantages of queries over a Form window's Filter window is that you can save a query as a database object. Then, the next time you want to run the query, you can simply double-click on the query object name rather than taking the trouble to recreate the query.

To save the design of a query from Datasheet view, you would follow these steps:

- Choose File, Save Query As (from Design view, choose File, Save As) to open the Save As dialog box.

- Type a name for the query. Query names are subject to the same rules as table and field names, and can't have the same name as an existing table.

- Click on OK.

Access will then automatically add your query name to the list of query object names in the Database window.

Let's save our query design:

1. Choose **File, Save Query As** to open the Save As dialog box.

2. In the Query Name text box, type **My Pay Rates**, and then click on **OK** to name and save the query.

3. Observe the title bar. It now displays your new query name.

4. Close the Query window; then observe the Database window. My Pay Rates now appears in the list of query object names.

 ADDING MULTIPLE FIELDS TO A QUERY

When you are adding multiple fields to a query's QBE grid, you can save yourself some effort by selecting all of the desired field names in field list, and then dragging them together to the QBE grid.

To add multiple field names to the QBE grid, you would follow these steps:

- In the Query window's Design view, select from the field list the first field name you wish to add.

- Press and hold Ctrl, click on the other field names you wish to add, and then release Ctrl.

- Place the mouse pointer over one of the selected field names in the field list, and then drag down to the next available Field cell in the QBE grid.

Access will add all of the selected field names, each in their own column, to the QBE grid, and will arrange the field names left to right in the order in which they are listed down in the field list.

Let's add multiple fields—First, Hours, and Pay Rate—to the QBE grid of an existing query:

1. Examine Figure 4.10. It pictures the Employee Rates table.

2. In the Database window, select the **Employee List** query object name; then click on **Design** to open the query in Design view.

3. Observe the field list in the Query window's upper pane. This query is based on the Employee Rates table.

4. In the field list, select **First**.

5. Press and hold down **Ctrl**, select **Hours** and **Pay Rate**, and then release **Ctrl**. All three field names—First, Hours, and Pay Rate—should now be selected.

Figure 4.10   **The Employee Rates table**

Last	First	ID	Dept	Hired	Hours	Pay Rate	Health
Abe	Marie	0012	CE	11/25/82	35.5	$6.75	Yes
Abot	Robert	0013	MK	9/18/84	40	$21.24	No
Beaton	Robert	0030	SS	11/23/83	35	$12.50	Yes
Bell	William	0028	MK	4/24/84	40	$22.50	Yoo
Binder	Julia	0004	MK	2/17/89	25	$25.00	Yes
Binga	Alice	0008	EE	9/1/85	15.5	$15.75	Yes
Binga	Dennis	0020	MK	5/12/84	40	$28.00	Yes
Binga	Jane	0007	EE	6/7/83	40	$17.00	Yes
Binga	Sam	0011	SS	7/5/80	35.5	$13.30	No
Carter	Andrea	0029	EE	8/23/84	40	$16.00	Yes
Chase	Wilma	0016	SS	8/17/84	40	$15.50	No
Conner	Bill	0009	CE	3/8/91	40	$6.30	Yes
DeMarco	Alice		ES	8/7/92	25.5	$8.90	Yes
Desoto	Frank	0018	MS	9/18/84	40	$16.00	No
Donaldson	Roger		EE	4/8/92	40	$12.00	No
Evans	Nancy	0006	EE	5/20/86	40	$15.00	No
Harper	Harry	0002	ES	4/19/88	40	$10.00	Yes
Haslam	David	0024	SS	5/13/87	40	$13.50	Yes
Henley	Albert	0019	ES	10/13/90	40	$10.75	No
James	Ted	0001	MK	4/1/87	38	$23.65	Yes
Jones	Homer	0022	CE	4/13/90	40	$17.25	Yes
Naylor	Ruth	0026	MK	9/1/83	40	$27.00	Yes
Osowski	Dominick	0010	MK	7/18/90	40	$22.00	Yes
Packer	Opal	0023	SS	3/31/85	25	$14.00	No
Packer	Penny	0003	MK	1/15/81	35	$24.00	Yes
Sanders	Maria	0005	ES	8/17/90	29.5	$17.00	Yes

6. Place the mouse pointer on one of the selected field names and drag the *multiple field icon* (which appears as multiple overlapping rectangles) to the QBE grid's fourth Field cell.

7. Observe the QBE grid (see Figure 4.11). You have just added all three field names simultaneously (you may need to scroll horizontally to see all of the columns).

Figure 4.11   **The Employee List query after adding multiple fields**

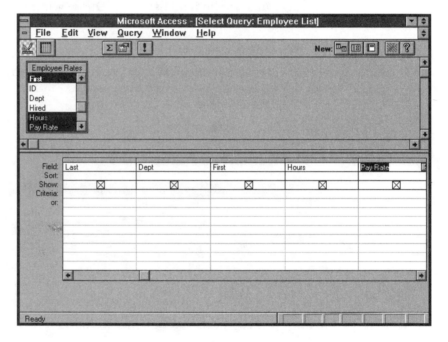

 REARRANGING THE QBE GRID

When you add multiple fields to a query's QBE grid at one time, Access inserts the field names in the order they have in the under-lying table or query's field list. Because the order of columns in a query's QBE grid determines the order of fields in the resulting dynaset, this can be disconcerting if you have logically connected fields that are not adjacent to each other in your dynaset (for example, if your dynaset lists first names, then pay rates, then last names, then hours).

However, you can rearrange the columns in a QBE grid much as you can rearrange the columns in a Table window's Datasheet view: Click on the column's field selector to select the column, point to the field selector, and then drag the selected column to the desired location. (As you drag, Access will display a dark line to indicate the new location of the selected column.) When you save the query design, the new order of the columns will become a permanent part of the design.

Let's rearrange the current QBE grid:

1. Observe the order of the columns in the QBE grid, then run the query (choose **Query, Run** or click on the **Datasheet View button**) and observe the dynaset. Fields appear in the dynaset in the order in which they are arranged in the QBE grid.

2. Return to Design view (choose **View, Query Design** or click on the **Design View button**).

3. Position the mouse pointer on the field selector for the First column (the button directly above the Field cell) until the mouse pointer changes to a downward-pointing arrow.

4. Click on the **field selector** to select the First column; then drag the selected column immediately to the left of the Last column (see Figure 4.12).

5. Run the query again, and then observe the dynaset. The First field now appears just before the Last field.

SETTING CRITERIA IN A QUERY

So far, the queries you have created and modified have enabled you only to limit visible fields and to sort records. In every case, though, the dynaset has displayed *every* record from the underlying table.

Another important feature of queries, however, is their ability to select only those records that meet certain criteria. For example, the MK Staff and Rates query selected only the records of Marketing Department employees.

Criteria can require an exact match for a specific value (for example, only records for employees who work exactly 40 hours per week) or a more general match (for example, the records of every employee whose last name begins with *B*, or the records of every employee who makes more than $10 per hour).

Figure 4.12   **Dragging the First column in the QBE grid**

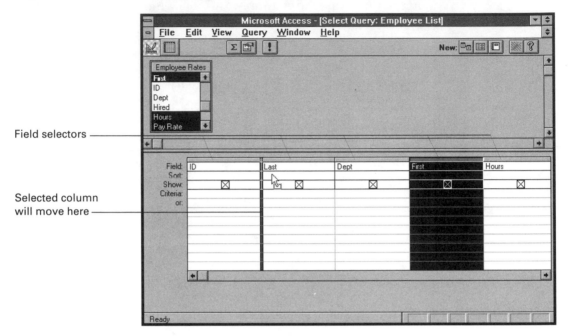

Field selectors

Selected column
will move here

SETTING CRITERIA

To set an exact criterion for a query, type the criterion in the appropriate Criteria cell. For example, in the MK Staff and Rates query, the query selected only records for Marketing department employees because the criterion "MK" (the two-letter code for the Marketing department) was set in the Dept column's Criteria cell. The query would not select records with MC or mk values in their Dept fields because those records would not exactly match the criterion (exact criteria are case sensitive).

When you enter criteria in a Criteria cell and then leave that cell, Access often adjusts the format of the criteria for the sake of conformity (much as it adjusted the format of a date you entered in Chapter 2 from 2-20-90 to 2/20/90). When you enter text as criteria, Access adds double quotation marks around that text; when you enter a date, Access adds pound signs (#) around the date. You can always add this punctuation yourself when you type the criteria, but it's usually easier to let Access do the job for you.

Let's add a criterion to your query so that the query will only select the records of Chemical Engineering department employees:

1. Return to Design view.

2. Click in the Dept column's Criteria cell (in the fourth row).

3. Type **CE** to specify that the query select only those records where the value in the Dept field is CE (Chemical Engineering).

4. Press **Tab**, and then observe the Criteria cell. Access automatically entered double quotation marks around CE.

5. Run the query, and then observe the dynaset. It displays only the records for the four Chemical Engineering (CE) department employees (see Figure 4.13).

6. Save the modified query as **My CE Employee List** (use the **File, Save Query As** command).

Figure 4.13   **The dynaset displaying records for Chemical Engineering Department employees**

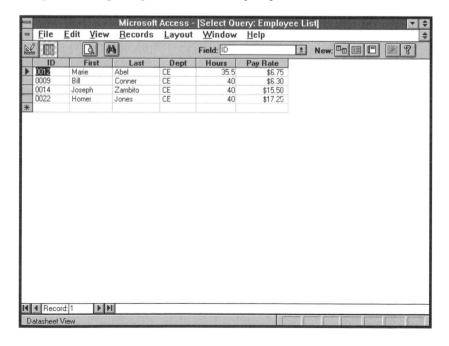

SETTING CRITERIA WITH A WILDCARD CHARACTER

To set criteria that are *not* exact, you can use the wildcard characters * (asterisk) and ? (question mark). You can use the asterisk to represent any number of characters. For example, B* in a last-name column's Criteria cell would specify any name of any length beginning with B. Use the question mark to represent any single character. For example, B??? could specify Bell or Bean, but would exclude Bon and Binga.

When you use a wildcard character in a criterion, Access adjusts the criterion by placing double quotation marks around what you typed and adds the *Like operator* and a space before the first quotation mark. The Like operator instructs Access to search for values that follow a certain pattern, rather than searching for exact matches. (You will learn about other criteria operators and their uses later in this chapter.) Criteria that use wildcard characters are not case sensitive.

Let's delete your current criterion for the Dept field and set a criterion that instructs your query to select the records of every employee whose last name begins with *B*:

1. Return to Design view; then delete "CE" from the Dept column's Criteria cell (select **"CE"**, and then press **Delete**).

2. In the Last column's Criteria cell, type **b***, and then press **Tab**.

3. Observe the Criteria cell. Access has automatically changed the criteria to Like "b*".

4. Run the query, and then compare the dynaset with Figure 4.14. The query selected only records for employees whose last names begin with *B*. Notice that the criterion is not case sensitive. In other words, although you entered a lowercase *b* in the Criteria cell, Access still found names that began with an uppercase *B*.

SETTING CRITERIA WITH COMPARISON OPERATORS

You can use *comparison operators* to set exact criteria (for example, every employee who works exactly 40 hours per week), *exclusionary* criteria (for example, every employee who does *not* work exactly 40 hours per week), or criteria for a *range* of values (for example, every employee who works *less* than 40 hours per week).

Figure 4.14   **The dynaset after setting a criterion with the Like operator**

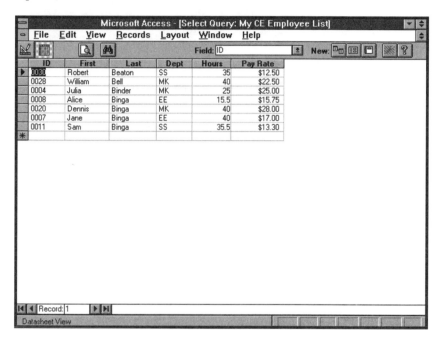

Here are Access' comparison operators and their meanings.

Operator	Meaning
<	Less than
>	Greater than
=	Equal to
<=	Less than or equal to
>=	Greater than or equal to
<>	Not equal to

Let's use a comparison operator to specify the records of employees who make more than $15 per hour:

1. Return to Design view, and then delete the criterion in the Last column.

2. In the Pay Rate column's Criteria cell, type **>15**.

3. Run the query, and then observe the dynaset. The query selected only the records of employees with a pay rate higher than $15 (see Figure 4.15).

Figure 4.15 **The dynaset after setting a criterion with a comparison operator**

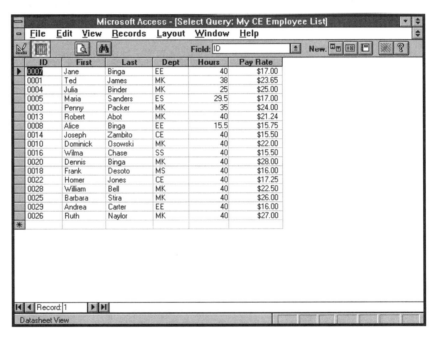

SETTING MULTIPLE CRITERIA WITH THE AND OPERATOR

You can use Access' *And operator* to set multiple criteria; for example, you could select employees who make more than $10 per hour *and* work 40 hours per week.

You can use the And operator to set criteria for two different fields by

- Entering those criteria in separate columns on the Criteria row of the QBE grid. For example, to specify only those records for employees who both work in the Marketing department and were hired in 1988, you could type the marketing-department code in the department column and */*/88 in the hired-date column.

- Using the And operator to set multiple criteria within a single field (by entering both criteria in a single Criteria cell and separating the criteria with And). For example, to specify the records for employees who both make more than $10 and less than $20 per hour, you could type *>10 And <20* in the pay-rate column.

There is practically no limit to the number of multiple criteria you can set at one time, and you can combine the two methods just described to specify records that meet multiple criteria both across and within fields. For example, you could specify records for employees who work in the Marketing Department, *and* were hired in 1988, *and* make more than $10 *and* less than $20 per hour by entering all of those criteria on the Criteria row.

Let's use the And operator to set some multiple criteria:

1. Return to Design view.

2. In the Dept column's Criteria cell, type **MK**.

3. Examine the Dept and Pay Rate columns. There are now criteria in both columns (see Figure 4.16).

Figure 4.16   **Setting multiple criteria**

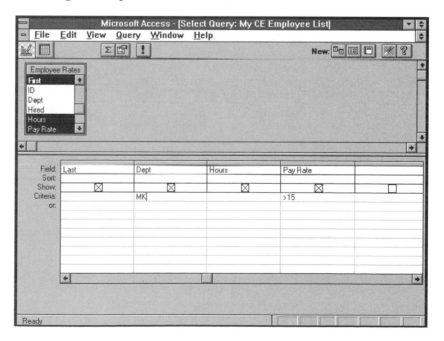

4. Run the query, and then observe the dynaset. The query has selected only the records of employees who both work in the Marketing Department *and* earn more than $15 per hour.

5. Return to Design view; then place the insertion point to the right of >15 in the Pay Rate column's Criteria cell.

6. Press **spacebar**, type **and <25**, and then press **Tab**. Access automatically changes your and to And, so the criterion now reads >15 And <25 (see Figure 4.17).

7. Run the query and observe the dynaset. The query selected only the five records for employees who work in the Marketing department, *and* earn more than $15 an hour *and* earn less than $25 per hour.

Figure 4.17   **Setting multiple criteria across and within fields**

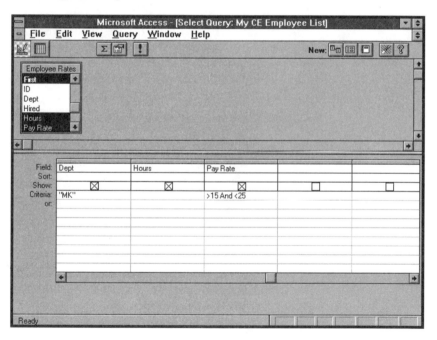

SETTING MULTIPLE CRITERIA WITH THE OR OPERATOR

In contrast to the And operator, you can use the *Or operator* to specify records that meet only part of a set of multiple criteria. For example, you can specify the records of employees who either work in the Marketing department *or* the Chemical Engineering department.

You can use the Or operator to set criteria for two different fields by setting one criterion on the Criteria row and the other criterion on the *Or row* (located just below the Criteria row). For example, to specify records for employees who either work in the Chemical Engineering department or make more than $20 per hour, you could type the department code in the department column's Criteria cell and >20 in the pay-rate column's Or cell.

You can also use the Or operator to set multiple criteria within a single Criteria cell by entering both criteria in a single Criteria cell, and separating the criteria with Or. For example, to specify the records for employees who work less than 25 hours or more than 40 hours per week, you could type <25 Or >40 in the hours-worked column's Criteria cell.

As with the And operator, there is practically no limit to the number of multiple criteria you can set at one time, and you can combine the two methods just described.

In addition, you can use both the And and Or operators in the same query; Access will select any record that meets all of the criteria on any single Criteria or Or row (although they are not labeled, every row that follows the first Or row is also an Or row).

Let's set some multiple criteria with the Or operator now:

1. Return to Design view, and then delete the criteria in the Pay Rate column.

2. In the Hours column's Or cell (the fifth row), type **<30**.

3. Observe the Dept and Hours columns. The criteria ("MK" for Dept and <30 for Hours) are on separate rows (see Figure 4.18).

4. Run the query and observe the dynaset. The query selected only those records for employees who work in the MK department *or* work fewer than 30 hours per week *or* both.

5. Return to Design view; then place the insertion point to the right of "MK" in the Dept column's Criteria cell.

Figure 4.18   **Setting multiple criteria with the Or operator**

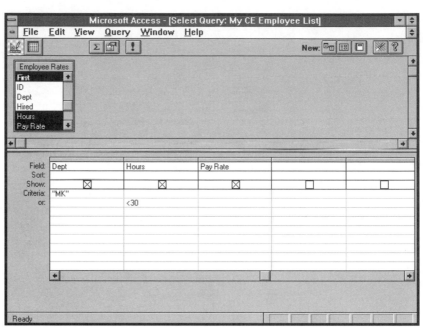

6. Press **spacebar**, type **or CE**, and then press **Tab**. Access automatically changes your or to Or and places double quotation marks around CE.

7. Run the query, and then observe the dynaset. The query selected only records for employees who work in the MK department, *or* the CE department, *or* who work fewer than 30 hours per week.

SETTING CRITERIA FOR RECORDS WITH EMPTY FIELDS

When you are responsible for managing a database, it is often useful to find records that have *no* data in certain fields. For example, when a number of new employees are hired, you may need immediately to create some incomplete records for them, and then go back later and fill in the rest of the data as it becomes available.

To select records with empty fields, you can set the Is Null expression as a criterion. (To find records that *don't* have empty fields, you can use the Is Not Null expression.)

Let's use the Is Null expression to find records with empty ID fields:

1. Return to Design view, and then delete the criteria in the Dept and Hours columns. There should now be no criteria set in the QBE grid.

2. In the ID column's Criteria cell, type **is null**, and then press **Tab**. Access changes your is null to Is Null.

3. Run the query, and then observe the dynaset. The query selected the three records with empty ID fields (see Figure 4.19).

4. Save the query as **My Missing IDs**.

Figure 4.19   **The dynaset of records with empty ID fields**

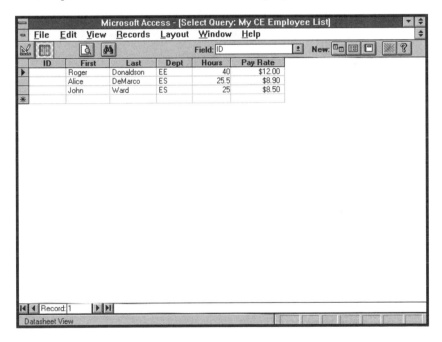

 EDITING RECORDS IN THE DYNASET

Earlier in this chapter, you learned that a dynaset is dynamic because it changes as the data in your tables change. The dynamics also work the other way: Changes you make in dynasets can change data in the underlying tables.

This feature makes queries even more useful because you can use them not only to *view* data, but also to *change* it. For example, in the last task you used a dynaset to find employee records that have empty ID fields. Now, you can add those ID numbers right in the dynaset to update the underlying table.

It's no coincidence that dynasets look just like tables; you can edit records in a dynaset just as you would in a table.

Let's use the dynaset from the My Missing IDs query to fill in some missing IDs, and then take a look at the underlying table, Employee Rates:

1. In the ID field for Roger Donaldson's record, type **0017** (see Figure 4.20). Notice as you type that the record selector displays a pencil indicator, just as it does when you're editing a record in a table.

2. In the ID field for Alice DeMarco's record, type **0027**.

3. Close the Query window.

Figure 4.20 **Editing records in a dynaset**

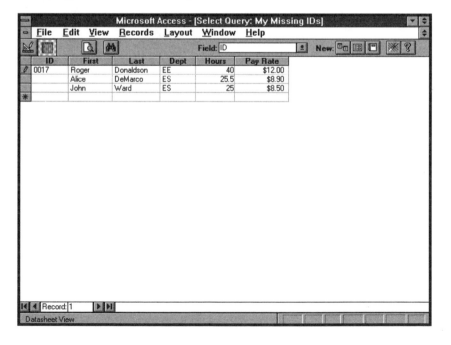

4. Open and observe the **Employee Rates** table. Access has saved the ID numbers you entered for Alice DeMarco and Roger Donaldson in this table.

5. Close the Table window.

PERFORMING CALCULATIONS IN QUERIES

In order to do "what-if" analysis, you can use a query to perform calculations on your data. For example, if you would like to see what everyone's pay rate would be if you raised the rates by 7 percent, you could use a query to calculate those new rates.

Unless you choose otherwise, Access will not use a calculation to change any existing data, but rather will add a field to the query's dynaset to display the calculation's result.

CREATING AND NAMING A CALCULATED FIELD

You can perform a *horizontal calculation* (that is, a calculation involving fields within the same record) by adding a *calculated field* to the QBE grid. To create a calculated field, enter a *calculation expression* in a blank Field cell.

To specify field names within a calculation expression, you must type square brackets around each field name. For example, to calculate an employee's gross pay (by multiplying the Hours and Pay Rate fields), you would type [Hours]*[Pay Rate] in a blank Field cell, and then run the query.

Here are some of the arithmetic operators you can use in calculated fields, and some sample expressions for those operators:

Operator	Expression	Action
+	[Hired Date]+30	Adds 30 days to the value in the Hired Date field
-	[Price]-[Discount]	Subtracts the value in the Discount field from the value in the Price field
*	[Hours]*[Pay Rate]	Multiplies the value in the Hours field by the value in the Pay Rate field
/	[Gross Pay]/[Hours]	Divides the value in the Gross Pay field by the value in the Hours field

When you enter a calculation expression in a Field cell, Access supplies a default field name, such as Expr1, to head the column in the resulting dynaset. For example, Access might change the [Hours]*[Pay Rate] expression to Expr1:[Hours]*[Pay Rate] and display the results of that calculation in the dynaset under Expr1. To replace this default name with a more meaningful name, such as Gross Pay, replace Access' default field name in the calculated expression.

Let's create a calculated field that calculates gross pay:

1. Open a new Query window in Design view. (In the Database window, display the list of query object names, and then click on **New**.)

2. Add the **Hours and Rates** table to the query, and then close the Add Table dialog box.

3. Add the **Dept**, **Hours**, and **Pay Rate** fields to the QBE grid.

4. Place the insertion point in the fourth Field cell, and then type **[hours]*[pay rate]** to create an expression that will calculate gross pay. (You must enclose field names within square brackets, but you can type them in any case.)

5. Press **Tab**, and then observe the QBE grid. Access has changed the calculated field to Expr1:[hours]*[pay rate]. (Because of the narrow column, you may not be able to see the entire field.)

6. Run the query, and then observe the dynaset (see Figure 4.21). The query has calculated the gross pay for each record and now displays this data in the Expr1 field. (Don't be concerned about the uneven number of decimal places displayed in the field; you'll learn how to format calculated fields in Chapter 9.)

7. Return to Design view, select **Expr1** (don't select the colon separating Expr1 from the calculation), and then type **Gross Pay** to replace Expr1.

8. Run the query, and then observe the dynaset. The calculated field now displays more meaningfully as Gross Pay.

9. Save the query as **My Gross Pay**.

Figure 4.21   **The dynaset with a calculated field**

```
─                    Microsoft Access - [Select Query: Query1]         ▼ ▲
─   File   Edit   View   Records   Layout   Window   Help                ▲
 ▨ ▦        ▧ ▨                        Field: Dept      ▲  New: ▫▫ ▣ ▫  ▧ ?
    Dept    Hours    Pay Rate      Expr1                                  ▲
 ▶ MK         38      $23.65        898.7
    ES        40      $10.00          400
    MK        35      $24.00          840
    MK        25      $25.00          625
    ES       29.5     $17.00        501.5
    EE        40      $15.00          600
    EE        40      $17.00          680
    EE       15.5     $15.75      244.125
    CE        40       $6.30          252
    MK        40      $22.00          880
    SS       35.5     $13.30       472.15
    CE       35.5      $6.75      239.625
    MK        40      $21.24        849.6
    CE        40      $15.50          620
    EE        40      $12.00          480
    SS        40      $15.50          620
    ES       25.5      $8.90       226.95
    MS        40      $16.00          640
    ES        40      $10.75          430
    MK        40      $28.00         1120
    EE       37.5     $14.00          525
    CE        40      $17.25          690
    SS        25      $14.00          350
    SS        40      $13.50          540
    MK        40      $26.00         1040
    MK        40      $27.00         1080                                 ▼
 ▮◀ Record: 1   ▶▮▶
  Two-letter code for department
```

 CALCULATING A TOTAL FOR A GROUP OF RECORDS

In addition to horizontal calculations, you can use queries to per-form *vertical calculations* (that is, calculations that involve the same field or fields down through groups of records) in order to calculate summary information, or *totals*. With Access, you can calculate totals for every record in a dynaset (for example, the average employee pay rate for the entire company) or totals for groups of records within a dynaset (for example, the average employee pay rates by department).

By default, Access does not provide a row in the QBE grid for calcu-lating totals for groups of records. However, when you choose View, Totals from the Query window (or click on the third button from the left on the tool bar, the Totals button), Access will add a *Totals row* to the QBE grid. In the Total row, Access will then place *Group By* in the Total cell under each regular field and *Expression* under each calculated field.

To then perform a calculation on a group of records, you would follow these steps:

- Verify that Group By is displayed only in the Total cell of the field by which you want to group records.

- In the Total cell of the column of the field by which you want to calculate a summary, select the appropriate *aggregate function* from the drop-down list(s). Aggregate functions enable you to calculate aggregate values, such as sums and averages, for a group of values.

- Run the query.

Here are Access' aggregate functions and their purposes:

Function	Use to Calculate
Sum	Total of the values within a field
Avg	Average of the values within a field
Min	Lowest value within a field
Max	Highest value within a field
Count	Number of values within a field (excluding fields with null values)
StDev	Standard deviation of the values within a field
Var	Variance of the values within a field
First	First value within a field
Last	Last value within field

It's important that you include in the QBE grid only those fields either by which you are grouping records or upon which you are calculating a total. For example, if you want to calculate the average hours worked by department, include only the hours-worked and department fields in the grid. If the QBE grid contains any other fields, delete them.

Note that Access calculates totals based on all of the records in a dynaset, not in the underlying table. Therefore, if you set criteria to select only certain records, Access will use only values from those records in the calculation.

Let's use Access' totals feature to calculate the total gross-pay costs by department:

1. Return to Design view, and then observe the QBE grid. The grid does not contain any row for totaling values for groups of records.

2. Choose **View, Totals** (or click on the **Totals button**); then observe the QBE grid again. Access has now added a Total row to the grid, and placed *Group By* under each regular field and *Expression* under the calculated field (see Figure 4.22).

3. Use the Hours column's **field selector** to select the column, and then press the **Delete** key to delete the column.

4. Select and delete the Pay Rate field. The QBE grid should now contain only Dept and Gross Pay columns.

Figure 4.22   **Displaying the Total row**

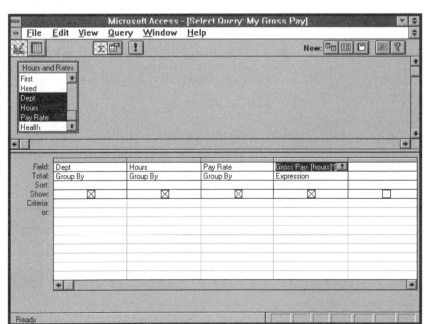

5. In the Gross Pay column's Total cell, click on the **drop-down list arrow** to open the drop-down list of aggregate functions.

6. From the list, select **Sum**, as shown in Figure 4.23 (you may need to scroll up).

7. Run the query; then observe the dynaset and compare it to the QBE grid pictured in Figure 4.23. In the query design, the Group By operator in the Dept column and the Sum operator in the Gross Pay column have instructed the query to group and calculate the sum of employees' gross pay by department.

8. Save the query as **My Dept Gross Pay Totals**.

9. Close the Query window.

Figure 4.23   **Selecting an aggregate function**

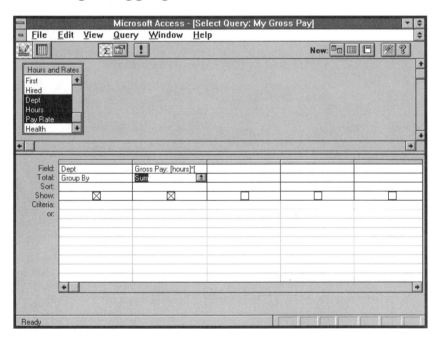

SUMMARY

In this chapter, you learned how to create and use select queries to limit the number of visible fields, sort records, select only those records that meet certain criteria, edit values, and perform calculations.

Here's a quick reference guide to the Access features introduced in this chapter:

Desired Result	How to Do It
View a query design	From the Database window, choose the query object name, and then click on **Design**; from a Query window in Datasheet view, choose **View, Query Design**, or click on the **Design View button**
Create a single-table query	From the Database window, click on the **Query object button**, click on **New**, select the table upon which you wish to base the query, click on **Add**, and then click on **Close**
Add a field to a query design	Open a Field cell's drop-down list box, and then select the field name; or, select the field name in the field list, and then drag the name to a Field cell
Run a select query	Choose **Query, Run**; or, click on the **Datasheet View button**
Sort records in a query	From a Sort cell's drop-down list box, select a sort option (**Ascending** or **Descending**), and then run the query
Save and name a new query, or rename an existing query	From a Query window, choose **File, Save Query As** or **File, Save As**, type a query name, and then click on **OK**
Save a modified query design	From a Query window, choose **File, Save Query** or **File, Save**

Desired Result	How to Do It
Add multiple fields to a query design	In the field list, select one field name, press and hold down **Ctrl**, click on the other field names, release **Ctrl**, and then drag the field names to a Field cell
Move a column in the QBE grid	Click on the column's **field selector**, and then drag the column to a new location
Set an exact query criterion	Type a value in a Criteria cell
Set a query criterion with a wildcard character	Type a value plus ***** (asterisk) to represent multiple characters and/or **?** (question mark) to represent a single character in a Criteria cell
Set a query criterion with a comparison operator	Type a value preceded by a comparison operator (**<, >, =, <=, >=,** or **<>**) in a Criteria cell
Set And criteria	Type criteria in more than one Criteria cell; and/or, type **And** between multiple criteria within a single Criteria cell
Set Or criteria	Type criteria in both Criteria and or cells; and/or, type **Or** between multiple criteria within a single Criteria cell
Set a criterion for empty fields	Type **Is Null** in the field's Criteria cell
Edit records in a dynaset	Directly edit values in the dynaset
Create a calculated field	Type a calculation expression in an empty Field cell
Rename a calculated field	Replace Access' default field name in the calculated field's Field cell
Calculate totals	Choose **View, Totals** (or click on the **Totals button**), select Group By and aggregate functions in the Total row, and then run the query

In Chapter 5, you'll learn how to create and customize a form to help you enter and view data.

IF YOU'RE STOPPING HERE

If you need to break off here, please exit Access. If you want to proceed directly to the next chapter, please do so now.

CHAPTER 5:
FORM BASICS

Viewing Data in
Forms

Creating a Form
with a FormWizard

Sorting and
Filtering Records
through a Form

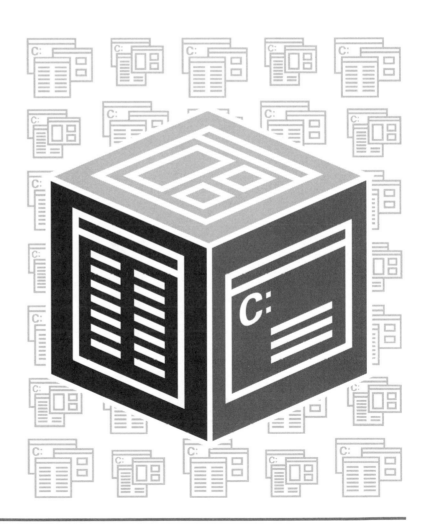

In Chapter 4, you learned how to use queries to ask questions about your data. In this chapter, you will learn how to create, modify, and use forms to control and customize the way you view and edit that data.

When you're done working through this chapter, you will know how to

- Use a form to view records in Form view and Datasheet view
- Create a form using a FormWizard
- Modify a form design
- Preview a form
- Sort and filter records through a form
- Edit and add records through a form

VIEWING DATA IN FORMS

In Chapter 1, you learned that forms enable you to view data in a customizable layout, rather than just in rows and columns. Forms also enable you to view limited fields, and often display only one record at a time.

Because of these features, forms are an excellent way to control and customize the way in which you view and edit data. For example, if you are editing home-address data in an employee-information table, you can use a form to view and edit

- Only the fields that are relevant to that task
- Only one record at a time so that you can focus on each individual employee

If you are entering data from paper forms, you can create an Access form to match the paper form, thus making your data-entry work that much easier.

 VIEWING DATA IN FORM VIEW

Every Form window offers you two ways to view your data: Form view and Datasheet view. In Form view, you view data in a customized layout, and can often view only one record at a time.

To switch to Form view from any other view in a Form window, choose View, Form, or click on the second button from the left on the tool bar, the Form View button.

If you do not have both the Access application and the EMPLOYEE Database windows opened and maximized, please do so now.

Take a look at a form in Form view:

1. Open and examine the Addresses and Extensions table. The table contains seven fields: Last, First, Adr, City, St, Zip, and Ext (see Figure 5.1).

Figure 5.1   **The Addresses and Extensions table**

Last	First	Adr	City	St	Zip	Ext
Martin	Jane	50 Beach Drive	Oceanside	CA	91762	349
James	Ted	34 Fields Street	Fort Worth	TX	76116	300
Abel	Marie	127 Ford Avenue	Shackelford	TX	76430	339
Binder	Julia	10 Cory Drive	Trenton	NJ	08753	324
Binga	Sam	50 Dallas Street	Pasadena	CA	91106	348
Sanders	Maria	12 East Avenue	Denton	TX	76201	310
Harper	Harry	82 East Avenue	Long Beach	CA	90745	395
Conner	Bill	32 Ash Lane	Allentown	NJ	08501	328
Donaldson	Roger	8165 Main Street	Trenton	NJ	08618	303
Packer	Penny	9929 Clearview	Vienna	VA	22181	346
Abot	Robert	99 Stonecreek Rd.	Trenton	NJ	08618	350
Evans	Nancy	21 Stonecreek Rd.	Trenton	NJ	08618	390
Zambito	Joseph	81 Pleasing Lane	Alhambra	CA	91801	311
Osowski	Dominick	23 Lakeside Ave.	S Granbury	TX	76048	368
Chase	Wilma	52 Pempleton Dr.	Albany	NY	12205	309
DeMarco	Alice	34 Sable Ave.	Bentwood	IL	61820	332
Kyler	Dennis	273 Fireside Dr.	Great Neck	NY	11023	362
Desoto	Frank	P.O. Box 7234	Trenton	NJ	07092	356
Henley	Albert	12 Divine Drive	San Pueblo	CO	80403	318
Beaton	Robert	391 State Street	West Seneca	NY	14224	323
Stira	Joe	200 Nester Street	Bath	NY	14708	315
Jones	Homer	466 Fairhaven St.	Los Alamos	MI	48104	337
Bell	William	66 Big Hill Rd.	Troy	NY	12182	340
Haslam	David	453 Lakeshore Dr.	Evans Mills	ND	58352	338
Carter	Andrea	718 Prole Road	Rockville	SC	29204	360
Naylor	Ruth	532 Union Street	Nashville	TN	38109	334

Record: 1

Datasheet View

2. Close the Table window.

3. Display the list of Form object names. (In the Database window, click on the **Form object button**.)

4. Double-click on **Address** to open the Address form.

5. Examine the form (see Figure 5.2). It is a modified single-column form based on the Addresses and Extensions table. The form currently displays six of the seven fields from Jane Martin's record (Record 1).

6. Click on the **Next Record navigation button** several times to view the next several records. For each record, the form displays the same six fields, but with different values.

Figure 5.2   **The Address form in Form view**

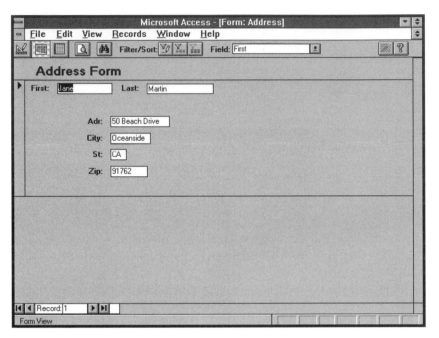

VIEWING DATA IN DATASHEET VIEW

If you want to view more than one record at a time in a form, you can use the Form window's Datasheet view. Datasheet view will display data in rows and columns, and can appear very similar to the form's underlying table or query dynaset. A Form window's Datasheet view, however, will display only the fields that are visible in Form view. For example, if a form is based on a table containing three fields—Name, Telephone #, and Extension—but the form in Form view displays only the Name and Telephone # fields, the Datasheet view of that form will also display only the Name and Telephone # fields.

To switch to Datasheet view from any other view in a Form window, choose View, Datasheet, or click on the Datasheet View button.

Now take a look at the Address form in Datasheet view:

1. Move to Maria Sanders' record (Record 6).

2. Observe the status bar. The Form window is currently in Form view.

3. Click on the **Datasheet View button** (the third button from the left on the tool bar) to switch to Datasheet view. The status bar now displays "Datasheet View."

4. Observe the form (see Figure 5.3). It now looks very similar to the Addresses and Extensions table, but still only displays six of the table's seven fields. Notice also that Maria Sanders' record is still the current record.

Figure 5.3   **The Address form in Datasheet view**

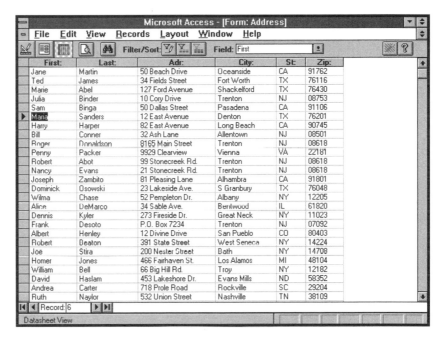

5. Click on the **Form View button** (the second button from the left on the tool bar) to return to Form view.

6. Close the Form window.

CREATING A FORM WITH A FORMWIZARD

To help you create your own forms, Access provides FormWizards. A *FormWizard* asks you questions about the form you want to create, and then builds the form for you based on your answers.

Access provides four FormWizards:

- The Single-column FormWizard builds forms that display fields from only one record at a time in a single column.

- The Tabular FormWizard builds forms that display fields from multiple records in a tabular (row-and-column) format.

- The Graph FormWizard builds forms that display data from fields as graphs (for example, as a bar chart or pie chart).

- The Main/Subform FormWizard builds forms that display data from two related tables or queries.

Whenever you start to create a new form, Access gives you the option of using a FormWizard.

 SELECTING A DATA SOURCE AND FORM TYPE

To start a FormWizard, you would follow these steps:

- In the Database window, click on the Form object button to display the list of form object names.

- Click on New to open the New Form dialog box.

- In the Select A Table/Query drop-down list box, select the table or query upon which you wish to base your new form.

- Click on FormWizards.

- In the Microsoft Access dialog box, select the name of the FormWizard you wish to use, and then click on OK.

Now start creating your own form, a form that will eventually resemble the Address form you just saw:

1. With the **Form object button** selected in the Database window, click on **New** to start creating a new form.

2. Observe the New Form dialog box. You can base a form upon a table or a query.

3. In the Select A Table/Query drop-down list box, select **Addresses and Extensions** to base your new form on the Addresses and Extensions table (see Figure 5.4).

Figure 5.4   **Creating a new form based on the Addresses and Extensions table**

4. Click on **FormWizards**.

5. Observe the Microsoft Access dialog box. As you can see, Access provides Single-column, Tabular, Graph, and Main/Subform FormWizards.

6. Click on **OK** to accept the default FormWizard: Single-column.

SPECIFYING FIELDS

You can choose to include on your form all of the fields from the underlying table or query, or just limited fields. This can help you focus on only relevant fields, and can also enable you to conceal certain data from other users of the form. For example, if you create a home-address entry form based on an employee-information table that contains everything from home addresses to salary information, you can hide the salary information simply by not placing salary-related fields on the form. (See your Access documentation for more information about data security.) After you start the Single-column FormWizard, it prompts you to specify the fields you want on the form, and the order in which to place them.

To add a single field to the form, select the field name in the Available Fields list box, and then click on >; to add all of the fields in the list box, click on >>. (To reverse field selections, click on < or <<.)

The FormWizard will place fields on the form in the order in which you select them.

Once you are done answering one set of FormWizard questions, click on Next to proceed to the next dialog box. (To change a previous answer, click on Back one or more times to return to previous dialog boxes.)

Now specify your form's fields and field order:

1. Observe the Microsoft Access FormWizard dialog box. You use this dialog box to select the fields that you want to appear on the form, and the order in which they should appear.

2. In the Available Fields list box, select **First**, and then click on **>** to instruct the FormWizard to place the First field in the uppermost position on the form (see Figure 5.5).

Figure 5.5   **Specifying fields**

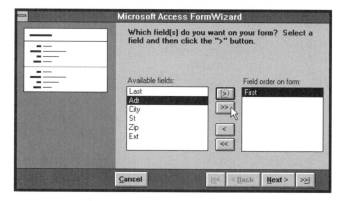

3. Click on **>>** to add the remaining fields to the form in the order in which they are listed in the Available Fields list box.

4. Click on **Next** to advance to the next dialog box.

 SELECTING A FORM LOOK AND ADDING A TITLE

The Single-column FormWizard offers five appearances, or looks, for forms: Standard, Chiseled, Shadowed, Boxed, and Embossed. These looks are purely cosmetic, affecting only the look, not the function, of forms.

After you select a look and click on Next, the Single-column Form-Wizard will ask you to specify a title for your form. This title is the text that will appear at the top of your form; don't confuse the title with the form's object name, which you specify with the File, Save As command.

Now select a look and specify a title for your form:

1. Observe the Microsoft Access FormWizard dialog box. By default, Access has already selected Standard, and the magnifying glass on the left displays an example of the Standard look (see Figure 5.6).

Figure 5.6   **Selecting a look for the form**

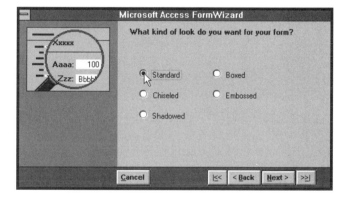

2. Select **Boxed**. The magnifying glass now displays an example of the Boxed look.

3. Select each of the remaining looks and observe the examples under the magnifying glass.

4. Select **Standard**, and then click on **Next** to advance to the next FormWizard dialog box.

5. Observe the dialog box. You can now enter a title to be displayed at the top of the form. By default, Access places the name of the table upon which the form is based in the Form Title text box. In this case it's Addresses and Extensions.

6. Type **My Address Form** to replace the selected text and specify a different title for the form (see Figure 5.7).

Figure 5.7   **Specifying a form title**

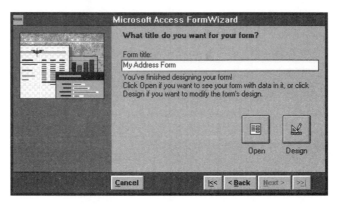

 OPENING THE FORM AND SAVING THE FORM DESIGN

Once you are finished working through all of the Single-column FormWizard's questions and are in the dialog box where you enter a form title, you can either open the form itself by clicking on Open or open the form's design by clicking on Design.

Once you have finished creating a form, you should save it by using the File, Save Form As (from Form or Datasheet view) or File, Save As (from Design view) command. Remember that the form title is different from the form object name, so the two need not match.

Now open your new form and save the design:

1. Observe the Microsoft Access FormWizard dialog box. You can now choose to view either the design of the form or the form itself.

2. Click on **Open** to open the form in Form view, and then, if necessary, maximize the Form window.

3. Observe the Form window. Access displays the title My Address Form at the top of the window, and displays the fields down the length of the window in the order in which you selected them (see Figure 5.8).

4. Click on the **Next Record navigation button** to view the next record. This form functions very much like the Address form you saw earlier in this chapter. Notice how the field names to the left of each field remain the same, while the data in the fields changes, as you move from record to record.

Figure 5.8   **The new form**

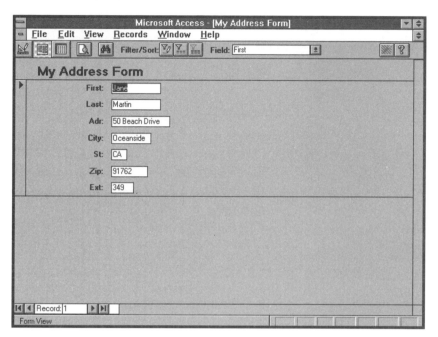

5. Choose **File, Save Form As** to open the Save As dialog box, type **My Address** in the Form Name text box, and then click on **OK** to name and save the form design.

MODIFYING THE FORM DESIGN

Using a FormWizard is often only the first step to creating a customized form. By working in a Form window's Design view, you can modify a FormWizard form design to suit your needs and tastes. To switch to Design view from any other view in a Form window, select View, Form Design, or click on the Design View button.

In Design view, you can view and manipulate the elements that determine how you see data in Form view. These elements are called *controls*.

Access provides three types of controls:

• A *bound control* is connected, or *bound*, to a field in a table or query; it displays the field's values, and enables you to edit those values in Form or Datasheet view.

- An *unbound control* is not bound to a field; rather, it displays information, such as a form title, that does not change from record to record. You cannot change an unbound control's information in Form or Datasheet view.

- A *calculated control* is bound to an expression rather than to a field. Like a query's calculated field, a calculated control can calculate values based on one or more fields. A calculated control can also display such information as the current date or page number.

A *label control*, or *label*, is a specialized type of unbound control that often serves to identify a related bound control in Form view by displaying that control's name.

In Design view, Access divides the Form window into three sections for controls:

- A Form Header section, which contains controls that appear once at the top of every form (such as the unbound control for the form title)

- A Detail section, which usually contains one or more sets of bound controls and their labels

- A Form Footer section, which contains controls that appear once at the bottom of every form

Among other things, you can select, delete, move, and size controls. Here are some ways to manipulate bound controls and labels:

- To select a bound control and its label, click on the bound control. When you do, Access will display five or seven (depending upon the size of the control) small *sizing handles,* a single, larger *move handle* around the bound control, and a single move handle in the upper-left corner of the control's label.

- To delete a selected bound control and its label, press the Delete key or choose Edit, Delete.

- To move a selected bound control by itself, place the mouse pointer over the control's move handle until the pointer changes to a *single-finger pointer*; then drag the control to anywhere else on the form.

- To move a selected bound control together with its label, place the mouse pointer over an edge of the bound control until the pointer changes to an *open-hand pointer*; then drag the control and label to anywhere else on the form.

- To resize a selected bound control or label, place the mouse pointer over one of the control's sizing handles until the pointer changes to a two-headed *arrow pointer*, then drag the control to a new size.

- To select multiple controls, select one control, press and hold down Shift, click on the other controls, and then release Shift.

- To align multiply selected controls with each other, choose Layout, Align, and then choose the desired alignment: Left, Right, Top, Bottom, or To Grid.

Now switch to Design view and modify your form layout:

1. Click on the **Design View button** (or choose **View, Form Design**) to switch to the Form window's Design view.

2. Choose **View, Toolbox** to hide the *toolbox*. (You will learn about the toolbox in Chapter 9.)

3. Observe the Form window's three sections: Form Header, Detail, and Form Footer.

4. Observe the controls in the Detail section. The left-hand, shaded boxes are labels; the right-hand, unshaded boxes are bound controls. By default, the Single-column FormWizard used the relevant field name followed by a colon for each label's text.

5. Click on the **Ext bound control** (the right-hand box) to select the bound control and its label (the left-hand box). Access should now display five sizing handles and one larger move handle around the bound control, and a single move handle in the upper-left corner of the label (see Figure 5.9).

6. Press the **Delete** key to delete the Ext bound control and its label.

7. Select the **Last bound control** and its label (click on the Last bound control).

8. Place the mouse pointer over the Last bound control's move handle. The pointer should now change to a hand with a single pointing finger.

9. Use the single-finger pointer to drag the bound control about 1 inch to the right (use the horizontal ruler to gauge distance); then observe the Form window. The single-finger pointer moves just the selected bound control, not its label.

10. Click on the **Undo button** (or choose **Edit, Undo Move**) to return the Last bound control to its original position.

Figure 5.9   **Selecting the Ext bound control and its label**

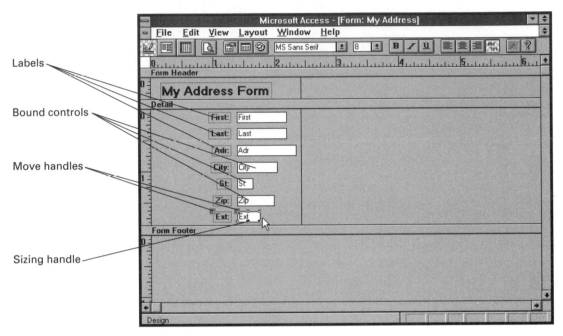

11. Place the mouse pointer on an edge of the Last bound control, away from any handles. The pointer should now change to an open hand.

12. Use the open-hand pointer to drag the last bound control about 3 inches to the right, and then observe the Form window (see Figure 5.10). The open-hand pointer moves the Last bound control and its label together. Also notice that Access expands the form's width to accommodate the new field placement.

13. Select the **First bound control** and its label; then use the open-hand pointer to drag the bound control and its label to the upper-left corner of the Detail section.

14. Place the mouse pointer on the First bound control's lower-right **sizing handle**. The pointer now changes to a two-headed arrow.

15. Use the arrow pointer to drag the edge of the bound control about $\frac{1}{2}$ inch to the right to enlarge the control (see Figure 5.11).

16. Move the **Last bound control** and its label to about $\frac{1}{4}$ inch to the right of the First bound control.

Figure 5.10   Moving the Last bound control and its label

Open-hand
pointer

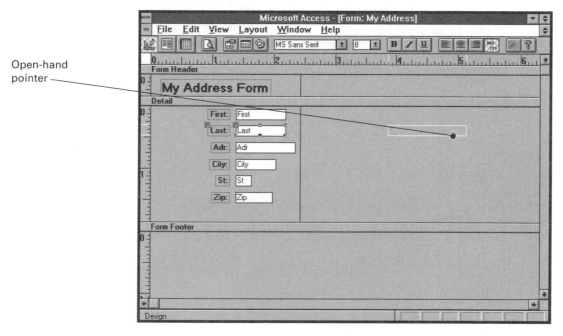

Figure 5.11   Enlarging the First bound control

Two-headed
arrow pointer

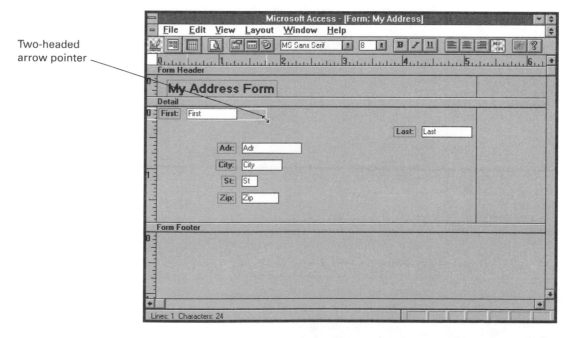

17. With the Last bound control and its label still selected, press **Shift**, click on the **First bound control**, and then release **Shift** to add the First bound control and its label to the selection.

18. Choose **Layout, Align, Bottom** to align the bottom edges of the selected bound controls and labels.

19. Choose **File, Save** to save the modified form design.

20. Switch to Form view; then observe the Form window. Access no longer displays the Ext field or its label, and it displays the First and Last fields and their labels in their new locations (see Figure 5.12).

Figure 5.12   **The modified form in Form view**

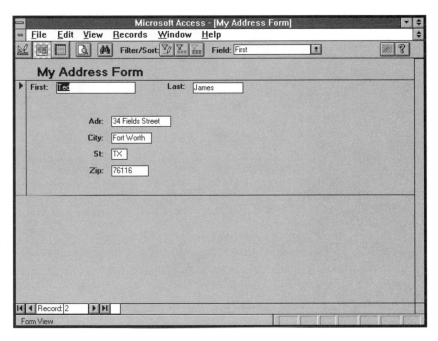

 PREVIEWING AND PRINTING THE FORM

Just as you can preview and print tables, queries, and reports, you can preview and print forms. When you preview or print a form, Access displays a separate copy of the form for each record in the underlying table or query dynaset, and tries to fit as many forms as it can on one sheet of paper.

You may also want to print the form for a blank record to distribute a paper data-collection form. This will make data entry easier because the paper form will match your electronic form exactly.

To preview a form from a Form window, choose File, Print Preview, or click on the Print Preview button. To then print the previewed form (or any previewed object for that matter), click on the Print button to open the Print dialog box; then click on OK.

Preview your form now:

1. Click on the **Print Preview button** (or choose **File, Print Preview**) to preview the printed form. When printing forms, Access will fit as many records as it can on a single page.

2. Change to a close-up view of the previewed form (click on **Zoom** or click on the previewed page with the magnifying-glass pointer). Each copy of the form displays data from a different record (see Figure 5.13).

3. Cancel the preview (click on Cancel).

Figure 5.13   **Previewing the form**

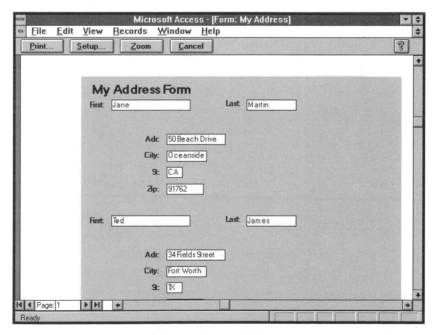

SORTING AND FILTERING RECORDS THROUGH A FORM

In Chapter 1, you learned that you can sort records through a Form window's Filter window. You can also use a Filter window to filter out records that do not meet certain criteria.

To help you work with the Filter window, Access supplies three Filter/Sort buttons on the tool bar when you have a Form window open in Form or Datasheet view: *Edit Filter/Sort*, *Apply Filter/Sort*, and *Show All Records*. These buttons are alternatives to the Records, Edit Filter/Sort, Records, Apply Filter/Sort, and Records, Show All Records commands.

As you saw in Chapter 4, a Form window's Filter window is very similar to a Query window in Design view. Both windows have an upper pane containing a field list and a lower pane containing a grid. A Filter window, however, is more limited than a Query window, and you cannot save its design (unless you save it as a query). However, for on-the-spot sorting and filtering, a Filter window is a valuable tool.

 SORTING RECORDS IN A FORM

As you saw in Chapter 1, you can use a Filter window to sort records in a form in a different order than they appear in the form's underlying table or query.

To sort records from a Form window in Form or Datasheet view, you would follow these steps:

- Click on the Edit Filter/Sort button (or choose Records, Edit Filter/Sort) to open the Filter window.

- For each field you want to sort by, drag the field name from the field list to one of the filter grid's Field cells (or select the field name from a Field cell's drop-down list box). As in a query design, Access will sort by fields according to their left-to-right order. Unlike a query, the form will always display the same set of fields, regardless of which fields you place in the filter grid.

- In the Sort cells under each field name, select a sort type of Ascending or Descending.

- Click on the Apply Filter/Sort button (or choose Records, Apply Filter/Sort) to apply the sort.

  Whenever you have a filter/sort in effect in Form or Datasheet view, Access will display a *FLTR indicator* in the status bar.

Now use the Filter window to sort your records by last and then first name:

1. From Form view, click on the **Next Record navigation button** several times and observe the records. The records display in the same unsorted order they have in the underlying table.

2. Observe the Filter/Sort buttons on the tool bar. They are, from left to right, the Edit Filter/Sort button, the Apply Filter/Sort button, and the Show All Records button.

3. Click on the **Edit Filter/Sort button** (the leftmost Filter/Sort button) to open the Form window's Filter window.

4. Observe the Filter window. Because this form is based on the Addresses and Extension table, Access displays that table's field list in the Filter window's upper pane.

5. From the field list, drag the **Last** and **First** field names, respectively, to the first and second Field cells of the filter grid.

6. In the Sort cells for both the Last and First columns, select **Ascending** to specify an ascending, two-level sort by those fields (see Figure 5.14).

7. Click on the **Apply Filter/Sort button** (the center Filter/Sort button) to perform the sort and return to the Form window.

8. Click on the **Next Record navigation button** several times. Access now displays the records in order by last and then first names.

9. Observe the status bar. FLTR indicates that a filter and/or sort is in effect.

 CREATING AND APPLYING A FILTER

Just as you can set criteria in a query, you can set criteria in a Filter window to filter your records and display in the Form window only those records that meet your criteria.

To filter records:

- Click on the Edit Filter/Sort button (or choose Records, Edit Filter/Sort) to open the Filter window.

Figure 5.14   **Specifying a two-level sort**

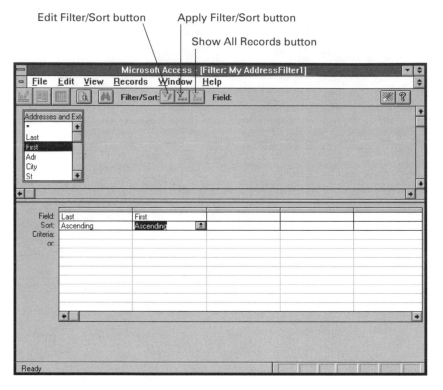

- For each field for which you want to set criteria, drag the field name from the field list to one of the filter grid's Field cells (or select the field name from the Field cell's drop-down list box).

- In the Criteria cell under any field name, set a criterion or criteria. You can use any of the criteria-setting options that you learned about when working with queries in Chapter 4.

- Click on the Apply Filter/Sort button (or choose Records, Apply Filter/Sort) to apply the filter.

You can use filters and sorts at the same time by setting both sort options and criteria in the filter grid.

Access will keep the filters and sorts you set in effect until you close the Form window or click on the Show All Records button (or choose Records, Show All Records).

Now apply a filter so that you view only records for employees who live in New York State, and then remove the filter/sort to view all of the records again:

1. Click on the **Edit Filter/Sort button** to switch to the Filter window. Notice that Access still displays the sort options you set.

2. Add the **St** field to the third Field cell.

3. In the St column's Criteria cell, type **NY** (see Figure 5.15).

Figure 5.15 **Setting a filter criterion**

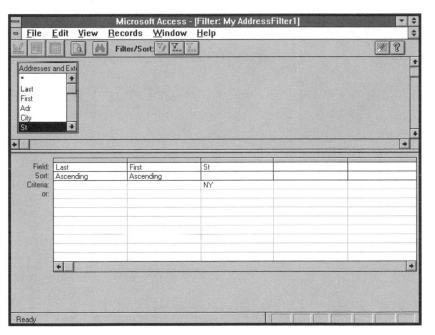

4. Click on the **Apply Filter/Sort button** to apply the filter/sort and return to the Form window.

5. Click on the **Next Record** and **Previous Record navigation buttons** several times and observe the records. The form still displays records in order by last and then first name, but now displays only those records where the St field is NY.

6. Switch to Datasheet view. You can now see the effect of the filter/sort more easily (see Figure 5.16).

Figure 5.16   **The sorted and filtered records in Datasheet view**

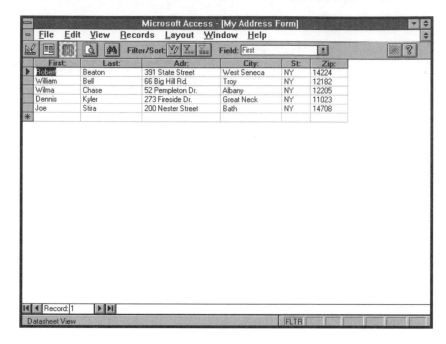

7. Click on the **Show All Records button** (the rightmost Filter/Sort button) to remove the filter/sort. Access now displays all of the records in their original order.

8. Observe the status bar. It no longer displays the FLTR indicator.

9. Return to Form view.

 EDITING AND ADDING RECORDS THROUGH A FORM

One of a form's primary purposes is for editing and adding records. Access will store edits made in a form in the form's underlying table.

Many of the selection and record-saving techniques you learned for tables in Chapter 2 also apply to forms. One nice shortcut in forms, though, is that you can select a field by clicking on the field's label.

Now use your new form to edit and add a record:

1. Click on the **First Record navigation button** to move to Jane Martin's record (Record 1).

2. Click on the **Adr** field's label to select the Adr field.

3. Type **140 Oak Street** to replace the selected text. Notice as you type that the large record selector on the left of the Form window displays a pencil indicator (see Figure 5.17).

Figure 5.17   **Editing a record in Form view**

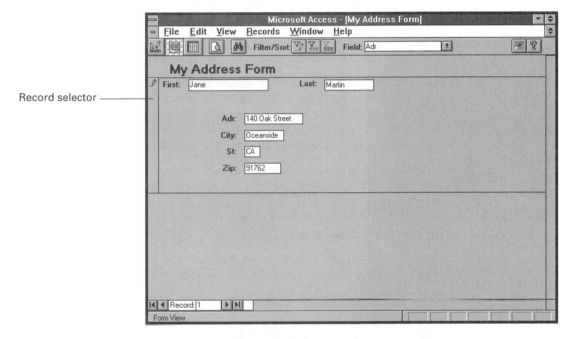

4. Click on the **Last Record navigation button**; then click on the **Next Record navigation button** to move to the blank record at the end of the underlying table.

5. Click on the First field's label to place the insertion point in the First field; then type your first name.

6. Press **Tab** to move to the Last field, and then type your last name.

PRACTICE YOUR SKILLS

1. Complete the current record with your address information.

2. Close the Form window.

3. Open your form's underlying table, Addresses and Extensions. Then observe that Access has stored in the table the data changes you made in the form.

4. Close the Table window, and then close the Database window.

PRACTICE YOUR SKILLS

In Chapter 4, you learned how to create and use queries to view limited fields and records, to edit records, and to perform calculations. In this chapter, you learned how to create a form using a Form-Wizard and how to apply sorts and filters to that form. The following two activities give you an opportunity to apply these techniques.

After each activity step, a chapter reference (in parentheses) informs you where we introduced the relevant technique for that step. Each step where you run a query or apply a filter/sort also includes within parentheses the number of records that should be in the dynaset or form.

In this activity, you will create a number of queries by specifying fields, setting sort orders and criteria, and creating calculated fields:

1. Open the **practice.mdb** database file, and then, if necessary, maximize the Database window (Chapter 1).

2. Create and run a new select query based on the Parking table to produce a dynaset that displays the ID, Park Lot, and Park Rate fields in descending order by Park Rate (52 records) (Chapter 4).

3. Return to Design view, set a criterion to select only those records where the Park Rate field is $55 or less, and then run the query (15 records) (Chapter 4).

4. Save the query design as **My Lowest Rates**; then close the Query window (Chapter 4).

5. Create and run a second new select query based on the Parking table to produce a dynaset that displays all of the fields in

the records for employees who park in the SE or NE lots (24 records) (Chapter 4).

6. Return to Design view, delete the current criteria, set criteria to select only those records for employees who park in the NE lot *and* pay a rate greater than $65, and then run the query (5 records) (Chapter 4).

7. Return to Design view, delete the current criteria, set criterion to select only those records for employees who are not assigned to a parking lot, and then run the query (4 records) (Chapter 4).

8. Save the query design as **My Unassigned Parking** (Chapter 4).

9. Return to Design view, delete the current criterion, and then create a calculated field to calculate a 5-percent rate increase for employees who park in the NW lot (multiply Park Rate by 1.05).

10. Name the calculated field **New NW Rate**, set a criterion to select only the records for employees who park in the NW lot, and then run the query (14 records) (Chapter 4).

11. Save the query design as **My NW Parking Increase**; then close the Query window (Chapter 4).

In this activity, you will use the Single-column FormWizard to create a new form, and then modify the form's design and apply a filter/sort:

1. Use the Single-column FormWizard to create a new form based on the Parking table. Include the Last, First, and Park Lot fields on the form (Chapter 5).

2. Give the form the Standard look; then entitle it **Lot Assignments** (Chapter 5).

3. Open the Form window in Design view; then maximize the window (Chapter 5).

4. Modify the form's design by putting the Last and First bound controls and labels on the same line (Chapter 5).

5. Save the form design as **My Parking Lot Assignments** (Chapter 5).

6. Switch to Form view; then open the Filter window and specify a two-level, ascending sort by last and then first name (Chapter 5).

7. Apply the filter/sort; then navigate through and observe the records (52 records) (Chapter 5).

8. Modify the filter/sort to specify only those records for employees who park in the SW lot, apply the filter/sort, and then navigate through and observe the records (10 records) (Chapter 5).

9. Switch to Datasheet view; then observe the records (Chapter 5).

10. Remove the filter/sort (Chapter 5).

11. Close the Form window; then close the Database window (Chapter 5).

SUMMARY

In this chapter, you learned how to use a Form window's Form and Datasheet views, create a form with a FormWizard, modify a form, preview a form, apply filter/sorts, and edit and add records through a form.

Here's a quick reference guide to the Access features introduced in this chapter:

Desired Result	How to Do It
View a form in Form view	From any other view in a Form window, choose **View, Form**; or, click on the **Form View button**
View a form in Datasheet view	From any other view in a Form window, choose **View, Datasheet**; or, click on the **Datasheet View button**
Create a new form with a FormWizard	From the Database window, display the list of form object names, click on **New**, select a table or query upon which to base the form, click on **FormWizards**, select the name of the FormWizard you wish to use, click on **OK**, and then answer the FormWizard's questions
Save and name a new form	From a Form window, choose **File, Save Form As** or **File, Save As**, type a form name, and then click on **OK**

Desired Result	How to Do It
View a form in Design view	From any other view in a Form window, choose **View, Form Design**; or, click on the **Design View button**
Select a bound control and its label	Click on the bound control
Delete a selected bound control and its label	Press the **Delete** key; or, choose **Edit, Delete**
Move a selected bound control	Place the mouse pointer over the control's **move handle** until the pointer changes to a single-finger pointer; then drag the control to a new location
Move a selected control and its label	Place the mouse pointer over one of the control's edges until the pointer changes to an open-hand pointer; then drag the control and its label to a new location
Resize a selected bound control	Place the mouse pointer over one of the control's **sizing handles** until the pointer changes to a double-headed arrow pointer, and then drag the control to a new size
Select multiple controls	Select one control, press and hold down **Ctrl**, select the other controls, and then release **Ctrl**
Align multiple selected controls	Choose **Layout, Align**, and then choose **Left**, **Right**, **Top**, **Bottom**, or **To Grid**
Save a modified form design	From a Form window, choose **File, Save Form** or **File, Save**
Preview a form	From a Form window, choose **File, Print Preview**; or, click on the **Print Preview button**
Sort records in a form	From a Form window in Form or Datasheet view, choose **Records, Edit Filter/Sort** (or click on the **Edit Filter/Sort button**), use the filter grid to specify fields and sort options, and then choose **Records, Apply Filter/Sort** (or click on the **Apply Filter/Sort button**)

Desired Result	How to Do It
Filter records in a form	From a Form window in Form or Datasheet view, choose **Records, Edit Filter/Sort** (or click on the **Edit Filter/Sort button**), use the filter grid to specify fields and filter criteria, and then choose **Records, Apply Filter/Sort** (or click on the **Apply Filter/Sort button**)
Remove a filter/sort	From a Form window in Form or Datasheet view, choose **Records, Show All Records** (or click on the **Show All Records button**)
Edit a record through a form	In Form or Datasheet view, directly edit the values
Add a record through a form	In Form or Datasheet view, move to the last, blank record, and then add values in the empty fields

In the next chapter, you'll learn how to create and use reports to present your data well on paper.

IF YOU'RE STOPPING HERE

If you need to break off here, please exit Access. If you want to proceed directly to the next chapter, please do so now.

CHAPTER 6:
REPORT BASICS

An Orientation to
Reports

Creating a Basic
Report

Creating a Groups
and Totals Report

In Chapter 5, you learned how to use forms to customize the arrangement of data on your computer screen. In this chapter, you will learn how to create, modify, and use reports to customize the arrangement of data on paper. You will also learn how to use reports to group and summarize your data.

When you're done working through this chapter, you will know how to:

- View a report's design
- Create reports using ReportWizards
- Preview a report
- Total fields and group records within a report
- Modify a report's design

AN ORIENTATION TO REPORTS

In Chapter 1, you learned that reports are the best way to present your data on paper. Although you can print your data directly from tables, query dynasets, and forms, reports give you greater control over how that data is printed.

Among other things, reports enable you to:

- Specify which fields you want printed
- Sort records
- Group records
- Calculate summary information
- Control the overall layout and appearance of your report

 ## PREVIEWING A BASIC REPORT

In Chapter 1, you previewed two reports: a basic report and a report with both groups and totals. In this chapter, you're going to preview those reports again with an eye towards creating similar reports yourself.

Note that when you preview a report (or when you preview any other Access object, for that matter), Access changes the object window's navigation buttons from record navigation buttons (First Record, Previous Record, and so on) to *page* navigation buttons (First Page, Previous Page, and so on). This change enables you to navigate more efficiently through a previewed report, moving you from page to page rather than from record to record. Access also changes the Specific Record Number box to a *Specific Page Number box*, which displays the number of the currently previewed page, and enables you to move directly to a specific page number.

If you do not have both the Access application and the EMPLOYEE Database windows opened and maximized, please open and maximize them now.

Now preview the same basic report you saw in Chapter 1, Employee Hours and Rates. This time, though, first take a look at the table upon which the report is based:

1. Open and examine the Pay Rates table (see Figure 6.1).

2. Close the Table window.

3. Display the list of report object names by clicking on the **Report object button** in the Database window.

4. Double-click on **Employee Hours and Rates** to preview the report (or select the object name, and then click on Preview).

Figure 6.1   **The Pay Rates table**

ID	First	Last	Hired	Dept	Hours	Pay Rate	Health
0007	Jane	Martin	6/7/83	EE	40	$17.00	Yes
0001	Ted	James	4/1/87	MK	38	$23.65	Yes
0012	Marie	Abel	11/25/82	CE	35.5	$6.75	Yes
0004	Julia	Binder	2/17/89	MK	25	$25.00	Yes
0011	Sam	Binga	7/5/80	SS	35.5	$13.30	No
0005	Maria	Sanders	8/17/90	ES	29.5	$17.00	Yes
0002	Harry	Harper	4/19/88	ES	40	$10.00	Yes
0009	Bill	Conner	3/8/91	CE	40	$6.30	Yes
0015	Roger	Donaldson	4/8/92	EE	40	$12.00	No
0003	Penny	Packer	1/15/81	MK	35	$24.00	Yes
0013	Robert	Abot	9/18/84	MK	40	$21.24	No
0008	Alice	Binga	9/1/85	EE	15.5	$15.75	Yes
0006	Nancy	Evans	5/20/86	EE	40	$15.00	No
0014	Joseph	Zambito	7/9/80	CE	40	$15.50	Yes
0010	Dominick	Osowski	7/18/90	MK	40	$22.00	Yes
0016	Wilma	Chase	8/17/84	SS	40	$15.50	No
0017	Alice	DeMarco	8/7/92	ES	25.5	$8.90	Yes
0020	Dennis	Binga	5/12/84	MK	40	$28.00	Yes
0018	Frank	Desoto	9/18/84	MS	40	$16.00	No
0019	Albert	Henley	10/13/90	ES	40	$10.75	No
0030	Robert	Beaton	11/23/83	SS	35	$12.50	Yes
0021	Joe	Stira	2/22/89	EE	37.5	$14.00	Yes
0022	Homer	Jones	4/13/90	CE	40	$17.25	Yes
0023	Opal	Packer	3/31/85	SS	25	$14.00	No
0028	William	Bell	4/24/84	MK	40	$22.50	Yes
0024	David	Haslam	5/13/87	SS	40	$13.50	Yes

5. If necessary, click on **Zoom** to zoom in on the report, then observe the report (see Figure 6.2). The report is tabular, is entitled Employee Hours and Rates, displays the current date, and lists employees alphabetically together with their hours and pay rates.

Figure 6.2   **Previewing the Employee Hours and Rates report**

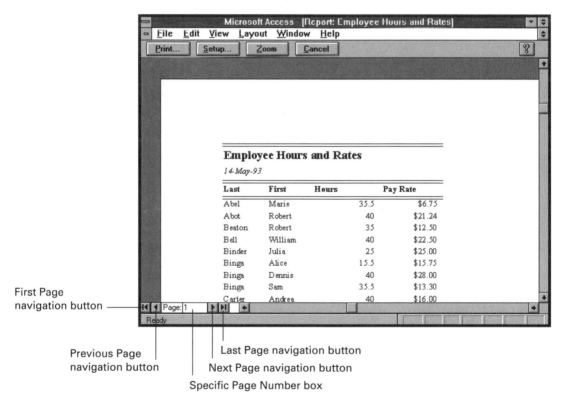

6. Observe the lower-left corner of the Report window. Instead of a Specific *Record* Number box and *record* navigation buttons, the window contains a Specific *Page* Number box and *page* navigation buttons.

7. Observe the Specific Page Number box. It shows that you are currently viewing the first page of the report.

8. Click on the **Last Page navigation button**; then observe the Specific Page Number box. Because you are still on page 1, this must be a single-page report.

9. Use the **vertical scroll bar** to scroll to and observe the end of the page. Here, the report displays grand totals for hours and pay rates. At the lower-right corner of the page, the report also displays a page number.

10. Cancel the preview.

 ORIENTATION TO A BASIC REPORT DESIGN

Like Table, Query, and Form windows, each Report window has a Design view that enables you to view and modify the report's design.

As with Form windows, Access divides a Report window's Design view into separate, specialized sections for containing controls. The number and type of these sections can vary in different report designs, but report designs commonly include

- A *Report Header section*, which contains controls for data that Access will print once at the beginning of the report (such as the report title and date).

- A *Page Header section*, which contains controls for data that Access will print at the top of each page of the report. (In a tabular report, this section will contain column-heading labels.)

- A *Detail section*, which contains controls for data that Access will print once for each record in the report's underlying table or query dynaset. (These repeating controls often comprise the bulk of reports.)

- A *Page Footer section*, which contains controls for data that Access will print at the bottom of each page of the report (such as a calculated control for page numbering).

- A *Report Footer section*, which contains controls for data that Access will print once at the end of the report. (Often, this section includes calculated controls that display summary information, such as sums and averages.)

Record sorting and grouping in a report is controlled through the Sorting and Grouping box. To open this box from a Report window's Design view, choose View, Sorting and Grouping, or click on the second button from the left on the tool bar, the Sorting and Grouping button. To open a Report window in Design view from the Database window, select the report object name, and then click on Design.

Let's view the design of the Employee Hours and Rates report you just previewed:

1. In the Database window, select **Employee Hours and Rates** (if necessary); then click on **Design** to open the Report window in Design view.

2. Observe the Report window. Access divides this window into five separate sections: Report Header, Page Header, Detail, Page Footer, and Report Footer (see Figure 6.3).

Figure 6.3   **The Employee Hours and Rates Report window in Design view**

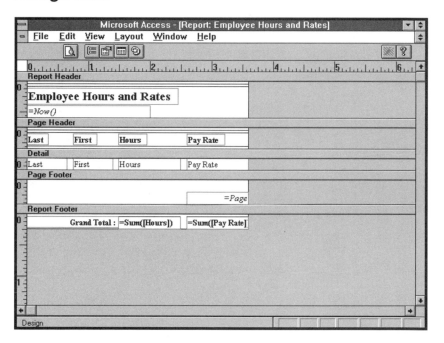

3. Observe the Report Header section. The section contains an unbound control for the report title, and a calculated control with the expression =Now() to display the current date. (Refer

back to Chapter 5 for a description of Access' control types. You'll learn how to create your own calculated controls in Chapter 9.)

4. Observe the Page Header section. Its unbound controls serve as column headings.

5. Observe the Detail section. It contains bound controls. Access will repeat these controls for each record in the report's underlying table.

6. Observe the Page Footer section. It contains a calculated control with the expression =Page. When you preview or print the report, this control will display the current page number.

7. Observe the Report Footer section. The calculated controls in this section contain expressions to sum the Hours and Pay Rate fields, =Sum([Hours]) and =Sum([Pay Rate]).

8. Compare the report design to the report shown in Figure 6.2. When printing the pictured report, Access used each of the controls in the Report Header, Page Header, Page Footer, and Report Footer sections once. (In a multiple-page report, Access would have used controls in the Page Header and Page Footer sections once for each page.) However, Access used the controls in the Detail section once for each record in the report's underlying table. In other words, the report displays the Last, First, Hours, and Pay Rate fields for each employee.

9. Choose **View, Sorting and Grouping** (or click on the Sorting and Grouping button, the second button from the left on the tool bar) to open the Sorting and Grouping box. A two-level, ascending sort by last, and then first name is specified here (see Figure 6.4).

10. Choose **View, Sorting and Grouping** again to close the box (or double-click on the box's Control menu box); then close the Report window.

 ## ORIENTATION TO A GROUPS AND TOTALS REPORT DESIGN

The basic report you previewed at the beginning of this chapter treated every record as part of a single group, and displayed grand totals at the end which summarized data from *every* record in the report.

Figure 6.4   **The Sorting and Grouping box**

Sorting and
Grouping button

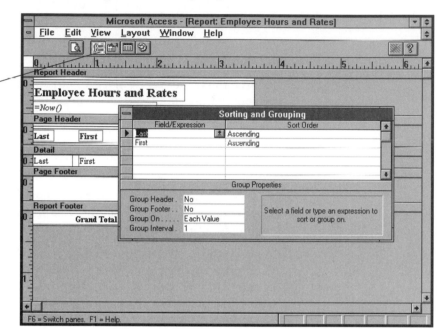

There may be times, however, when you want to break your records down into smaller groups within a single report, and provide summary information for each of those groups (as well as grand totals summarizing data from all of the groups). For example, if you are creating an employee-gross-pay report, you may want to group employees and calculate gross-pay subtotals by department. To accomplish this, you would instruct Access to group your report on the underlying table or query dynaset's department field.

You can include up to ten levels of sorting and/or grouping in a report. For each level of grouping within a report, Access adds two *group sections* to the report's design:

• A *group header section*, which contains controls for data that Access will print at the beginning of each group (such as the name of the group)

• A *group footer section*, which contains controls for data that Access will print at the end of each group (such as group summary information)

In Design view, group header and footer sections will bear the name of the field or the expression upon which the group is based. For example, in a report grouped by the Dept field, the group header will display as Dept Header.

When sorting records in a report that incorporates both grouping and sorting, Access automatically sorts the groups themselves first, and then sorts the records within those groups.

Let's preview a report with both groups and totals, and then examine its design:

1. Preview the Dept Gross Pay report (double-click on the object name).

2. Observe the Report window. In this report, records are grouped by department, with the department name displayed at the beginning of each group and a gross-pay subtotal at the end of each group (see Figure 6.5).

3. Observe the Specific Page Number box. It indicates that you are currently viewing page 1.

Figure 6.5 **Previewing the Dept Gross Pay report**

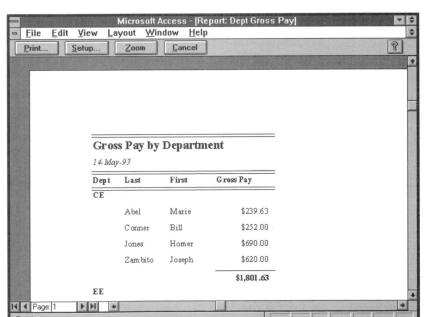

4. Click on the **Last Page navigation button** to move to the last page of the report, page 2.

5. Scroll to and observe the end of the page. The report displays a gross-pay grand total. Notice also the page number (2) at the very bottom of the page.

6. Cancel the preview and return to the Database window.

7. Open the Dept Gross Pay report in Design view (select the object name, and then click on **Design**).

8. Observe the Report window. In addition to the sections you saw in the basic report design, this report includes Dept Header and Dept Footer sections that instruct the report to group records by department.

9. Observe the controls in the Dept Header and Dept Footer sections. The unbound control in the Dept Header section serves to display the department name, while the calculated control in the Dept Footer section contains an expression to sum gross pay by department.

10. Close the Report window.

CREATING A BASIC REPORT

You can avoid most of the detail work of creating your own reports by using Access' ReportWizards. Much like FormWizards, ReportWizards ask you questions about the report you want to create, and then build a new report for you based on your answers.

Access provides three ReportWizards:

- The *Single-column* ReportWizard builds single-column reports much like the Single-column FormWizard builds single-column forms: It arranges fields and their labels in a single column down the page, with each field on a separate line.

- The *Groups/Totals* ReportWizard builds reports that present data in a tabular format. This ReportWizard can build reports with anywhere from zero to three levels of grouping, and automatically creates calculated controls to display summary information for the overall report and for each grouping level.

- The *Mailing Labels* ReportWizard builds reports to print data in a customized format suitable for your particular size of mailing labels.

Whenever you start to create a new report, Access gives you the option of using a ReportWizard.

SELECTING THE DATA SOURCE AND REPORTWIZARD

To start a ReportWizard, you would follow these steps:

- In the Database window, click on the Report object button to display the list of report object names.

- Click on New to open the New Report dialog box.

- In the Select A Table/Query drop-down list box, select the table or query upon which you wish to base your new report.

- Click on ReportWizards.

- In the Microsoft Access dialog box, select the name of the ReportWizard you wish to use, and then click on OK.

Now start creating a basic report that will look much like the basic Employee Hours and Rates report you previewed at the beginning of this chapter:

1. In the Database window, click on **New** to begin creating a new report.

2. Observe the New Report dialog box. You can base a report on a table or a query.

3. In the Select A Table/Query drop-down list box, select **Pay Rates** to base your new report on the Pay Rates table (see Figure 6.6).

Figure 6.6   **Selecting the report's data source**

4. Click on **ReportWizards**.

5. Observe the Microsoft Access dialog box. Access provides three ReportWizards: Single-column, Groups/Totals, and Mailing Labels.

6. Select **Groups/Totals** (see Figure 6.7), and then click on **OK**.

Figure 6.7　　　**Selecting the Groups/Totals ReportWizard**

 SPECIFYING FIELDS AND THE SORT ORDER

With reports, as with forms, you can choose to include only limited fields from the underlying table or query. Careful field selection will produce a report that is both readable and informative. For example, if you are creating an employee-gross-pay report, you probably won't want to include fields for each employee's home address; this information would clutter the report and confuse the reader.

After you start the Groups/Totals ReportWizard, it prompts you to specify the fields you want on the report, and the order in which to place them. To add a single field to the report, select the field's name in the Available Fields list box; then click on > (or, double-click on the field name). To add all of the fields, click on >>. Like a Form-Wizard, the ReportWizard will place fields on your report in the order in which you select them here.

Once you are done selecting fields, click on Next to advance to the ReportWizard's next dialog box. This dialog box asks you to specify from zero to three fields by which to group records. To create a basic report with no groups, simply click on Next.

The next ReportWizard dialog box asks you to specify the fields by which to sort your records. To specify fields for sorting, you can use the same techniques you used for specifying fields to include on the report. If you choose to sort by more than one field, Access will perform a multiple-level sort in the final report according to the order in which you select fields here. Once you have specified a sort order, click on Next to advance to the next dialog box. (To specify no sorting in your report, simply click on Next to bypass the dialog box.)

Now add four fields to your report, choose to have no groups, and specify a two-level sort by last and then first names:

1. Observe the Microsoft Access ReportWizard dialog box. You use this dialog box to specify the fields that you want to appear on the report, and the order in which you want them to appear.

2. In the Available Fields list box, double-click on **Last** to add the field to the report (or select Last, and then click on >).

3. Add the **First**, **Hours**, and **Pay Rate** fields to the report, in that order (see Figure 6.8), and then click on **Next** to advance to the next dialog box.

Figure 6.8   **Specifying fields**

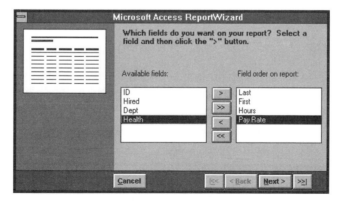

4. Observe the dialog box. You can group records in your report on anywhere from zero to three fields. Because you are creating a basic report with no groups, click on **Next** to advance to the next dialog box.

5. Observe the dialog box. This dialog box enables you to sort records in your report.

6. From the Available Fields list box, add **Last** and then **First** to the Sort Order Of Records In Groups list box (see Figure 6.9). When you preview or print this report, Access will now automatically sort records by last, and then first name.

7. Click on **Next** to advance to the next dialog box.

Figure 6.9   **Setting a sort order**

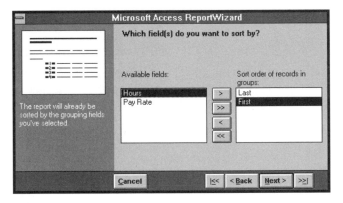

 SELECTING THE REPORT LOOK AND ADDING A TITLE

Once you've finished selecting a sort order and moved to the next dialog box, you just need to select an appropriate look for your report and give the report a title.

The Groups/Totals ReportWizard offers three looks for reports: Executive, Presentation, and Ledger. As with forms, these looks are purely cosmetic; they don't affect the contents of your report, just the report's overall appearance.

After you select a look and click on Next, the Groups/Totals ReportWizard asks you to specify a title for your report. As with forms, this title is not the same as the report's object name (which you specify by using the File, Save As command).

Now select a look and specify a title for your report:

1. Observe the new dialog box. This ReportWizard offers three report looks: Executive, Presentation, and Ledger. The magnifying glass on the left-hand side of the dialog box displays an example of the selected style, Executive (see Figure 6.10).

Figure 6.10   **Report looks**

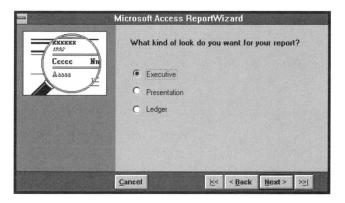

2. While observing the magnifying glass, select **Presentation** and then **Ledger** to view examples of those looks.

3. Select **Executive**; then click on **Next** to advance to the next dialog box.

4. Observe the new dialog box. Here, you can enter a report title. (By default, Access suggests the name of the table upon which you based your report: Pay Rates.)

5. Type **Hours and Rates** to replace the selected text in the Report Title text box and specify a custom report title (see Figure 6.11).

PREVIEWING THE REPORT AND SAVING THE REPORT DESIGN

Once you are finished working through all of the Groups/Totals ReportWizard's questions, you can either preview the report by clicking on Print Preview or open the report's design by clicking on Design. If you click on Print Preview, and then click on Cancel to cancel the preview, Access takes you directly to the Report window's Design view.

Figure 6.11   **Adding a report title**

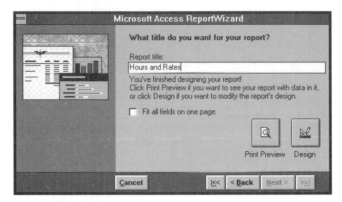

As with any newly created object, you should save your new report design as soon as possible. You can save reports either from the Report window's preview or Design view by using the File, Save As command.

Now preview your new report, observe its design, and then save the report and close the Report window:

1. Observe the dialog box. You can now choose either to preview the report or to view the report's design.

2. Click on **Print Preview** to preview your new report. Then, if necessary, maximize the Report window.

3. Observe the Report window. Your new report is much like the basic report you saw earlier: It has a title, displays the current date, and lists employees alphabetically together with their hours and rates (see Figure 6.12).

4. Scroll to the end of the report. You should see grand totals for the Hours and Pay Rate fields.

5. Click on **Cancel** to cancel the preview and switch to the Report window's Design view.

6. Observe the report design. It is similar to the basic report design you saw earlier in this chapter. Note that the Report-Wizard automatically created a calculated control in the Report Header section to display the current date, a calculated control in the Page Footer section to display page numbers, and calculated controls in the Report Footer section to sum the report's two numeric fields, Hours and Pay Rate (see Figure 6.13).

Figure 6.12   **Previewing the report**

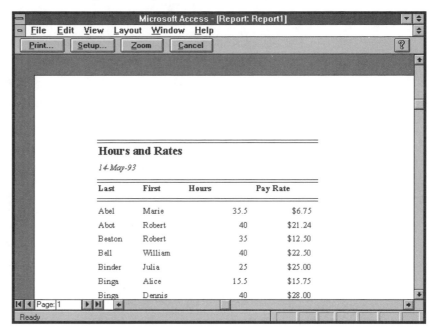

Figure 6.13   **The new report's design**

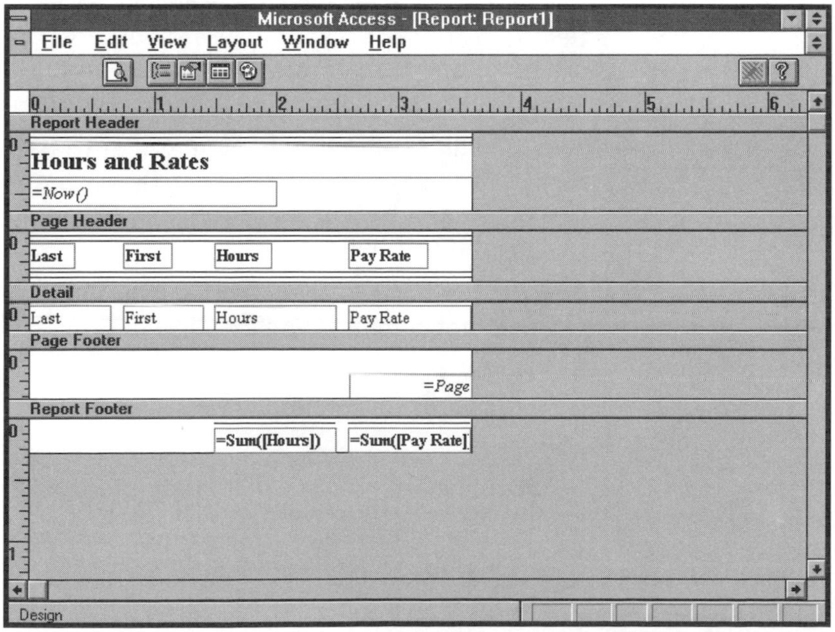

7. Click on the **Sorting and Grouping button** (or, choose View, Sorting and Grouping) to open the Sorting and Grouping box. Access displays here the two-level sort you specified through the ReportWizard.

8. Close the Sorting and Grouping box.

9. Choose **File, Save As**, type **My Hours and Rates**, and then click on **OK** to name and save the report design.

10. Close the Report window.

CREATING A GROUPS AND TOTALS REPORT

You've just learned how to create a basic report using the Groups/-Totals ReportWizard. This time around, you'll use the same ReportWizard to create a report with both groups and totals, and you'll base your report not on a table but on a query.

This second report will be an employee-gross-pay report that groups employee records by department, and provides summary information both for each group and for the overall report.

Because you need a gross-pay field for this report—a field which is not available in the Pay Rates table—you will base the report not on the Pay Rates table itself but on the Concatenated Gross Pay query; this query is based on the Pay Rates table, and includes a calculated field for gross pay. (ReportWizards do not provide any option for creating calculated fields, but they *do* enable you to use a calculated field from an underlying query like any regular field.)

You may find over time that you prefer to base your reports (and forms, for that matter) on queries rather than tables because queries are more flexible. Here are some advantages of basing a report (or form) on a query:

- You can create calculated fields in the query, and then easily use those fields when creating the report.

- You can limit not just the fields but also the records you use for your report by setting criteria in the query.

- You can create reports that use data from more than one table. (You'll learn how to create multiple-table queries in Chapter 7.)

- You can specialize existing reports by modifying the report's underlying query.

Once you've finished creating this second report, you'll learn how to modify the design that the ReportWizard provides.

STARTING REPORTWIZARD AND SPECIFYING FIELDS

The first steps in creating this second report are quite similar to the steps you followed to create your first report.

First examine the Concatenated Gross Pay query upon which you will base the report, and then start creating the report itself:

1. Run the Concatenated Gross Pay query, and then observe the query's dynaset. It contains the Dept, Name, and Gross Pay fields (see Figure 6.14).

Figure 6.14   **The Concatenated Gross Pay query's dynaset**

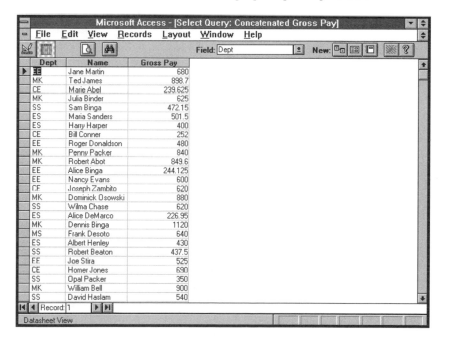

2. Switch to the Query window's Design view, and then observe the query's design. (You may not be able to view the entire expressions for the Name and Gross Pay fields. To view each one of these expressions, place the insertion point in the

appropriate Field cell, and then use the Home and End keys.) The query is based on the Pay Rates table, and Gross Pay is a calculated field that multiplies Hours by Pay Rate. Notice also that the Name calculated field *concatenates* (combines) the First and Last fields. (You'll learn more about concatenated fields in Chapter 7.)

3. Close the Query window.

4. Begin creating a new report by displaying the list of Report object names, and then clicking on **New**.

5. In the Select A Table/Query drop-down list box, select **Concatenated Gross Pay** to base this report on the Concatenated Gross Pay query. (Notice that it's impossible to tell a table from a query in this dialog box. For this reason, it's a good idea to examine the proposed table or query *before* creating a new report.)

6. Click on **ReportWizards**.

7. Select **Groups/Totals**, and then click on **OK** to start the Groups/Totals ReportWizard.

8. Observe the Microsoft Access ReportWizard dialog box. The Available Fields list box lists all of the query's fields.

9. Click on **>>** to add all of the available fields to the report in the order in which they are listed (see Figure 6.15). Then click on **Next** to advance to the next dialog box.

Figure 6.15   **Adding all available fields to the report**

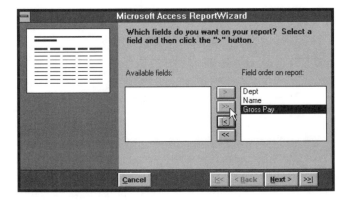

DESIGNATING A GROUP

As you learned earlier in this chapter, you can include up to ten levels of sorting and/or grouping in a report. However, because most reports need far less than ten groups, the Groups/Totals ReportWizard only enables you to group by up to three fields. (To group by more than three fields, you can use the Sorting and Grouping box from the Report window's Design view.) To specify a field or fields for grouping, you can use the same techniques that you used to specify fields in other ReportWizard dialog boxes.

Once you have specified a field or fields for grouping, and have clicked on Next to advance to the next dialog box, the Groups/Totals ReportWizard asks you to specify the grouping method. At this point, you can choose to have your report group records by the entire value within your grouping field or fields (Normal), or by anywhere from the first to the first five characters within that field. For example, if your company uses product codes where the first digit of the code identifies each product's category, you could select 1st Character to group those products by category. This option, then, would remove the need to have a separate field just for product category.

Because you want Access to use the entire value within your grouping field, you will choose the default Normal grouping method.

Now specify Dept as the grouping field, and Normal as the grouping method:

1. Observe the Microsoft Access ReportWizard dialog box. You can select anywhere from zero to three fields by which to group in the report.

2. Add **Dept** to the Records Will Be Grouped By list box to instruct Access to group records in your new report by department (see Figure 6.16).

3. Click on **Next** to advance to the next dialog box.

4. Observe the dialog box. Access can group records by the entire value within the Dept field (Normal), or by only a number of leading characters within the field.

5. Verify that Normal is selected (see Figure 6.17); then click on **Next**.

Figure 6.16   **Designating a grouping field**

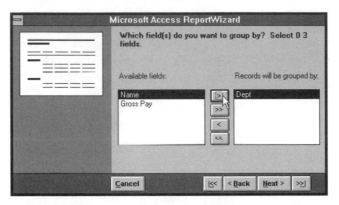

Figure 6.17   **Specifying a grouping method**

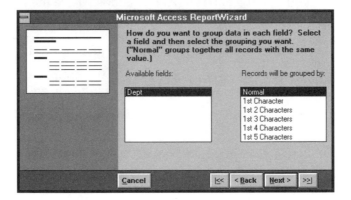

SPECIFYING A SORT ORDER, STYLE, AND TITLE

You learned earlier that when sorting records in a report with both groups and sorting, Access automatically sorts the groups themselves first, and then sorts the records within those groups.

After you specify grouping fields and methods to the Groups/Totals ReportWizard, the ReportWizard's next dialog box enables you to specify sorting fields within your groups. Because it would be redundant to sort by a field that you've already specified as a grouping field, the dialog box lists only nongrouping fields in its

Available Fields list box. Once you've specified a sorting field or fields, the only tasks left are to select a report look and specify a report title.

Now finish your report by specifying a single-level sort by the Gross Pay field, selecting the Executive report look, and specifying a report title:

1. Observe the left-hand side of the new dialog box. Because you chose to group records by department, Access automatically sorts those groups alphabetically by department name. However, you can also instruct Access to sort records *within* those groups. (Note that because you specified Dept as a grouping field for this report, the dialog box does not list Dept in its Available Fields list box.)

2. Add **Gross Pay** to the Sort Order Of Records In Groups list box (see Figure 6.18).

Figure 6.18 **Specifying a sort order**

3. Click on **Next** to advance to the next dialog box.

4. Click on **Next** again to accept the Executive look and advance to the next dialog box.

5. In the Report Title text box, type **Gross Pay by Department** as the report name.

PREVIEWING THE REPORT AND EXAMINING THE REPORT DESIGN

Now that you've completed the ReportWizard's questions, you can preview the report:

1. Click on **Print Preview**. Then, if necessary, maximize the Report window.

2. Examine the previewed report. Records are grouped by department, and there is a gross-pay subtotal for each group. Within each group, records are sorted by gross pay (see Figure 6.19).

Figure 6.19   **Previewing the new report**

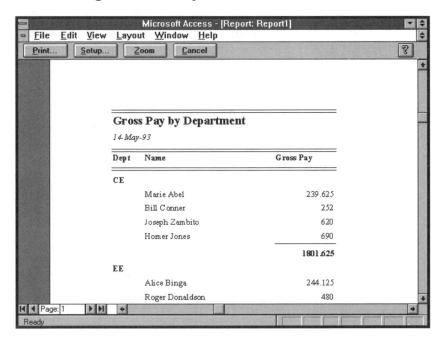

3. Scroll to the end of the report by clicking on the **Last Page navigation button**, and then using the **vertical scroll bar**. The report includes a gross-pay grand total.

4. Cancel the preview and switch to the Report window's Design view by clicking on **Cancel**.

5. Examine the report design. Like the groups and totals report design you saw earlier in this chapter, this design includes

Dept Header and Dept Footer sections for grouping records by the Dept field. The Dept Header section contains an unbound control to display each department name, while the Dept Footer section contains a calculated control to sum the gross pay for each department (see Figure 6.20).

6. Use the **File, Save As** command to save the report design as **My Dept Total Gross Pay**.

Figure 6.20 **The new report's design**

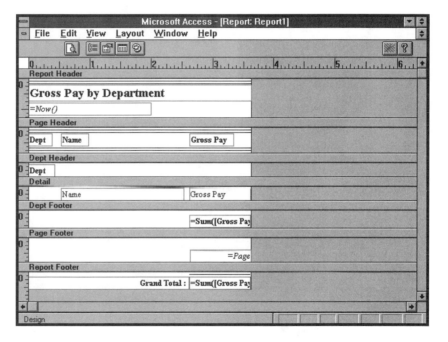

MODIFYING THE REPORT DESIGN

If a ReportWizard does not build a report to suit your needs and tastes exactly, you can modify the design through the Report window's Design view. To modify a report's design, you can use many of the techniques you learned in the last chapter when modifying a form's design, including those to delete, move, size, and align controls.

You can also modify a report's (or form's) design by changing the properties of the controls comprising the design. (*Control properties* are akin to properties for other Access elements; they determine the appearance and behavior of each control.)

In a Report window's Design view, you can display on the tool bar—by selecting any control or controls—two drop-down list boxes and seven buttons that enable you to change some control properties, as shown in Figure 6.21. Any changes you then make using the tool bar will affect only the selected control or controls.

Figure 6.21   **Control-property boxes and buttons on the tool bar**

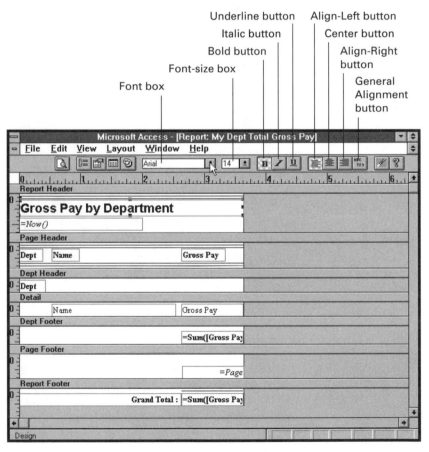

These tool-bar boxes and buttons are

- The *Font box*, which enables you to specify the *font*, or shape and appearance, of a control's contents. (Notice that this book uses two fonts, one for the headings and page headers, and another for the body text.)

- The *Font-size box*, which enables you to specify the size of a control's contents. (Notice that this book's headings and page headers use text that has a larger font size than the rest of the book's text.)

- The *Bold button*, which enables you to *boldface*, or darken, a control's contents. (**This text is bold.**)

- The *Italic button*, which enables you to *italicize*, or slant, a control's contents. (*This text is italic.*)

- The *Underline button*, which enables you to *underline* a control's contents. (<u>This text is underlined.</u>)

- The *Align-Left button*, which enables you to align the control's contents against the control's left edge.

- The *Center button*, which enables you to center the control's contents between the control's left and right edges.

- The *Align-Right button*, which enables you to align the control's contents against the control's right edge.

- The *General Alignment button*, which enables you to align the control's contents against the left edge if the contents are text and against the right edge if the contents are numbers.

In Chapter 9, you'll learn how to change control properties using other methods.

Now use some of these tool-bar boxes and buttons to improve your report's design:

1. Click on the **Print Preview button** to preview the report. Then scroll to the top of the report by clicking on the **First Page navigation button**, and then using the **vertical scroll bar**.

2. Compare your report to the finished report pictured in Figure 6.22. In the figure, the report title and column headings have a different font, and the Gross Pay column heading is right-aligned in order to line up better with the gross-pay values.

Figure 6.22   **The previewed report after modifying control properties**

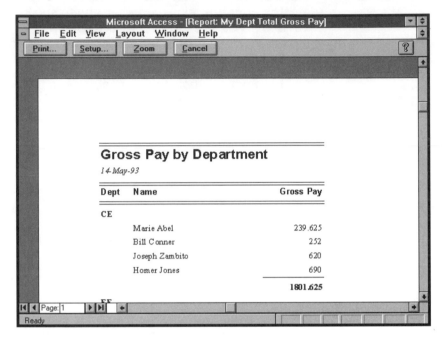

3. Cancel the preview and return to Design view.

4. In the Report Header section, select the unbound control containing the report title **Gross Pay by Department**.

5. Observe the tool bar. When you selected the control, Access added two drop-down list boxes and seven buttons for changing control properties.

6. Observe the tool bar's Font box. It shows that the report title font is currently set to Times New Roman (it may instead be set to Tms Rmn or Times).

7. Open the Font box's drop-down list, and then select **Arial** to change the title's font (see Figure 6.21). (If Arial is not listed, choose Helv or Helvetica.)

8. Observe the Font-size box on the tool bar. The title's current size is 14.

9. Open the Font-size box's drop-down list, and then select **16** to increase the title's font size.

10. In the Page Header section, select the unbound control containing the **Gross Pay** column heading; then observe the tool bar. The selected alignment button is the General Alignment button (the third button from the right on the tool bar), which aligns text to the left.

11. Click on the **Align-Right button** (the fourth button from the right on the tool bar) to right-align the heading within its control.

12. Place the mouse pointer over one of the selected control's edges until the pointer changes to an open-hand pointer; then drag the control about 1/4 inch to the right edge of the Page Header section (see Figure 6.23).

Figure 6.23   **Moving the Gross Pay column heading**

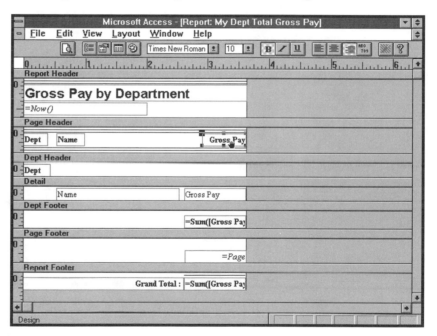

PRACTICE YOUR SKILLS

1. Change the font for each control in the Page Header section to **Arial** (or Helv or Helvetica).

2. Preview the report, then compare it to Figure 6.22.

3. Save the changes to the report design using the **File, Save** command.

4. Close the Report and Database windows.

SUMMARY

In this chapter, you learned how to view and modify a report's design, preview reports, and create reports using ReportWizards.

Here's a quick reference guide to the Access features introduced in this chapter:

Desired Result	How to Do It
Preview a report	From the Database window, select the report object name and then click on **Preview**; or, double-click on the report object name. From the Report window, click on the **Print Preview button**
Move to the last page of a previewed report	Click on the **Last Page navigation button**
Move to the first page of a previewed report	Click on the **First Page navigation button**
Move to the end of a report	Click on the **Last Page navigation button**, and then use the **vertical scroll bar** to scroll to the end of the last page
Open a Report window in Design view	From the Database window, select the report object name, and then click on **Design**
Open and close the Sorting and Grouping box	In a Report window's Design view, choose **View, Sorting and Grouping**; or, click on the **Sorting and Grouping button**

Create a new report with a ReportWizard	From the Database window, click on the **Report object button** to display report object names, click on **New**, select a table or query upon which to base the report, click on **ReportWizards**, select the name of the ReportWizard you wish to use, click on **OK**, and then answer the ReportWizard's questions, clicking on **Next** to move from dialog box to dialog box
Save and name a report	From the Report window, choose **File, Save As**, type a report object name, and then click on **OK**
Save a modified report	From the Report window, choose **File, Save**
Change a report control's font	In the Report window's Design view, select the control, and then select a new font name from the **Font box**
Change a report control's font size	In the Report window's Design view, select the control, and then select a new font size from the **Font-Size box**
Right-align a report control's contents	In the Report window's Design view, select the control, and then click on the **Align-Right button**

In Chapter 7, you'll learn how to create and run select queries more efficiently, how to create advanced select queries, and how to create and run parameter, action, and multiple-table queries.

IF YOU'RE STOPPING HERE

If you need to break off here, please exit Access. If you want to proceed directly to the next chapter, please do so now.

CHAPTER 7: ENHANCED QUERY DESIGN

Reviewing Select
Queries

Creating Advanced
Select Queries

Creating Parameter
Queries

Creating Action
Queries

Creating Multiple-
Table Queries

Back in Chapter 4, you learned how to create and run single-table select queries. In this chapter, you will first review and then expand on that knowledge in order to construct queries more efficiently and to create more advanced single-table select queries. Then, you'll go on to devise some additional types of queries, including parameter, action, and multiple-table queries.

When you are done working through this chapter you will know how to:

- Create a query with a single click

- *Concatenate* (that is, combine) values from two fields into a single field

- Work more easily with lengthy expressions in the QBE grid

- Specify records with unique values

- Create and run a *parameter query* in order to specify criteria conveniently

- Create and run an *update query* in order to change values in multiple records

- Create and run an *append query* in order to copy records from one table to another

- Create and run a *delete query* in order to delete multiple records

- Create a *multiple-table query* in order to combine data from multiple tables

- Create a *make-table query* in order to create a new table

REVIEWING SELECT QUERIES

Throughout Chapter 4, you learned the basics of creating, running, and using select queries to view data. Because that was three chapters ago, let's take the time now to work with some select queries again as a review.

We'll also take this opportunity to demonstrate how to create and work with queries more efficiently. Access offers a lot of shortcuts that become useful once you are comfortable working with the program. While we can't possibly show you all of these shortcuts, we will try to reveal some of the best ones.

CREATING AND RUNNING A SELECT QUERY

In Chapter 4, you created new queries from the Database window by following these steps:

- Clicking on the Query object button to display the list of query object names
- Clicking on New
- Selecting a table or query name in the Add Table dialog box
- Clicking on Add
- Clicking on Close

However, you can create a new query more quickly—and directly from a Table or Query window—by clicking on the fifth button from the right on the toolbar, the *New Query button*. (This button displays the same icon as the Database window's Query object button.) When you click on the New Query button, Access creates a new query based on the current table or query, and does not open the Add Table dialog box. You can also create a new query from the Database window by selecting the table or query object name you want to base the new query upon, and then clicking on the New Query button.

In this chapter, we're going to start using a third database file (besides the employee.mdb and practice.mdb files that you've used so far) called company.mdb. Rather than containing just employee data, company.mdb contains company-wide data.

If you do not have the Access application window opened and maximized, please open and maximize it now. If you have a Database window open, please close it.

Now, open your new database and create a new select query with the New Query button:

1. Open the company.mdb database file (it's stored in the same place as the employee.mdb and practice.mdb database files) and maximize the COMPANY Database window.

2. From the Database window, open and examine the Payroll Data table (see Figure 7.1). Note that the table contains 11 fields and 51 records, and the records are in order by ID (ID is the table's primary-key field).

Figure 7.1   **The Payroll Data table**

New Query button

ID	Last	First	Dept	Hired	Hours	Pay Rate	Health	Park Lot	Park Rate	Comment
EN01	James	Ted	MK	01-Apr-81	38	$15.50	A2	SW	$50.00	
EN03	Harper	Hanna	ES	19-Apr-80	40	$21.50	A2	NW	$65.00	
EN04	Packer	Penny	MK	15-Jan-85	35	$24.00	A1	NW	$55.00	
EN05	Binder	Julia	MS	17-Feb-83	25	$8.52	B			Julia works v
EN07	Sanders	Maria	ES	17-Aug-83	29.5	$7.25	B			
EN08	Faster	Connie	EE	20-May-90	40	$15.00	A1	NW	$62.00	
EN10	Martin	Jane	CC	07-Jun-07	40	$8.75	A2	SE	$55.50	Jane Martin's
EN11	Binga	Allison	EE	01-Sep-89	15.5	$7.25	B	SW	$55.75	
EN12	Conner	Bill	CE	08-Mar-80	40	$19.50	B			
EN13	Osowski	Dominick	SA	18-Jul-92	40	$22.00	A1	NE	$65.00	
EN14	Binga	Sam	SS	05-Jul-84	35.5	$13.30	A1	NW	$60.00	
EN15	Abel	Murray	CE	25-Nov-86	35.5	$12.50	A1	NE	$62.00	
EN16	Abot	Robert	MK	18-Sep-82	40	$12.60	A1	NW	$65.00	Bob is due fo
EN17	Zambito	Joseph	CE	09-Jul-84	40	$15.50	A2	NE	$67.75	
EN18	McDonald	Peter	EE	08-Apr-83	40	$21.50	C	NE	$60.00	
EN19	Chase	Wilma	SS	17-Aug-88	40	$15.50	A1	SE	$52.00	
EN20	DeMarco	Arlene	ES	07-Aug-86	25.5	$8.90	B	SW	$55.00	
EN23	Desoto	Frank	MS	18-Sep-88	40	$21.50	A2	NE	$67.75	
EN24	Henley	Albert	ES	13-Oct-80	40	$17.80	B	SE	$52.50	
EN26	Kyler	Dennis	MK	12-May-88	40	$17.80	C			
EN27	Zangari	Nick	EE	22-Feb-92	37.5	$32.50	B	NE	$67.75	Nick has con
EN30	Jones	Hugh	CE	13-Apr-82	40	$17.25	A1	SE	$55.00	
EN32	Vetch	Randall	SS	31-Mar-89	25	$14.00	A1	SW	$50.00	
EN34	Horn	Jason	SS	13-May-91	40	$13.50	A1	SE	$52.50	
EN36	Castile	Abraham	MK	01-Nov-82	40	$18.00	A1	NW	$60.50	
EN38	Wilson	Judy	MK	01-Sep-87	40	$16.00	B	NW	$65.50	

Record: 1

Employee identification code

3. Click on the **New Query button** to open a new Query window in Design view and automatically add the current table, Payroll Data, to the query design.

4. Add **Last**, **First**, **Dept**, and **Pay Rate**, respectively, to the first four Field cells of the QBE grid. (Chapter 4 covers adding multiple fields to a QBE grid.)

5. In the Last column's Sort cell, select **Ascending** from the drop-down list.

6. Open and examine the **Query** menu. Access makes all new queries select queries by default.

7. Close the **Query** menu.

8. Run the query (click on the **Datasheet View button** or choose **Query, Run**), and then observe the dynaset (see Figure 7.2). It displays only 4 of the table's 11 fields (Last, First, Dept, and

Pay Rate), it has sorted records not by ID (as in the underlying Payroll Data table) but by last name, and it has included all 51 records (because you set no criteria).

Figure 7.2   **The new query's dynaset**

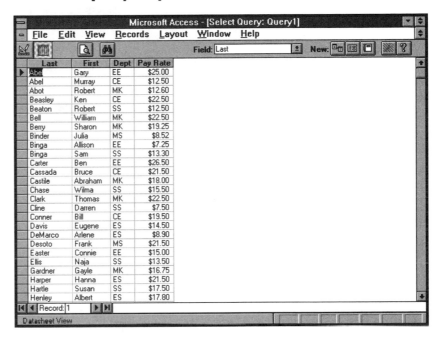

 CALCULATING A 7 PERCENT PAY INCREASE

In Chapter 4, when you created a calculated field in a query to calculate gross pay, remember that Access automatically named the field Expr1. Later, you changed Expr1 to a more meaningful name: Gross Pay. You can avoid a little of this work, however, by naming the calculated field as you create it. To do so, first type the calculated field's name followed by a colon (:), and then type your calculation expression (do not type any spaces before or after the colon). For example, if you wanted to create a calculated field named Gross Pay by multiplying the Hours and Pay Rate fields, you would type Gross Pay:[hours]*[pay rate] in an empty Field cell.

As you start to work with longer expressions in the QBE grid, you may find that the grid's default column widths are not wide enough to display your entire expression at once. However, you can manually widen or narrow QBE-grid columns using the technique you used in Chapter 2 to resize a column in a Table window's Datasheet view:

- In the QBE grid, place the mouse pointer on the right edge of the column's field selector until the pointer changes to a cross with a horizontal, two-headed arrow.

- Drag the column boundary to the right to widen the column or to the left to narrow the column.

- Release the mouse button when the column is the desired width.

Note that, unlike in a Table window, you cannot save your customized QBE-grid column widths. Once you close a Query window and then reopen it, Access sets all of your columns to the default width. (You can, however, use the View, Options command to set a new default width for all QBE-grid columns.)

Now create a calculated field, New Pay Rate, that calculates a 7 percent increase over the current pay rate, and then widen the calculated field's QBE-grid column so that you can view the entire field:

1. Return to the Query window's Design view (click on the **Design View button** or choose **View, Query Design**).

2. In the QBE grid's fifth Field cell, type **New Pay Rate:[pay rate]*1.07** to both create a calculated field and provide a custom name for that calculated field (remember that you must enclose field names within square brackets).

3. Observe the QBE grid. You cannot view the entire calculated field.

4. Place the mouse pointer on the right edge of the calculated field's field selector until the pointer changes to a cross with a horizontal two-headed arrow. Then drag the column boundary about half a column width to the right (see Figure 7.3). This should widen the column enough so that you can view the entire field.

5. Run the query, and then observe the dynaset. The dynaset now includes a New Pay Rate field that calculates a 7 percent increase over the Pay Rate field (see Figure 7.4).

Figure 7.3   **Widening a QBE-grid column**

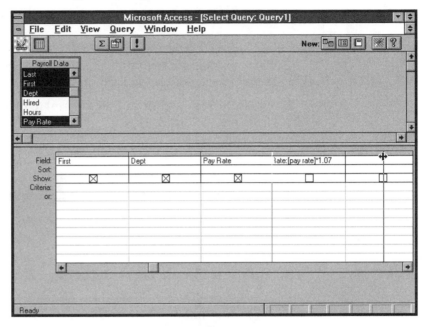

Figure 7.4   **The query dynaset with the New Pay Rate field**

Last	First	Dept	Pay Rate	New Pay Rate
Abel	Gary	EE	$25.00	26.75
Abel	Murray	CE	$12.50	13.375
Abot	Robert	MK	$12.60	13.482
Beasley	Ken	CE	$22.50	24.075
Beaton	Robert	SS	$12.50	13.375
Bell	William	MK	$22.50	24.075
Berry	Sharon	MK	$19.25	20.5975
Binder	Julia	MS	$8.52	9.1164
Binga	Allison	EE	$7.25	7.7575
Binga	Sam	SS	$13.30	14.231
Carter	Ben	EE	$26.50	28.355
Cassada	Bruce	CE	$21.50	23.005
Castile	Abraham	MK	$18.00	19.26
Chase	Wilma	SS	$15.50	16.585
Clark	Thomas	MK	$22.50	24.075
Cline	Darren	SS	$7.50	8.025
Conner	Bill	CE	$19.50	20.865
Davis	Eugene	ES	$14.50	15.515
DeMarco	Arlene	ES	$8.90	9.523
Desoto	Frank	MS	$21.50	23.005
Easter	Connie	EE	$15.00	16.05
Ellis	Naja	SS	$13.50	14.445
Gardner	Gayle	MK	$16.75	17.9225
Harper	Hanna	ES	$21.50	23.005
Hartle	Susan	SS	$17.50	18.725
Henley	Albert	ES	$17.80	19.046

DELETING FIELDS FROM THE QBE GRID

Let's review how to delete a field from the QBE grid:

1. Return to Design view.

2. Click on the Last column's field selector (you may need to scroll to the left on the QBE grid) to select the column.

3. Press **Delete** (or choose Edit, Delete) to delete the Last column from the QBE grid.

PRACTICE YOUR SKILLS

1. Delete the First column from the QBE grid.

2. Run the query, and then compare the dynaset to Figure 7.5.

Figure 7.5   **The query dynaset after deleting two fields**

Dept	Pay Rate	New Pay Rate
MK	$15.50	16.585
ES	$21.50	23.005
MK	$24.00	25.68
MS	$8.52	9.1164
ES	$7.25	7.7575
EE	$15.00	16.05
EE	$8.75	9.3625
EE	$7.25	7.7575
CE	$19.50	20.865
SA	$22.00	23.54
SS	$13.30	14.231
CE	$12.50	13.375
MK	$12.60	13.482
CE	$15.50	16.585
EE	$21.50	23.005
SS	$15.50	16.585
ES	$8.90	9.523
MS	$21.50	23.005
ES	$17.80	19.046
MK	$17.80	19.046
EE	$32.50	34.775
CE	$17.25	18.4575
SS	$14.00	14.98
SS	$13.50	14.445
MK	$18.00	19.26
MK	$16.00	17.12

Microsoft Access - [Select Query: Query1]

File Edit View Records Layout Window Help

Field: Dept   New:

Record: 1

2-character department code

CREATING ADVANCED SELECT QUERIES

By the time you completed Chapter 4, you had started to use some fairly advanced techniques with select queries. We're now going to review two of those advanced techniques: calculating totals for groups of records and using a criterion with wildcard characters. Then we'll take a look at two new techniques: concatenating fields and specifying records with unique values.

 GROUPING RECORDS AND AVERAGING PAY RATES

At the end of Chapter 4, you used Access' totals feature to group employee records by department and calculate the total employee gross-pay cost for each department (using the Sum aggregate function).

Let's use Access' totals feature this time to group employee records by department and calculate averages (using the Avg aggregate function) for both the current pay rate and the new pay rate:

1. Return to Design view.

2. Click on the **Totals button** (or choose View, Totals) to add a Total row to the QBE grid. Note that Access automatically adds the Group By operator under each regular field, and the Expression operator under the calculated field, New Pay Rate (see Figure 7.6).

3. In the Pay Rate column's Total cell, use the cell's drop-down list to change the operator from Group By to **Avg**. Because the Group By operator remains under only the Dept field, this instructs the query to average pay rates by department.

4. In the New Pay Rate column's Total cell, change the operator from Expression to **Avg**. Your query will now also average the *new* pay rates by department.

5. Run the query, and then observe the dynaset. It displays only seven records, one for each department, and has calculated averages for both the Pay Rate and the New Pay Rate fields (see Figure 7.7).

6. Double-click on the Query window's **Control menu box** to close the Query window. Because you have not yet saved the query, Access asks if you want to save the query now.

Figure 7.6   **Displaying the Total row**

Totals button

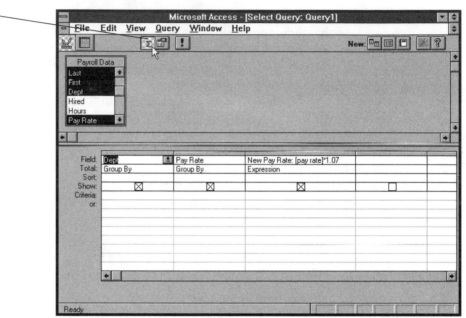

Figure 7.7   **The query dynaset that groups records and averages pay rates**

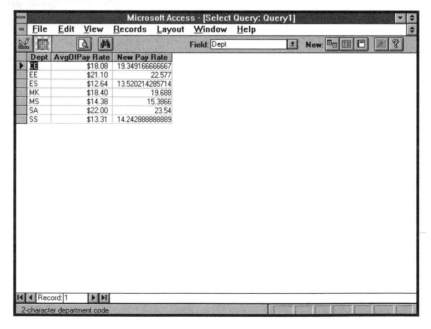

7. Click on **No** to close the Query window without saving the query and return to the Payroll Data Table window. (Remember that you started from this Table window when you first created your new query.)

CREATING A CONCATENATION EXPRESSION

When you store people's names in a table, it is usually best for sorting purposes to store first and last names in separate fields. If you then want to combine the two names temporarily for items such as mailing labels and form letters, you can use a query to concatenate (combine) values from two text fields into one by using a *concatenation expression*. You can create a concatenation expression by using the *concatenation operator*, &, to separate the field names within a QBE-grid Field cell. For example, if you wanted to create a new field to concatenate the First and Last fields, you could type [First]&[Last].

When you create a concatenated field, Access runs together the values from the two fields with no space in between. For example, if a record's First field contains Alice and the Last field contains Binga, the concatenated field just listed will result in AliceBinga.

To solve this problem, you can add a space to your concatenation expression by enclosing the space within double quotation marks (") and separating the quotation marks and space from other elements in the expression with concatenation operators. For example, to concatenate the First and Last fields with a space in between, you could use the expression [First]&" "&[Last].

Another potential problem is that Access sorts concatenated fields by the fields' combined values. In the preceding example, Access will sort records primarily by first name. But what if you want to sort by last name? To concatenate fields but still sort by only one of those fields, place that one field (in this case, the Last field) in a separate Field cell in the QBE grid, select a sort order in the Sort cell, and then uncheck that field's Show box. This way, the query will sort records by the separate field, but will not display the otherwise redundant field in its dynaset. (Remember from Chapter 4 that the Show box tells a query whether or not to display the field in the dynaset.)

Create a calculated field that concatenates the First and Last fields, and instruct the query to sort records only by last name:

1. From the Payroll Data Table window, create a new query based on the Payroll Data table (click on the **New Query button**).

2. Add **Last, First**, and **Hired** to the first three Field cells of the QBE grid, in that order.

3. Run the query, and then observe the dynaset. The query displays last and first names in two separate fields. Notice also that the dynaset displays the records in the order in which they are stored in the underlying table (sorted by ID).

4. Return to Design view.

5. In the First field cell, select First (do *not* select the entire column).

6. Type **[first]&" "&[last]** to replace First. (Be sure to include square brackets around each field name, and no spaces in the expression except for the single space between the two double quotation marks.) Then press **Tab**.

7. Widen the calculated field's column and observe the field. Access automatically named this field Expr1 (see Figure 7.8).

Figure 7.8   **Viewing the concatenated field**

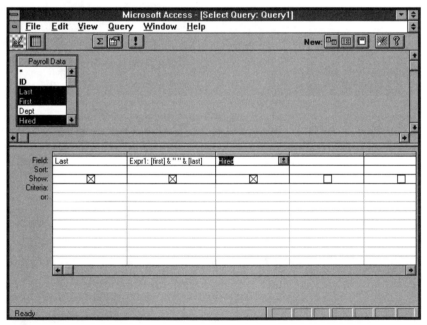

8. In the Last column's Sort cell, select **Ascending** to instruct the query to sort records in ascending order by last name.

9. Run the query, and then observe the dynaset. The query has sorted records by last name, and has successfully concatenated first and last names into a single field. However, the calculated field is entitled Expr1, and the information in the Last field is redundant.

10. Return to Design view.

11. Uncheck the Last column's Show box.

12. Change the calculated field's name to Name (double-click on **Expr1** to select the default name, and then type **Name**).

13. Run the query, and then observe the dynaset. The calculated field is now entitled Name, and records are still sorted by last name even though the dynaset does not display the Last field (see Figure 7.9).

Figure 7.9   **The final query dynaset**

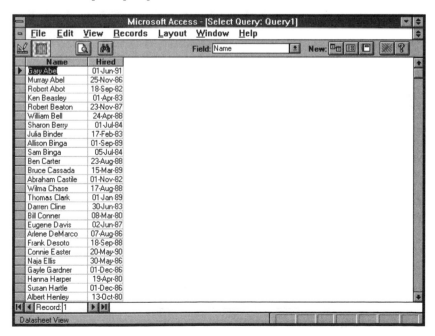

SETTING CRITERIA WITH WILDCARD CHARACTERS

You learned in Chapter 4 that you can use the wildcard characters *
and ? to set criteria for values that match a certain *pattern* rather
than for exact values.

In Chapter 4, you set a criterion to search for records of employees
whose last names began with *B.* This time, you'll set a criterion to
search for records of employees who were hired in 1988:

1. Return to Design view.

2. In the Hired column's Criteria cell, type ***/*/88**, and then press
   Tab. Access automatically changes your criteria to Like "*/*/88".

3. Run the query, and then observe the dynaset. It displays records
   only for the six employees hired in 1988 (see Figure 7.10).

4. Save the query as **My 1988 Hires**, and then close the Query
   window and return to the Payroll Data Table window.

Figure 7.10   **The query dynaset displaying only 1988 hires**

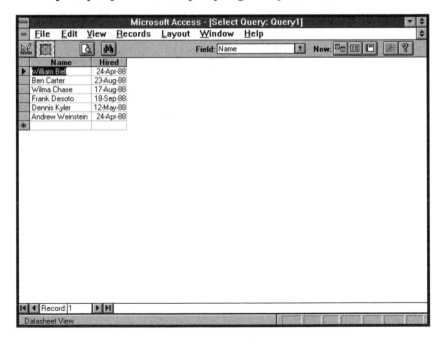

SPECIFYING RECORDS WITH UNIQUE VALUES

When you run queries that use only one or very few fields, your dynaset may display the same exact value or set of values for multiple records. For example, if you generate a list of department codes from an employee-information table that contains a department code for each record, you will probably get long lists of duplicate department codes.

You can, however, instruct your query to display duplicate values only once by specifying that your dynaset include unique values only. To specify that a query includes unique values only, you would follow these steps:

- From the Query window's Design view, choose View, Query Properties to open the Query Properties dialog box. (Alternatively, you can click on the fourth button from the left on the tool bar, the *Properties button*, which displays a pointing hand.)

- Check Unique Values Only.

- Click on OK to close the dialog box.

Let's create a dynaset that displays unique values only:

1. From the Payroll Data Table window, create a new query based on the Payroll Data table.

2. Add **Dept** to the QBE grid's first Field cell.

3. In the Dept column's Sort cell, select **Ascending**.

4. Run the query, and then observe the dynaset. It displays all 51 records from the underlying table, often repeating department codes (see Figure 7.11).

5. Return to Design view; then choose **View, Query Properties** (or click on the Properties button on the tool bar) to open the Query Properties dialog box (see Figure 7.12).

6. In the Query Properties dialog box, check **Unique Values Only**, and then click on **OK**.

7. Run the query, and then observe the dynaset. It displays the seven department codes only once each (see Figure 7.13).

8. Close the Query window without saving the query (double-click on the window's **Control menu box**, and then click on **No**).

Figure 7.11   **The query dynaset displaying repeated values**

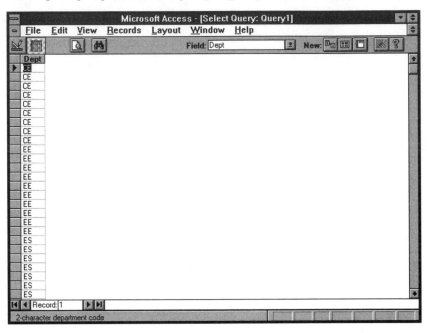

Figure 7.12   **The Query Properties dialog box**

Properties button

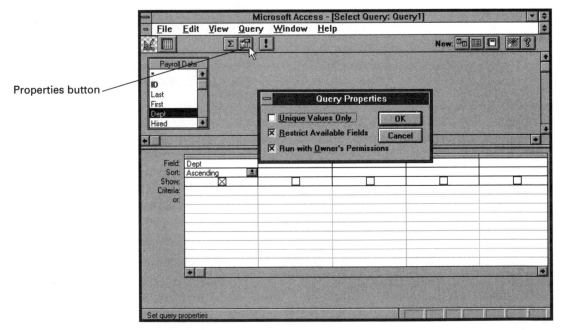

Figure 7.13   **The query dynaset displaying unique values only**

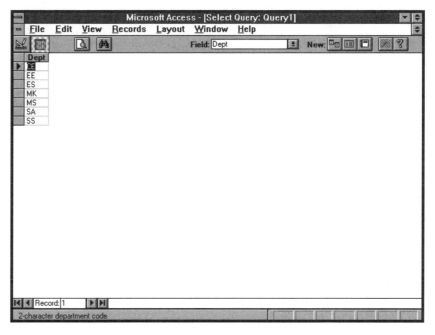

CREATING PARAMETER QUERIES

As you work with your data, you may need to run certain queries on a regular basis, but with different criteria each time you run them. Or, perhaps more importantly, you may need to design a query with changing criteria for a fellow user who isn't familiar with query design. For example, you may need to design a query to show current sales figures for any given salesperson.

To meet this need, you could use one of the following strategies:

* Manually change the salesperson criterion before running the query each time (this won't help your fellow user, though).

* Design and save a separate query for every salesperson (which could clutter up your Database window, waste space on your computer's hard drive, and require additional work every time a new salesperson is hired).

* Create a parameter query that, when run, automatically opens a dialog box asking for the salesperson's name, and then displays that salesperson's data.

CREATING A SINGLE-PARAMETER QUERY

A *single-parameter query* asks for only one criterion. To create a single-parameter query from an existing query, you first need to determine two things:

• For which field do you want to set a parameter?

• What dialog-box text, or *parameter name*, do you want Access to use when it requests the criterion for that parameter's field?

Parameters are a specialized type of criteria expression, so you enter parameter names in the QBE grid's Criteria row. To set a parameter, type your parameter name in the appropriate Criteria cell, enclosing it within square brackets to enable Access to distinguish it from simple criteria. You can use any name for a parameter except the name of an existing field.

Create and run a parameter query that asks for a department code, and then lists that department's employees:

1. From the Payroll Data Table window, create a new query based on the Payroll Data table.

2. Add **Last**, **First**, and **Dept**, respectively, to the first three Field cells of the QBE grid.

3. In the Dept column's Criteria cell, type **[Enter a Dept Code]**, making sure to include the square brackets.

4. Click on the **Datasheet View button** (or choose Query, Run) to start to run the query. Instead of displaying a dynaset, Access now displays an Enter Parameter Value dialog box that prompts you with the parameter name you typed in the Dept column's Criteria cell (see Figure 7.14).

Figure 7.14   **The Enter Parameter Value dialog box**

5. In the Enter a Dept Code text box, type **mk**, and then click on **OK** to finish running the query.

6. Observe the dynaset. Because you specified mk in the Enter Parameter Value dialog box, the dynaset displays only records for Marketing (MK) department employees. (Remember that by default criteria are not case sensitive.)

PRACTICE YOUR SKILLS

1. Return to Design view.

2. Run the query, specifying records for Chemical Engineering (CE) department employees.

3. Compare your dynaset to Figure 7.15.

Figure 7.15 **The query dynaset for Chemical Engineering Department employees**

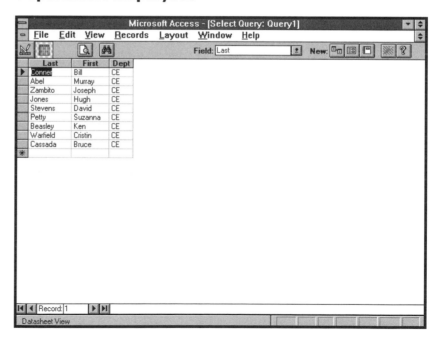

CREATING A MULTIPLE-PARAMETER QUERY

You can also create parameter queries that request multiple criteria. In a *multiple-parameter query*, you can set multiple parameters within a single field, separate parameters for separate fields, or a combination of the two. For example, you might want to design a query that asks both for a salesperson's name and for a given time period, and then displays that salesperson's sales figures for that period. To accomplish this, you could set three parameters: one in the last-name field to ask for the salesperson's last name, and two in the sales-date field to ask for the beginning and ending dates.

For each parameter you set, Access will open a separate Enter Parameter Value dialog box. Therefore, you need to provide an appropriate parameter name for each dialog box.

Remember that parameters are a type of criteria expression; therefore, you can set multiple parameters using any of the techniques for setting multiple criteria you learned in Chapter 4, including setting multiple parameters within a single field using the And and Or comparison operators.

Now change your single-parameter query to a multiple-parameter query that asks for a department code and a hired-date time period, and then displays the records for every employee in that department who was hired during that time period:

1. Return to Design view.

2. Add **Hired** to the QBE grid's fourth Field cell.

3. Place the insertion point in the Hired column's Criteria cell, and then press **Shift+F2** to open the cell's Zoom box. (Using the Zoom box is an alternative to widening a QBE-grid column; it provides you with more room to type and view expressions.)

4. In the Zoom box, type **>= [Enter a Beginning Date] and <= [Enter an Ending Date]** (see Figure 7.16); then click on **OK** to close the Zoom box. (When comparing dates, Access assigns lower mathematical values to earlier dates than to later dates. Thus, >= finds dates from that date forward while <= finds dates from that date back.)

Figure 7.16   **Entering multiple parameters through the Zoom box**

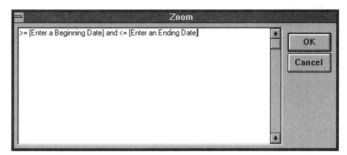

5. Observe the Hired column's Criteria cell, which now contains the entire expression you typed in the Zoom box (even though you can see only part of the expression).

6. Observe the QBE grid. You now have three parameters set: one in the Dept column and two in the Hired column.

7. Start to run the query (click on the **Datasheet View Button** or choose **Query Run**). Access opens an Enter Parameter Value dialog box to prompt you for a department code.

8. In the Enter a Dept Code text box, type **mk**, and then click on **OK** to close the dialog box.

9. Access opens a second Enter Parameter Value dialog box to prompt you for a beginning hire date. In the Enter a Beginning Date text box, type **1/1/88**, and then click on **OK** to close the dialog box.

10. Access opens a third Enter Parameter Value dialog box to prompt you for an ending hire date. In the Enter an Ending Date text box, type **12/31/88**, and then click on **OK** to close the dialog box.

11. Observe the dynaset. It contains the only two records that meet the three parameters you specified: Marketing (MK) Department employees hired between January 1 and December 31, 1988 (see Figure 7.17).

12. Save the query as **My Parameter Query**, and then close the Query window and return to the Payroll Data Table window.

Figure 7.17   **The dynaset of the multiple-parameter query**

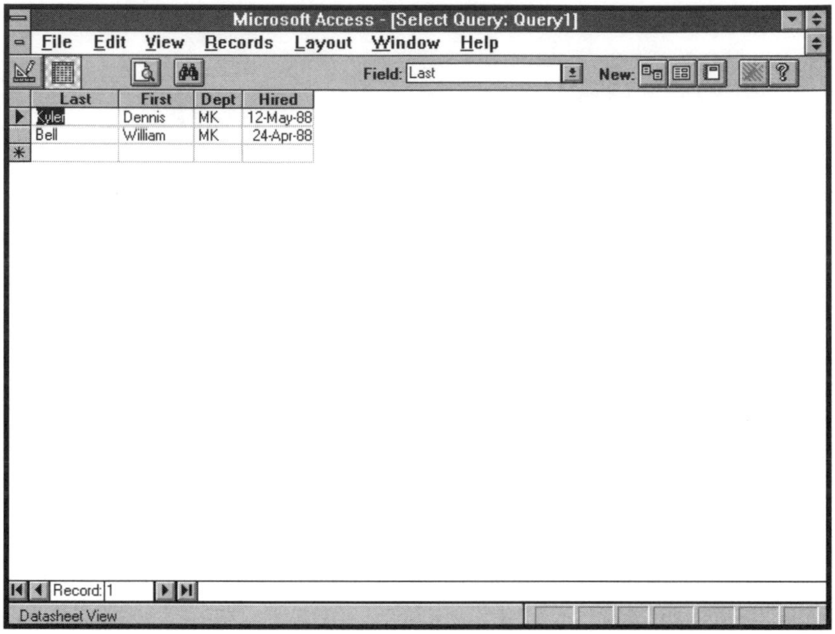

CREATING ACTION QUERIES

Up until this point, you have created only select queries—that is, queries that select and display records in a dynaset, but do not change the records themselves in any way. For queries that actually *change* records, you must use *action queries*.

Action queries are most useful for making similar changes to a group of records. For example, if you want to raise every Marketing department employee's salary by 7 percent, you can use an action query to calculate the raises and change the pay-rate fields. This way, you needn't open your employee-information table and change each employee's pay-rate field manually.

You can also incorporate parameters into action queries in order to make them more flexible. Using the pay-raise example, you could use parameters to ask for the department and pay-raise percentage, thus enabling you to raise the pay in each department by different rates.

Action queries change data instead of displaying dynasets, and you cannot use the Edit, Undo command to undo these changes. For this reason, it's a good idea to first review a dynaset by designing and running the query as a select query, and then convert and run the query as an action query. Also, you may want to make a backup copy of your database file before running any action queries.

Action queries can be both helpful and destructive, so Access provides three types of warnings to prevent you from inadvertently changing data:

- In the Database window, Access displays an exclamation point before each action query's object name to indicate that the query will change data rather than just show it.

- Because action queries do not display dynasets, Access disables the Query window's Datasheet View button. To run an action query, you must either choose Query, Run, or click on the *Run button* (the fifth button from the left on the tool bar, it displays an exclamation point).

- After you start to run the query, Access displays a dialog box to inform you of how many records will be affected by the query, and to ask you to confirm the action. At this point, you can stop the query by clicking on Cancel; if you want Access to proceed, click on OK.

When you work with an action query, you may find it useful to check the query's underlying table both before and after running the query. As you may have already discovered, Access enables you to have more than one window open at a time. (In fact, when you are working in any Access database, the Database window is always open somewhere in Access' application window.) So, rather than closing and reopening Table and Query windows, you can keep all of the related windows open and simply switch between windows. You can switch between windows by using the Window menu, which displays every open window and places a check mark next to the current (or *active*) window. To switch to another window, select that window's name.

One disadvantage of switching between open windows, however, is that Access does not always automatically display the latest changes to data, even though it has already made those changes. To refresh the contents of an open window and ensure that you are viewing the latest data, choose Records, Show All Records. (Alternatively, you can close and reopen the window.)

Access enables you to create four types of action queries:

- Update queries, which can update values in multiple records

- Append queries, which can copy records from one table to another

- Delete queries, which can delete multiple records

- Make-table queries, which can create new tables

CREATING AN UPDATE QUERY

Update queries enable you to change values in multiple records. For example, you can use an update query to raise the parking rate for every employee who uses the SE or SW parking lots.

To create and run an update query, you would follow these steps:

- Create a select query based on the table that contains the records you want to update.

- Add any regular fields that you need to help you identify your records, and set any criterion that you need to specify the correct records to update.

- For each field that you want to update, add that field *and* create a calculated field that will supply the updated value.

- Run the query to make sure that the dynaset displays the correct records and that your calculated fields have produced the correct values.

- When your select query produces the correct dynaset, return to Design view and choose Query, Update to convert the select query to an update query. When you do, Access removes the Sort and Show rows from the QBE grid (because they are irrelevant to update queries), and adds an Update To row that enables you to define how to update what fields.

- In the Update To cells for the fields you want to update, copy the appropriate calculation expressions from the query's calculated fields (don't include the calculated fields' field names).

- Because you no longer need the query's calculated fields, delete their columns from the QBE grid.

- Run the query and confirm the update.

Create an update query to increase by 3 percent the annual parking-rate fees for all employees who use the SE or SW lot:

1. In the Payroll Data table, observe the parking rates for employees who use the SE or SW parking lot. The rates range from $50.00 to $57.75.

2. Open and examine the **Window** menu. The bottom of the menu lists the two windows open within the Access application window: the COMPANY Database window and the Payroll Data Table window. Because the Table window is currently the *active window* (that is, the window in which you are currently working), its name is checked.

3. From the Window menu, select **1 Database: COMPANY** (see Figure 7.18) to activate and view the Database window.

4. From the Database window, open the SE and SW Parking Rate Increase Query window in Design view by clicking on the **Query object button**, selecting the query object name, and then clicking on **Design**.

Figure 7.18   **Switching windows**

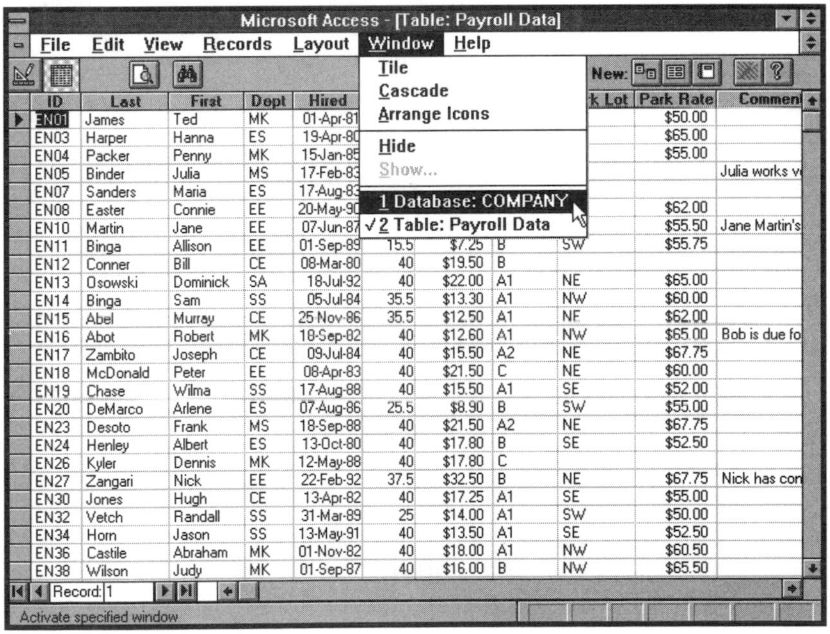

5. Examine the query design. The query includes the four regular fields Park Lot, Park Rate, Last, and First, as well as a fifth calculated field called New Park Rate. Records are set to be sorted in ascending order by Park Lot, and then Park Rate, and the criteria of "SE" Or "SW" is set in the Park Lot column.

6. Place the insertion point in the New Park Rate column's Field cell, and then open the Zoom box (press **Shift+F2**) and examine the entire calculated field. This field will calculate a 3 percent parking-rate increase by multiplying the current parking rate by 1.03. Click on **Cancel** to close the Zoom box.

7. Observe the title bar. This is a select query.

8. Run the query, and then observe the dynaset. It displays only the records for the 20 employees who use the SE or SW parking lots, in ascending order by parking lot, and then the current park rates, and lists both the current and calculated park rates (see Figure 7.19).

Figure 7.19   **The dynaset displaying employees who use the SE or SW parking lots**

Park Lot	Park Rate	Last	First	New Park Rate
SE	$50.00	Ellis	Naja	51.5
SE	$52.00	Chase	Wilma	53.56
SE	$52.50	Henley	Albert	54.075
SE	$52.50	Horn	Jason	54.075
SE	$52.50	Stevens	David	54.075
SE	$52.75	McCarthy	Kathryn	54.3325
SE	$55.00	Jones	Hugh	56.65
SE	$55.50	Martin	Jane	57.165
SE	$57.50	Pierce	Edward	59.225
SE	$57.75	Petty	Suzanna	59.4825
SW	$50.00	Ward	Rodney	51.5
SW	$50.00	James	Ted	51.5
SW	$50.00	Vetch	Randall	51.5
SW	$52.50	Cline	Darren	54.075
SW	$52.50	Smith	Patricia	54.075
SW	$55.00	Berry	Sharon	56.65
SW	$55.00	Hartle	Susan	56.65
SW	$55.00	DeMarco	Arlene	56.65
SW	$55.75	Binga	Allison	57.4225
SW	$57.75	Gardner	Gayle	59.4825

9. Choose **Window, 2 Table: Payroll Data** to switch to the Payroll Data Table window, and then observe the table. The query has not changed any of the table's park rates.

10. Choose **Window, 3 Select Query: SE and SW Parking Rate Increase** to return to the Query window, and then switch to the Query window's Design view.

11. Choose **Query, Update** to change the query from a select query to an update query. Notice that the title bar reflects this change.

12. Observe the QBE grid. Access has removed the Sort and Show rows, and has added an Update To row.

13. In the Park Rate column's Update To cell, type **[park rate]*1.03** to specify a 3 percent increase for the field (see Figure 7.20).

14. Delete the New Park Rate column from the QBE grid because it is no longer needed.

Figure 7.20   **Adding an expression to update the Park Rate field**

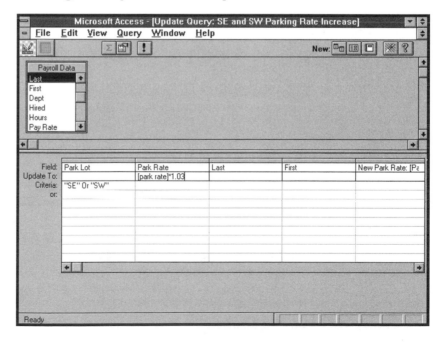

15. Click on the **Run button** (the fifth button from the left on the tool bar) to start running the query. (Because this is an action query, you cannot use the Datasheet View button to run the query.) Access opens a dialog box asking you to confirm that your query should update 20 rows (that is, records), as shown in Figure 7.21.

Figure 7.21   **The dialog box asking for confirmation**

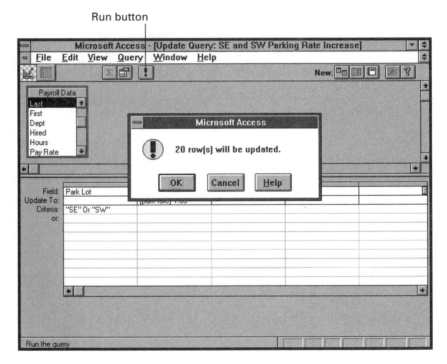

16. Click on **OK** to update the records. Notice that because this is an action rather than a select query, Access does not display a datasheet after running the query.

17. Switch to the Payroll Data Table window (choose **Window, 2 Table: Payroll Data**) and observe the updated table. The query has increased by 3 percent the park rates for all the employees who use the SE or SW parking lots.

18. Switch back to the Query window (choose **Window, 3 Update Query: SE and SW Parking Rate Increase**), save your modified query design with the query's original name (choose **File, Save**), and then close the Query window.

19. Switch to the Database window and observe the object name for the SE and SW Parking Rate Increase query. Because this is now an action query, an exclamation point precedes the name. (You may want to select another query object name so that you can see the exclamation point more easily.)

CREATING AN APPEND QUERY

Append queries enable you to copy records from a *source table* to a *destination table*. For example, if you receive a table containing records for new customers (the source table), you can use an append query to copy some of those new customers to your existing customer-information table (the destination table).

You can choose to append only specific fields from one table to another. However, if you want to append *entire* records from a source table, you can use the asterisk displayed at the top of that table's field list to represent every field in the table. When you add the asterisk to one of the QBE grid's Field cells, Access displays in that single Field cell the table's name followed by a period and an asterisk (rather than placing each of the table's field names in a separate Field cell). For example, if you add the asterisk from the New Data field list to the QBE grid, Access displays New Data.* in a single Field cell. In this way, the asterisk can save you both effort and QBE-grid space.

In a query that uses the asterisk, if you want to append only those records that meet certain criteria, add the appropriate fields to the grid separately, set criteria in their Criteria cells, and uncheck their Show boxes. This enables your query to use the criteria without duplicating the fields.

Then, run the query to make sure that the dynaset displays the correct records and fields. When the dynaset is correct, return to Design view and choose Query, Append to convert the select query to an append query. When you do, Access opens the Query Properties dialog box so you can specify your destination table. Specify the destination table, and then click on OK to close the dialog box.

Once you have converted the query, Access removes the QBE grid's Sort and Show rows, and adds an Append To row. If you are using the asterisk, Access adds to the asterisk column's Append To cell an asterisk expression for your destination table; if you have used any other columns in the QBE grid, Access also copies the field names from those column's Field cells to their Append To cells. Because Access cannot append the same field twice in a single query, you should delete the contents of those Append To cells.

When you run an append query that uses the asterisk on tables that share the same field names and data types, the query appends every field from the source table into the destination table. If, on the other hand, certain field names or data types do not match, Access attempts to append the fields that *do* match, ignoring the fields that don't. (See your Access documentation for information on appending records between tables with different designs.)

Let's create a query now that appends records for Systems Administration department employees from the New Department Records table to the Payroll Data table:

1. From the Database window, open and observe the New Department Records table. This table's design is identical to that of the Payroll Data table, but contains only ten records (see Figure 7.22). The records are for the employees of the Systems Administration (SA) and Shipping and Receiving (SR) departments (these employees are not included in the Payroll Data table).

2. Close the Table window. Then, from the Database window, create a new query based on the New Department Records table. (With the New Department Records table object name selected, click on the **New Query button**.)

3. Drag the asterisk at the top of the field list to the QBE grid's first Field cell to specify every field in the table. Then widen the column so you can view the Field cell's entire contents. In the QBE grid, Access displays the asterisk as New Department Records.*.

4. Add the **Dept** field to the QBE grid's second Field cell.

5. In the Dept column's Criteria cell, type **SA**.

6. Uncheck the Dept column's Show box so that the Dept field is included only once in the dynaset (see Figure 7.23).

7. Run the select query (because this is still a select query, you can use the Datasheet View button). Then observe the dynaset. It displays only records for the six Systems Administration (SA) department employees.

Figure 7.22   **The New Department Records table**

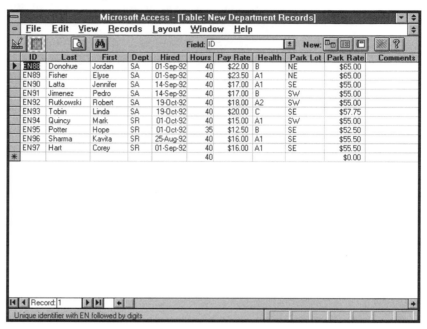

Figure 7.23   **Excluding the redundant Dept field from the dynaset**

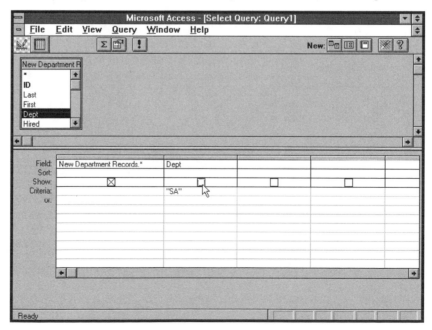

8. Return to Design view, and then choose **Query, Append** to start changing your select query to an append query. Access opens the Query Properties dialog box so you can specify your destination table.

9. From the Append To Table Name drop-down list box, select **Payroll Data** to specify that the query should append records from the New Department Records table to the Payroll Data table (see Figure 7.24). Then click on **OK** to close the dialog box. Notice that the title bar shows that your query is now an append query.

Figure 7.24   **Specifying a destination table**

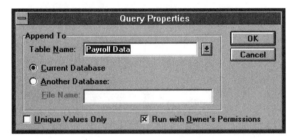

10. Observe the QBE grid. Access has removed the Sort and Show rows from the QBE grid, and has added an Append To row. In the Append To cell for the asterisk column, Access has added Payroll Data.*, and in the Append To cell for the Dept column, Access has added Dept (see Figure 7.25).

11. In the Dept column's Append To cell, delete Dept (do not delete Dept from the Field cell or "SA" from the Criteria cell). When running an append query, you cannot append to the same field twice (Payroll Data.* in the New Department Records.* column already includes the Dept field). However, you still need the Dept column to specify records for Systems Administration department employees.

12. Click on the **Run button** (or choose Query, Run) to start running your append query. Access opens a dialog box asking you to confirm that your query should append six records. Click on **OK** to append the records.

Figure 7.25   **The query design after converting the query**

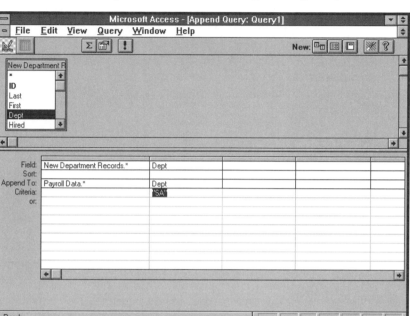

13. Switch to the Payroll Data Table window, and then scroll through and observe the table. It does not appear that your query has added the six records for the Systems Administration Department employees.

14. Choose **Records, Show All Records**, and then reexamine the table. The end of the table now displays the six appended records (see Figure 7.26).

15. Switch back to the Query window, and then close the window without saving your query.

 CREATING A DELETE QUERY

When you want to delete multiple records from a table, you can use a delete query. For example, now that you have just appended six records to your destination table (Payroll Data), you can use a delete query to delete the now-duplicate records from your source table (New Department Records).

Figure 7.26   **The Payroll Data table with the appended records**

ID	Last	First	Dept	Hired	Hours	Pay Rate	Health	Park Lot	Park Rate	Commen
EN78	Russell	Larry	MS	01-Apr-84	40	$13.50	B	NE	$60.00	
EN79	Pierce	Edward	SS	01-Apr-81	40	$12.50	A2	SE	$59.23	
EN80	Nelson	Luke	MK	20-Jun-87	40	$17.50	B			
EN81	Davis	Eugene	ES	02-Jun-87	40	$14.50	B	NE	$60.00	
EN83	Warfield	Cristin	CE	30-Jun-82	40	$17.50	C	NE	$62.50	
EN85	Cassada	Bruce	CE	15-Mar-89	40	$21.50	A2	NW	$65.50	
EN86	Murray	Nancy	EE	15-Mar-83	40	$23.00	B	NW	$62.75	
EN87	Gardner	Gayle	MK	01-Dec-86	40	$16.75	B	SW	$59.48	
EN00	Donohue	Jordan	SA	01-Sep-92	40	$22.00	B	NE	$65.00	
EN89	Fisher	Elyse	SA	01-Sep-92	40	$23.50	A1	NE	$65.00	
EN90	Latta	Jennifer	SA	14-Sep-92	40	$17.00	A1	SE	$55.00	
EN91	Jimenez	Pedro	SA	14-Sep-92	40	$17.00	B	SW	$55.00	
EN92	Rutkowski	Robert	SA	19-Oct-92	40	$18.00	A2	SW	$55.00	
EN93	Tobin	Linda	SA	19-Oct-92	40	$20.00	C	SE	$57.75	
									$0.00	

Unique identifier with EN followed by digits

To create and run a delete query, you would follow these steps:

- Create a select query based on the table from which you want to delete your records.

- Use the asterisk in the QBE grid to specify all of the table's fields (a delete query will only delete entire records at a time).

- If you want to specify criteria, also add those fields to the QBE grid and then set your criteria.

- Run the query to make sure that your query will delete the correct records.

- When your select query produces the correct dynaset, return to Design view and choose Query, Delete to convert your select query to a delete query. When you do, Access removes the Sort and Show rows from the QBE grid, and adds a Delete row that enables you to specify the table from which you want to delete your records. In this Delete row, Access places a From operator under the asterisk to indicate that records will be deleted from that table, and a Where operator under any fields that you have used to set criteria.

- Run the query, and then confirm the deletion.

Let's create and run a delete query to delete the Systems Administration department employee records from the New Department Records table:

1. From the Database window, open and observe the New Department Records table. The table still contains the six Systems Administration department employee records you appended to the Payroll Data table.

2. Create a new query based on the New Department Records table.

3. In the Query window, drag the asterisk from the New Department Records field iist to the QBE grid's first Field cell to add all of the table's fields to the query.

4. Add **Dept** to the QBE grid's second Field cell.

5. In the Dept column's Criteria cell, type **SA**.

6. Run the query, and then observe the dynaset. It displays only the records for the Systems Administration department employees.

7. Return to Design view, and then choose **Query, Delete** to change the your select query to a delete query.

8. Observe the QBE grid (see Figure 7.27). Access has removed the Sort and Show rows, and has added a Delete row. The From in the New Department Records.* column instructs the query to delete records from the New Department Records table. The Where in the Dept column instructs the query to delete only those records that meet the criterion in the column's Criteria cell (that is, records for Systems Administration employees).

9. Start to run the query by clicking on the **Run button** (or choosing Query, Run). Access opens a dialog box that asks you to confirm that the query should delete six rows (records).

10. Click on **OK** to delete the records.

11. Switch to and observe the New Department Records Table window. The table displays #Deleted in every field of the first six records (see Figure 7.28).

Figure 7.27   **The query design after converting the query**

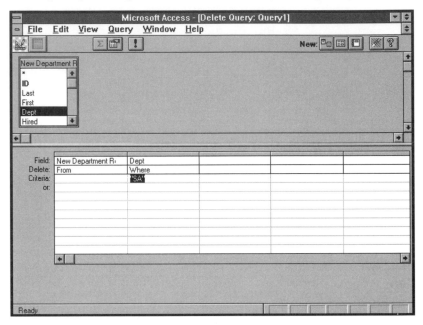

Figure 7.28   **The New Department Records table indicating deleted records**

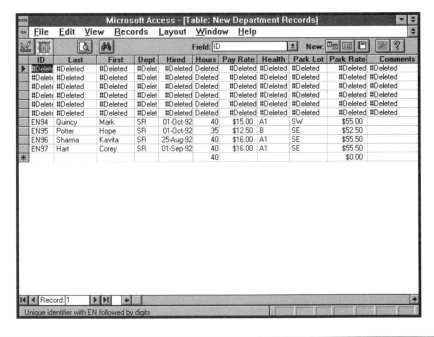

12. Choose **Records, Show All Records**. The Table window now displays only the records for the four Shipping and Receiving (SR) department employees.

13. Close the New Department Records Table window; then close the Query window without saving your delete query.

CREATING MULTIPLE-TABLE QUERIES

Through multiple-table queries, you can use data from more than one table at a time by combining that data into a single dynaset. For example, you can store employee names in one table and their addresses in another table, but combine that data when you need to generate an employee mailing list.

EXAMINING THE DESIGN OF A MULTIPLE-TABLE QUERY

Before you create your own multiple-table query, take a look at the design of an existing one:

1. Switch to and observe the Payroll Data Table window. The table contains employee names, but no addresses.

2. Switch to the Database window; then open and observe the Addresses table. This table includes employee addresses, but no first or last names.

3. Close both Table windows.

4. Open the Home Addresses Query window in Design view, and then observe the window's upper pane (see Figure 7.29). The pane holds field lists from both the Addresses and Payroll Data tables. Notice that these field lists are joined by a line connecting their common ID fields.

5. Observe the QBE grid. It includes a Table row that indicates from which table the query will obtain the values for each field. The First and Last fields are from the Payroll Data table; the Address, City, St, and Zip fields are from the Addresses table (you may need to scroll to the right on the QBE grid to see all the fields).

6. Run the query, and then observe the dynaset. It displays data combined from both tables.

7. Close the Query window.

Figure 7.29   **The Home Addresses query design**

Microsoft Access - [Select Query: Home Addresses]

File   Edit   View   Query   Window   Help

Field:	First	Last	Address	City	St
Table:	Payroll Data	Payroll Data	Addresses	Addresses	Addresses
Sort:					
Show:	☒	☒	☒	☒	☒
Criteria:					
or:					

Ready

JOINING TABLES

To obtain a meaningful dynaset from a multiple-table query, you
may need to *join* your tables—that is, show Access which fields in
each table share common values. For example, you could join an
employee-name table with an employee-address table using an
employee-ID field stored in each table. (If you want to create multiple-table queries, you should include in every table a field that re-
lates to a field in at least one other table. We'll take a closer look at
using fields to establish table relationships in Chapter 8.)

Before you can join tables, you need to add multiple field lists to the
upper pane of the Query window's Design view through the Add
Table dialog box. (If you create a new query from the Database window by clicking on the New button, Access opens the Add Table dialog box automatically; to open the dialog box from an existing
Query window, choose Query, Add Table.) In the Add Table dialog
box for each table you want to add, click on the table's name, and
then click on Add. Once you've added all of the desired tables, click
on Close to close the dialog box.

After you've added the tables, you can join them by creating *join lines* between related fields in each of the tables' field lists. To create a join line, select and drag one field name over to its companion field name in another field list.

Once you've joined the tables in your query design, you can add fields to the QBE grid from any of the field lists. For example, if you wanted to create a mailing list, you could add first- and last-name fields from one table, and address fields from another. When adding fields to the QBE grid from multiple tables, you may want to choose View, Table Names to add a Table row to the grid where Access can display the source table for each field.

Let's create a multiple-table select query based on the Payroll Data and Addresses tables in order to combine employee names, parking-lot data, and addresses into a single dynaset:

1. In the Database window, click on **New** to start creating a new query. Access opens the Add Table dialog box.

2. Select **Payroll Data**, and then click on **Add** to add the Payroll Data table's field list to the query design.

3. Select **Addresses**, and then click on **Add** to add the Addresses table's field list to the query design.

4. Click on **Close** to close the dialog box, and then observe the Query window's upper pane. The upper pane holds both tables, but there is no join line between the two tables.

5. Drag **ID** from the Payroll Data field list to ID in the Addresses field list to create a join line between the two field lists (see Figure 7.30).

6. From the Payroll Data field list, add **First**, **Last**, **Park Lot**, and **Park Rate**, respectively, to the QBE grid's first four Field cells.

7. From the Addresses field list, add **Address**, **City**, **St**, and **Zip**, respectively, to the QBE grid's next four Field cells.

8. Observe the QBE grid. You cannot see which fields belong to which table.

9. Choose **View, Table Names** to add a Table row to the QBE grid. Now you *can* see which fields belong to which table.

10. Run the query, and then observe the dynaset. It displays data from both tables (see Figure 7.31).

Figure 7.30   **Creating a join line**

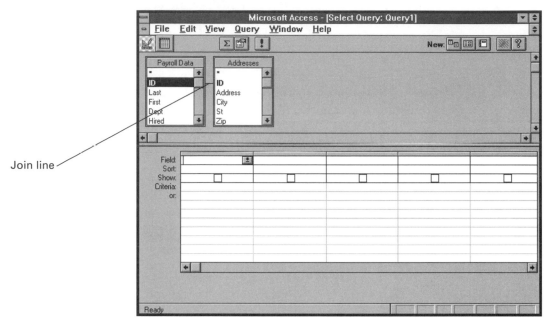

Join line

Figure 7.31   **The combined dynaset**

First	Last	Park Lot	Park Rate	Address	City	St	Zip
Ted	James	SW	$51.50	34 Fields Street	Walworth	NY	14568
Hanna	Harper	NW	$65.00	82 East Avenue	Adams Basin	NY	14410
Penny	Packer	NW	$55.00	450 N. Madison St.	Holley	NY	14470
Julia	Binder			10 Cory Drive	Hulberton	NY	14473
Maria	Sanders			12 East Avenue	Leicester	NY	14481
Connie	Easter	NW	$62.00	21 Stonecreek Rd.	Shortsville	NY	14548
Jane	Martin	SE	$57.17	50 Smart Drive	Knowlesville	NY	14479
Allison	Binga	SW	$57.42	50 Dallas Street	South Byron	NY	14557
Bill	Conner			32 Ash Lane	Perkinsville	NY	14529
Dominick	Osowski	NE	$65.00	23 Lakeside Ave	Pultneyville	NY	14538
Sam	Binga	NW	$60.00	50 Dallas Street	South Byron	NY	14557
Murray	Abel	NE	$62.00	127 Ford Avenue	Lakeville	NY	14480
Robert	Abot	NW	$65.00	99 Stonecreek Rd.	Gorham	NY	14461
Joseph	Zambito	NE	$67.75	81 Pleasing Lane	Rose	NY	14542
Peter	McDonald	NE	$60.00	8165 Main Street	Oaks Corners	NY	14518
Wilma	Chase	SE	$53.56	52 Pempleton Dr.	Wyoming	NY	14591
Arlene	DeMarco	SW	$56.65	34 Sable Ave.	Gorham	NY	14461
Frank	Desoto	NE	$67.75	P.O. Box 7234	Wayland	NY	14572
Albert	Henley	SE	$54.08	12 Divine Drive	Holley	NY	14470
Dennis	Kyler			273 Fireside Dr.	Dresden	NY	14441
Nick	Zangari	NE	$67.75	34 Park Street	Retsof	NY	14539
Hugh	Jones	SE	$56.65	466 Fairhaven St.	Leicester	NY	14481
Randall	Vetch	SW	$51.50	45 Central Blvd.	Hall	NY	14463
Jason	Horn	SE	$54.08	453 Lakeshore Dr.	Pultneyville	NY	14538
Abraham	Castile	NW	$60.50	67 Fargo Road	Ionia	NY	14475
Judy	Wilson	NW	$65.50	532 Union Street	Waterport	NY	14571

CREATING A MAKE-TABLE QUERY

Once you've created a multiple-table select query (or any other type of select query, for that matter), you can create a new table that duplicates the query's dynaset by converting and running that query as a make-table query.

Creating a new table can be useful when you need to supply data to another user, but you want to supply only limited fields or records, or need to combine the data from multiple tables into a single table.

Once you've created a select query that produces the dynaset that you want to save as your new table, return to Design view and choose Query, Make Table to convert the query to a make-table query. Access then opens the Query Properties dialog box, enabling you to provide a name for your new table. Specify a name, and then click on OK to close the dialog box.

When you run the query, Access opens a dialog box indicating how many records the query will copy into your new table. Click on OK to confirm the copy.

Now modify your query so that it finds only those records for employees who use the company parking lots, and then convert the query and use it to create a new table:

1. Observe the Query window. Some of the records do not have values in the Park Lot and Park Rate fields.

2. Return to Design view. Then, in the Park Lot column's Criteria cell, type **is not null** to specify records that *do not* have an empty Park Lot field. (Remember from Chapter 4 that you used the is null expression to find records that *did* have empty fields; is not null finds just the opposite.)

3. Press **Tab**, and then observe your criterion. Access automatically changed your expression to Is Not Null.

4. In the Zip column's Sort cell, select **Ascending**.

5. Run the query, and then observe the dynaset. It displays only those records that have values in the Park Lot field, and has sorted the records by zip code (see Figure 7.32).

6. Return to Design view, and then choose **Query, Make Table** to start changing your select query into a make-table query. Access opens the Query Properties dialog box so you can specify a name for the table you wish to make.

7. In the Table Name drop-down list box, type **My Parking and Addresses** (see Figure 7.33); then click on **OK** to close the dialog box.

8. Start to run the query. (Because this is an action query, click on the **Run button**, or choose **Query, Run**.) Access opens a dialog box asking you to confirm that the query should copy 46 records into a new table.

Figure 7.32   **The dynaset displaying only employees who use the company parking lots**

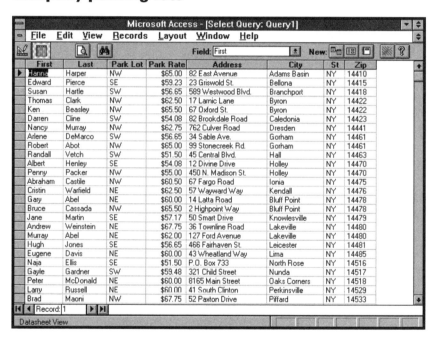

Figure 7.33   **Specifying a table name**

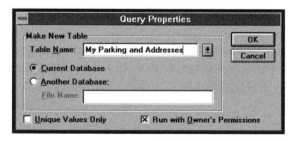

9. Click on **OK** to create the new table.

10. Close the Query window without saving your query.

11. From the Database window, open and observe the My Parking and Addresses table. The records in the table are identical to those in your query's dynaset (compare Figure 7.34 with Figure 7.32).

12. Close the Table window.

Figure 7.34   **The My Parking and Addresses table**

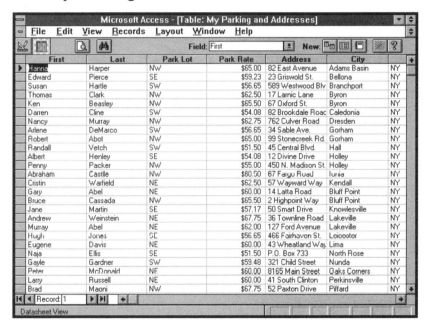

SUMMARY

In this chapter, you learned how to create and run queries more efficiently, how to create advanced select queries, and how to create and run parameter, action, and multiple-table queries.

Here's a quick reference guide to the Access features introduced in this chapter:

Desired Result	How to Do It
Create a select query with a single click	From a Table or Query window, click on the **New Query button**
Widen a QBE-grid column	Place the mouse pointer on the right edge of the column's field selector until the pointer changes to a cross with a horizontal, two-headed arrow, drag the column boundary to the right, and then release the mouse button
Create a concatenation expression	In a QBE-grid's Field cell, type field names within brackets and text within double quotation marks, separating each item with the concatenation operator &
Open the Zoom box	Place the focus in a cell, and then press **Shift+F2**
Specify records with unique values only	From a Query window's Design view, choose **View, Query Properties** (or click on the **Query Properties button**), check **Unique Values Only**, and then click on **OK**
Create a parameter query	Within a QBE-grid Criteria cell, type a parameter name enclosed within square brackets
Run an action query	Choose **Query, Run**, or click on the **Run button**
Refresh the contents of an open window	Choose **Records, Show All Records**
Convert a select query to an update query	From the Query window's Design view, choose **Query, Update**
Add all of a table's fields to the QBE grid	From the table's field list, drag the asterisk to a QBE-grid Field cell

Desired Result	How to Do It
Convert a select query to an append query	From the Query window's Design view, choose **Query, Append**
Convert a select query to a delete query	From the Query window's Design view, choose **Query, Delete**
Convert a select query to a make-table query	From the Query window's Design view, choose **Query, Make Table**
Create a multiple-table query	Use the query design's Add Table dialog box to add multiple tables to the query design
Join tables	In the upper pane of a Query window in Design view, drag a field name from one field list to its companion field in another field list
View source-table names in the QBE grid	From the Query window's Design view, choose **View, Table Names**
Specify fields that contain values	In a QBE-grid's Criteria row, type **is not null** under the appropriate field names

In the next chapter, you'll learn how to use new methods of modifying a table's Datasheet-view layout, how to change field properties, how to work with keyed tables, and how to create table relationships.

IF YOU'RE STOPPING HERE

If you need to break off here, please exit Access. If you want to proceed directly to the next chapter, please do so now.

CHAPTER 8: ENHANCED TABLE DESIGN

Changing Field
Properties

Working with Keyed
Tables

Creating
Relationships
between Tables

In Chapter 2, you learned the basics of creating a table and defining a table's fields. In this chapter, you will learn how to refine your tables' designs in order to make your tables easier to use and your data more reliable and consistent. You'll also learn more about a table's primary key, and how to use primary-key fields to establish relationships between tables.

When you're done working through this chapter, you will know how to:

- Examine and modify field properties
- Change the display formats of fields
- Set default values
- Set validation rules and validation text
- Remove, add, and change a table's primary key
- Create and use table relationships

CHANGING FIELD PROPERTIES

Field properties determine the appearance and behavior of fields. Among other things, field properties can determine how Access displays values in a field, limit the range of values or the number of characters in a field, and/or establish a field's default value. (When you created text fields in Chapter 2, you changed the Field Size property to limit the number of characters allowed in that field. For example, when you created an ID field and set that field's Field Size property to 4, you limited the number of characters in that field to four. For all other fields and field properties, however, you accepted all of Access' field-property defaults.)

When you create a form or report using a table's fields, those fields' properties are duplicated in to those objects as *control properties*. However, if you change field properties in a table, you may *not* automatically affect existing control properties on forms and reports. Therefore, if you want to set field properties that will affect control properties in forms and reports, you should set those properties in your table *before* creating objects based on that table. (You will learn more about control properties and their relationships to field properties in Chapter 9.)

 EXAMINING FIELD PROPERTIES

To view or modify a table's field properties, open that table's window in Design view, place the focus in the row of the field for which you want to change field properties, and then make changes in that field's property boxes (located on the left side of the Table window's lower pane).

Each field data type (Text, Number, Currency, Date/Time, and so on) has its own set of field properties, and each of those field properties has unique capabilities relative to the data type and to other field properties. For this reason, you may find it difficult to memorize all of the possible choices for every field property in every situation. Rather than try to learn every possibility, you can turn to Access' Help system. Access often displays brief help messages relevant to the task at hand in the status bar or somewhere in an object window. To get more detailed *context-sensitive* help, open Access' Help window with the F1 key. For example, if the focus is in a text field's Field Size property, you can press F1 to open the Help window pertaining to the Field Size property for text fields.

In this task, you are going to examine field properties in an existing table. Some of these field properties are the same default field properties you saw in Chapter 2; others are custom properties that serve a specific purpose. One custom setting that you'll look at in particular instructs Access to capitalize values automatically when you enter lowercase text; you'll use context-sensitive Help to view the other possible settings for that field property.

If you do not have both the Access application and the COMPANY Database windows opened and maximized, please open and maximize them now.

Now let's start:

1. Open the Payroll Data table in Design view and observe the Table window's upper pane. The ID text field is selected.

2. Observe the left side of the Table window's lower pane. It displays the field properties for the ID field.

3. Observe the right side of the window's lower pane. Because the focus is in the ID row's Field Name box, Access displays a brief help message on naming fields.

4. Move the focus to the ID field's Field Size property box (press **F6** or click in the property box); then observe the right side of the lower pane. It now displays a brief help message on a text field's Field Size property (see Figure 8.1).

5. Move the focus to the Format property box and observe the brief help message for this property. The Format property determines how Access displays values in the ID field.

Figure 8.1   **Displaying a brief help message on a text field's Field Size property**

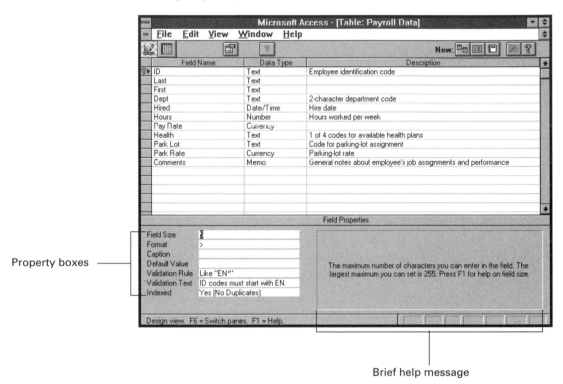

Property boxes ———

Brief help message

6. Observe the Format property box. It contains the format >, which is not explained in the brief help message.

7. Press **F1** to open the Help window for the Format property, and then maximize the Help window.

8. Because ID is a text field, click on **Text and Memo Data Types** to view help on the Format property relative to text and memo fields. (You'll learn about memo fields later in this chapter.)

9. Observe the Help window (see Figure 8.2). The > Format property changes all characters to uppercase if they aren't already.

10. Close the Help window.

11. Switch to Datasheet view, and then observe the values in the ID field. All characters display in uppercase.

Figure 8.2　　**The Help window for the Format property of text and memo fields**

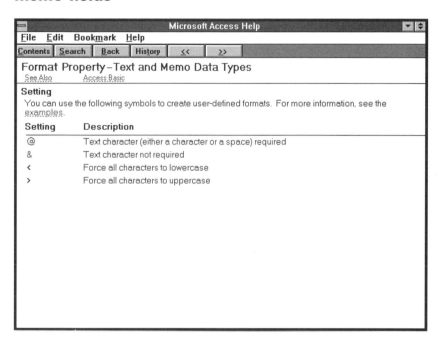

12. Select **EN03** in the ID field for Hanna Harper (Record 2), and then type **en03** to replace the value.

13. Press **Tab** to move from the field, and then observe the value. Because of the > Format property, Access displays the value as EN03.

MODIFYING THE DISPLAY FORMAT OF A DATE/TIME FIELD

To help you determine possible settings for a field property, Access often supplies a list of settings right in the Table window. If there is a list for a particular field property, Access displays a drop-down list arrow whenever the focus is in that property's box, enabling you to select a setting from that property box's drop-down list rather than typing the setting manually.

For the Format property of date/time fields, Access provides a list of seven possible settings:

• *General Date,* for example, 11/15/93 04:30 PM

- *Long Date,* for example, Monday, November 15, 1993
- *Medium Date,* for example, 14-Nov-93
- *Short Date,* for example, 11/14/93
- *Long Time,* for example, 4:30:00 PM
- *Medium Time,* for example, 04:30 PM
- *Short Time,* for example, 16:30

(Note that for some date/time formats, Access depends on the settings in the International section of the Windows Control Panel. For more information on viewing or changing these settings, refer to your Microsoft Windows documentation.)

You can enter dates and times in any of these formats; Access automatically displays that date or time in the format specified by that date/time field's Format property. For example, if you type 14-Nov-93 in a date/time field set with the Short Date Format property, Access displays your date as 11/14/93. One of the advantages of field properties is that they ensure data conformity while allowing for flexibility in data entry.

Let's change the Format property for the Hired date/time field from Medium Date to Short Date:

1. Return to Design view, move the focus to the Hired row, and then observe the window's lower pane. It now displays properties for the Hired field.

2. Observe the Format property for Hired. It is set to Medium Date.

3. Switch to Datasheet view and observe the values in the Hired field. Dates display in the Medium Date format *dd-mmm-yy* (see Figure 8.3).

4. Return to Design view; then move the focus to the Hired field's Format property box to display the property box's drop-down list arrow.

5. Click on the **drop-down list arrow** to open the property box's drop-down list, and then observe the list. Access provides seven formats for date/time fields.

6. Select **Short Date**.

7. Save your change to the table design (choose **File, Save**).

Figure 8.3   **Hired values displayed in the Medium Date format**

ID	Last	First	Dept	Hired	Hours	Pay Rate	Health	Park Lot	Park Rate	Comment
EN01	James	Ted	MK	01-Apr-81	38	$15.50	A2	SW	$51.50	
EN03	Harper	Hanna	ES	19-Apr-80	40	$21.50	A2	NW	$65.00	
EN04	Packer	Penny	MK	15-Jan-85	35	$24.00	A1	NW	$55.00	
EN05	Binder	Julia	MS	17-Feb-83	25	$8.52	B			Julia works v
EN07	Sanders	Maria	ES	17-Aug-83	29.5	$7.25	B			
EN08	Easter	Connie	EE	20-May-90	40	$15.00	A1	NW	$62.00	
EN10	Martin	Jane	EE	07-Jun-87	40	$8.75	A2	SE	$57.17	Jane Martin's
EN11	Binga	Allison	EE	01-Sep-89	15.5	$7.25	B	SW	$57.42	
EN12	Conner	Bill	CE	08-Mar-80	40	$19.50	B			
EN13	Osowski	Dominick	SA	18-Jul-92	40	$22.00	A1	NE	$65.00	
EN14	Binga	Sam	SS	05-Jul-84	35.5	$13.30	A1	NW	$60.00	
EN15	Abel	Murray	CE	25-Nov-86	35.5	$12.50	A1	NE	$62.00	
EN16	Abot	Robert	MK	18-Sep-82	40	$12.60	A1	NW	$65.00	Bob is due fo
EN17	Zambito	Joseph	CE	09-Jul-84	40	$15.50	A2	NE	$67.75	
EN18	McDonald	Peter	EE	08-Apr-83	40	$21.50	C	NE	$60.00	
EN19	Chase	Wilma	SS	17-Aug-88	40	$15.50	A1	SE	$53.56	
EN20	DeMarco	Arlene	ES	07-Aug-86	25.5	$8.90	B	SW	$56.65	
EN23	Desoto	Frank	MS	18-Sep-88	40	$21.50	A2	NE	$67.75	
EN24	Henley	Albert	ES	13-Oct-80	40	$17.80	B	SE	$54.08	
EN26	Kyler	Dennis	MK	12-May-88	40	$17.80	C			
EN27	Zangari	Nick	EE	22-Feb-92	37.5	$32.50	B	NE	$67.75	Nick has con
EN30	Jones	Hugh	CE	13-Apr-82	40	$17.25	A1	SE	$56.65	
EN32	Vetch	Randall	SS	31-Mar-89	25	$14.00	A1	SW	$51.50	
EN34	Horn	Jason	SS	13-May-91	40	$13.50	A1	SE	$54.08	
EN36	Castile	Abraham	MK	01-Nov-82	40	$18.00	A1	NW	$60.50	
EN38	Wilson	Judy	MK	01-Sep-87	40	$16.00	B	NW	$65.50	

Record: 2

Employee identification code

8. Switch to Datasheet view, and then observe the values in the Hired field. The dates now display in the Short Date format *mm/dd/yy* (see Figure 8.4).

MODIFYING THE DISPLAY FORMAT OF A NUMBER FIELD

It is important to note that the Format property does not actually change the values that you enter in a field; it just changes the way Access *displays* those values. For example, when you typed en03 earlier in this chapter and Access displayed the value as EN03, the underlying value was still en03.

This difference between what you type and what Access displays may seem minor for text values; however, it can be very significant for numbers that you use in calculations. For example, you could type 40.5 in a number field, only to have Access display that value as 40. What happens, then, when you use that field in a calculation? Because Access stored the value as you typed it (40.5), rest assured that Access will use that entire number in any calculations.

Figure 8.4   **Hired values displayed in the Short Date format**

ID	Last	First	Dept	Hired	Hours	Pay Rate	Health	Park Lot	Park Rate	Comment
EN01	James	Ted	MK	4/1/81	38	$15.50	A2	SW	$51.50	
EN03	Harper	Hanna	ES	4/19/80	40	$21.50	A2	NW	$65.00	
EN04	Packer	Penny	MK	1/15/85	35	$24.00	A1	NW	$55.00	
EN05	Binder	Julia	MS	2/17/83	25	$8.52	B			Julia works v
EN07	Sanders	Maria	ES	8/17/83	29.5	$7.25	B			
EN08	Easter	Connie	EE	5/20/90	40	$15.00	A1	NW	$62.00	
EN10	Martin	Jane	EE	6/7/87	40	$8.75	A2	SE	$57.17	Jane Martin's
EN11	Binga	Allison	EE	9/1/89	15.5	$7.25	B	SW	$57.42	
EN12	Conner	Bill	CE	3/8/80	40	$19.50	B			
EN13	Osowski	Dominick	SA	7/18/92	40	$22.00	A1	NE	$65.00	
EN14	Binga	Sam	SS	7/5/84	35.5	$13.30	A1	NW	$60.00	
EN15	Abel	Murray	CE	11/25/86	35.5	$12.50	A1	NE	$62.00	
EN16	Abot	Robert	MK	9/18/82	40	$12.60	A1	NW	$65.00	Bob is due fo
EN17	Zambito	Joseph	CE	7/9/84	40	$15.50	A2	NE	$67.75	
EN18	McDonald	Peter	EE	4/8/83	40	$21.50	C	NE	$60.00	
EN19	Chase	Wilma	SS	8/17/88	40	$15.50	A1	SE	$53.56	
EN20	DeMarco	Arlene	ES	8/7/86	25.5	$8.90	B	SW	$56.65	
EN23	Desoto	Frank	MS	9/18/88	40	$21.50	A2	NE	$67.75	
EN24	Henley	Albert	ES	10/13/80	40	$17.80	B	SE	$54.08	
EN26	Kyler	Dennis	MK	5/12/88	40	$17.80	C			
EN27	Zangari	Nick	EE	2/22/92	37.5	$32.50	B	NE	$67.75	Nick has con
EN30	Jones	Hugh	CE	4/13/82	40	$17.25	A1	SE	$56.65	
EN32	Vetch	Randall	SS	3/31/89	25	$14.00	A1	SW	$51.50	
EN34	Horn	Jason	SS	5/13/91	40	$13.50	A1	SE	$54.08	
EN36	Castile	Abraham	MK	11/1/82	40	$18.00	A1	NW	$60.50	
EN38	Wilson	Judy	MK	9/1/87	40	$16.00	B	NW	$65.50	

Why would you want to display only part of a number's value? To make that number easier to read. If, for example, you are creating a report that contains multimillion-dollar figures, displaying numbers to the second decimal place might be distracting. Changing a number's display enables you to temporarily round off numbers.

Because number and currency fields are similar, they have similar field properties and field-property settings. There are six standard settings for the Format property of number and currency fields:

- *General Number* displays values as entered, using as many or as few decimal places as necessary. An example is 5425.6.

- *Currency* precedes values with a dollar sign, includes thousand separators as necessary, and always displays two decimal places. An example is $5,425.60. If the value is negative, Access encloses that value within parentheses and displays the value in red.

- *Fixed* displays values with a fixed number of decimal places from 0 to 15. The default number of decimal places is 2. An example is 5425.60.

- *Standard* displays values as entered, but adds thousand separators as needed. An example is 5,245.6.

- *Percent* displays values multiplied by 100 and followed by a percent sign. An example is 524560%.

- *Scientific* displays numbers in standard scientific notation. An example is 5.24E+03.

If the Format cell is blank for a number field, Access displays numbers using the General Number setting.

When you use any number format other than General Number, you can use the Decimal Places property to determine how many decimal places to display. When the Decimal Places property is set to Auto, Access uses the Format property setting's default to determine the number of decimal places. For example, if you set a field's format property to Fixed and its Decimal Places property to Auto, Access will display values with two decimal places because the default number of decimal places for the Fixed format is two.

Let's change the Format property for the Hours field to Fixed, and then set the Decimal Places property so that every value in the Hours field displays one decimal place:

1. Observe the values in the Hours field. Decimal places are displayed only as needed (refer back to Figure 8.4).

2. Switch to Design view, move the focus to the Hours row, and then observe the Hours field's Format property box. It is empty.

3. Open and observe the Format property box's drop-down list. Access provides six formats for number fields.

4. Select **Fixed**, and then save the table design.

5. Return to Datasheet view, and then observe the values in the Hours field. Each now displays two decimal places (see Figure 8.5).

6. Switch to Design view, and then observe the Hours field's Decimal Places property box. It is set to Auto.

7. Move the focus to the Decimal Places property box; then observe the right side of the lower pane. The brief help message explains that this property determines the number of digits displayed to the right of the decimal separator (that is, the decimal point).

Figure 8.5 **Hours values displayed in the Fixed format**

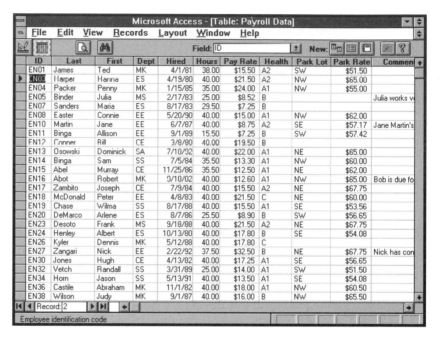

ID	Last	First	Dept	Hired	Hours	Pay Rate	Health	Park Lot	Park Rate	Comment
EN01	James	Ted	MK	4/1/81	38.00	$15.50	A2	SW	$51.50	
EN03	Harper	Hanna	ES	4/19/80	40.00	$21.50	A2	NW	$65.00	
EN04	Packer	Penny	MK	1/15/85	35.00	$24.00	A1	NW	$55.00	
EN05	Binder	Julia	MS	2/17/83	25.00	$8.52	B			Julia works w
EN07	Sanders	Maria	ES	8/17/83	29.50	$7.25	B			
EN08	Easter	Connie	EE	5/20/90	40.00	$15.00	A1	NW	$62.00	
EN10	Martin	Jane	EE	6/7/87	40.00	$8.75	A2	SE	$57.17	Jane Martin's
EN11	Binga	Allison	EE	9/1/89	15.50	$7.25	B	SW	$57.42	
EN12	Conner	Bill	CE	3/8/80	40.00	$19.50	B			
EN13	Osowski	Dominick	SA	7/10/92	40.00	$22.00	A1	NE	$65.00	
EN14	Binga	Sam	SS	7/5/84	35.50	$13.30	A1	NW	$60.00	
EN15	Abel	Murray	CE	11/25/86	35.50	$12.50	A1	NE	$62.00	
EN16	Abot	Robert	MK	9/10/02	40.00	$12.60	A1	NW	$65.00	Bob is due fo
EN17	Zambito	Joseph	CE	7/9/84	40.00	$15.50	A2	NE	$67.75	
EN18	McDonald	Peter	EE	4/8/83	40.00	$21.50	C	NE	$60.00	
EN19	Chase	Wilma	SS	8/17/88	40.00	$15.50	A1	SE	$53.56	
EN20	DeMarco	Arlene	ES	8/7/86	25.50	$8.90	B	SW	$56.65	
EN23	Desoto	Frank	MS	9/18/88	40.00	$21.50	A2	NE	$67.75	
EN24	Henley	Albert	ES	10/13/80	40.00	$17.80	B	SE	$54.08	
EN26	Kyler	Dennis	MK	5/12/88	40.00	$17.80	C			
EN27	Zangari	Nick	EE	2/22/92	37.50	$32.50	B	NE	$67.75	Nick has con
EN30	Jones	Hugh	CE	4/13/82	40.00	$17.25	A1	SE	$56.65	
EN32	Vetch	Randall	SS	3/31/89	25.00	$14.00	A1	SW	$51.50	
EN34	Horn	Jason	SS	5/13/91	40.00	$13.50	A1	SE	$54.08	
EN36	Castile	Abraham	MK	11/1/82	40.00	$18.00	A1	NW	$60.50	
EN38	Wilson	Judy	MK	9/1/87	40.00	$16.00	B	NW	$65.50	

Employee identification code

8. Open and observe the Decimal Places property box's drop-down list. You can use this list to specify any number of decimal places from 0 to 15.

9. Select **1**, and then save the table design.

10. Switch to Datasheet view, and then observe the values in the Hours field. Each now displays one decimal place (see Figure 8.6).

SETTING DEFAULT VALUES

If you enter the same value in a field for a majority of records, you can speed data entry by specifying that value as a default value. Once you do, Access enters that value automatically when you enter a new record. For example, if you expect that most new employees will work 40 hours per week, you can set a default value of 40 in the hours-worked field. For the infrequent employee who doesn't work 40 hours per week, you can simply replace the default value with another value as you enter that employee's record.

Figure 8.6   **Hours values displayed in the Fixed format with one decimal place**

ID	Last	First	Dept	Hired	Hours	Pay Rate	Health	Park Lot	Park Rate	Comment
EN01	James	Ted	MK	4/1/81	38.0	$15.50	A2	SW	$51.50	
EN03	Harper	Hanna	ES	4/19/80	40.0	$21.50	A2	NW	$65.00	
EN04	Packer	Penny	MK	1/15/85	35.0	$24.00	A1	NW	$55.00	
EN05	Binder	Julia	MS	2/17/83	25.0	$8.52	B			Julia works v
EN07	Sanders	Maria	ES	8/17/83	29.5	$7.25	B			
EN08	Easter	Connie	EE	5/20/90	40.0	$15.00	A1	NW	$62.00	
EN10	Martin	Jane	EE	6/7/87	40.0	$8.75	A2	SE	$57.17	Jane Martin's
EN11	Binga	Allison	EE	9/1/89	15.5	$7.25	B	SW	$57.42	
EN12	Conner	Bill	CE	3/8/80	40.0	$19.50	B			
EN13	Osowski	Dominick	SA	7/18/92	40.0	$22.00	A1	NE	$65.00	
EN14	Binga	Sam	SS	7/5/84	35.5	$13.30	A1	NW	$60.00	
EN15	Abel	Murray	CE	11/25/86	35.5	$12.50	A1	NE	$62.00	
EN16	Abot	Robert	MK	9/18/82	40.0	$12.60	A1	NW	$65.00	Bob is due fo
EN17	Zambito	Joseph	CE	7/9/84	40.0	$15.50	A2	NE	$67.75	
EN18	McDonald	Peter	EE	4/8/83	40.0	$21.50	C	NE	$60.00	
EN19	Chase	Wilma	SS	8/17/88	40.0	$15.50	A1	SE	$53.56	
EN20	DeMarco	Arlene	ES	8/7/86	25.5	$8.90	B	SW	$56.65	
EN23	Desoto	Frank	MS	9/18/88	40.0	$21.50	A2	NE	$67.75	
EN24	Henley	Albert	ES	10/13/80	40.0	$17.80	B	SE	$54.08	
EN26	Kyler	Dennis	MK	5/12/88	40.0	$17.80	C			
EN27	Zangari	Nick	EE	2/22/92	37.5	$32.50	B	NE	$67.75	Nick has con
EN30	Jones	Hugh	CE	4/13/82	40.0	$17.25	A1	SE	$56.65	
EN32	Vetch	Randall	SS	3/31/89	25.0	$14.00	A1	SW	$51.50	
EN34	Horn	Jason	SS	5/13/91	40.0	$13.50	A1	SE	$54.08	
EN36	Castile	Abraham	MK	11/1/82	40.0	$18.00	A1	NW	$60.50	
EN38	Wilson	Judy	MK	9/1/87	40.0	$16.00	B	NW	$65.50	

Record: 2

Employee identification code

Default values provide a convenient shortcut when you enter new records; however, setting a default value does not affect values in existing records.

In Chapter 2, you saw Access automatically set a default value of 0 for number and currency fields as you created those fields. In this task, you'll see a default value of 0 that Access has already set in the Park Rate field, and then you'll set your own default value in the Hours field:

1. Move to and observe the blank record at the end of the table (click on the **Last Record navigation button**, and then click on the **Next Record navigation button**). Access has already placed a default value of 0, displayed as $0.00, in the Park Rate field (see Figure 8.7).

2. Switch to Design view; then display and observe the Park Rate field's properties (move the focus to the Park Rate row). The Default Value property is set to 0.

Figure 8.7   **A blank record with a default value in the Park Rate field**

ID	Last	First	Dept	Hired	Hours	Pay Rate	Health	Park Lot	Park Rate	Comment
EN57	Carter	Ben	EE	8/23/88	40.0	$26.50	C	NW	$65.00	
EN62	Beaton	Robert	SS	11/23/87	35.0	$12.50	B	NW	$67.75	
EN66	McCarthy	Kathryn	MS	3/21/90	40.0	$14.00	A1	SE	$54.33	
EN68	Stevens	David	CE	9/30/84	40.0	$15.00	A2	SE	$54.08	David is curre
EN69	Petty	Suzanna	CE	3/31/84	40.0	$21.50	C	SE	$59.48	
EN71	Beasley	Ken	CE	4/1/83	40.0	$22.50	C	NW	$65.50	Ken demonst
EN72	Weinstein	Andrew	EE	4/24/88	40.0	$32.50	C	NE	$67.75	
EN73	Berry	Sharon	MK	7/1/84	40.0	$19.25	A2	SW	$56.65	
FN74	Hartle	Susan	SS	12/1/86	25.0	$17.50	B	SW	$56.65	
EN76	Smith	Patricia	ES	4/6/90	40.0	$10.00	B	SW	$54.08	
EN77	Clark	Thomas	MK	1/1/89	40.0	$22.50	C	NW	$62.50	
EN78	Russell	Larry	MS	4/1/84	40.0	$13.50	B	NE	$60.00	
EN79	Pierce	Edward	SS	4/1/81	40.0	$12.50	A2	SE	$59.23	
EN80	Nelson	Luke	MK	6/20/87	40.0	$17.50	B			
EN81	Davis	Eugene	ES	6/2/87	40.0	$14.50	B	NE	$60.00	
EN83	Warfield	Cristin	CE	6/30/82	40.0	$17.50	C	NE	$62.50	
EN85	Cassada	Bruce	CE	3/15/89	40.0	$21.50	A2	NW	$65.50	
EN86	Murray	Nancy	EE	3/15/83	40.0	$23.00	B	NW	$62.75	
EN87	Gardner	Gayle	MK	12/1/86	40.0	$16.75	B	SW	$59.48	
EN88	Donohue	Jordan	SA	9/1/92	40.0	$22.00	B	NE	$65.00	
EN89	Fisher	Elyse	SA	9/1/92	40.0	$23.50	A1	NE	$65.00	
EN90	Latta	Jennifer	SA	9/14/92	40.0	$17.00	A1	SE	$55.00	
EN91	Jimenez	Pedro	SA	9/14/92	40.0	$17.00	B	SW	$55.00	
EN92	Rutkowski	Robert	SA	10/19/92	40.0	$18.00	A2	SW	$55.00	
EN93	Tobin	Linda	SA	10/19/92	40.0	$20.00	C	SE	$57.75	
									$0.00	

Microsoft Access - [Table: Payroll Data]
File   Edit   View   Records   Layout   Window   Help
Field: ID   New:
Record: 58
Employee identification code

Default value

3. Display and observe the Hours field's properties. The Default Value property box is empty.

4. Type **40** in the Default Value property box.

5. Save the table design, and then return to Datasheet view.

6. Observe the table's last, blank record. The Hours field now displays your default value (see Figure 8.8).

SETTING VALIDATION RULES AND VALIDATION TEXT

Validation rules are field properties you can set to require or prevent certain values or patterns of values in a field. For example, with validation rules you can require that an employee-ID code begin with specific characters, or prohibit a pay rate from exceeding a certain dollar amount.

Figure 8.8   **A blank record with your default value in the Hours field**

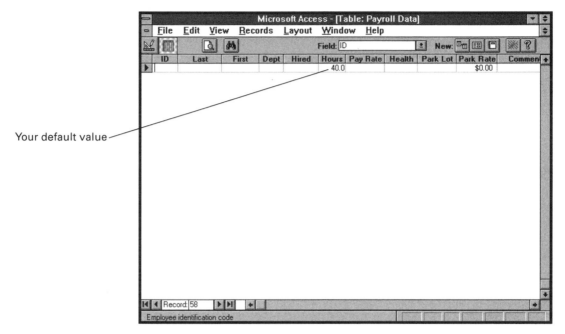

Your default value

Validation rules help to promote data conformity, and can help prevent data-entry errors. Like default values, though, validation rules do not affect existing records (unless you attempt to change existing values within those records).

Whenever you set a validation rule, you should also set validation text that explains that rule. Access uses this validation text in a dialog box that it opens whenever data entered into that field does not follow the validation rule. For example, if you set a validation rule preventing a value in an hours-worked field from exceeding 60, your validation text might be *Employees cannot be scheduled to work more than 60 hours per week.* When you then enter a value greater than 60 in that field, Access opens a dialog box containing your text to explain the validation rule, and prevents you from saving that record until the value adheres to the validation rule.

To set a validation rule and text in a Table window's Design view, display the field properties of the field for which you want to set the rule and text. Then type a validation expression in the Validation Rule property box and type some validation text in the Validation Text property box. You can use the same techniques for setting validation expressions as you have used for criteria expressions. For example, if you want to prevent hours-worked values from exceeding 60, type <=60 in the hours-worked field's Validation Rule property box.

Let's look at a field that has a validation rule and text set already, and then set and test a validation rule and text for a second field:

1. In the ID field of the table's last, blank record, type **in99**; then press **Tab** to leave the field. Access opens a dialog box to inform you that ID codes must start with EN (see Figure 8.9).

Figure 8.9   **Validation text in a dialog box**

2. Click on **OK**, and then replace in99 with **en99**.

3. Press **Tab**. Access accepts your new ID code and displays it in uppercase. (Remember that the ID field employs the > Format property.)

4. Switch to Design view; then display and observe the ID field's properties (see Figure 8.10). The Validation Rule property requires that ID numbers start with EN; the Validation Text property provides text for the dialog box that Access opens when the Validation Rule property is violated (as you saw in step 1).

5. Display and observe the Pay Rate field's properties. Both the Validation Rule and Validation Text property boxes are empty.

6. In the Validation Rule property box, type **<=45** to disallow new pay rates greater than $45.00.

7. In the Validation Text property box, type **You cannot enter a pay rate greater than $45.00**.

8. Save the table design, and then switch to Datasheet view.

Figure 8.10 **The ID field's properties**

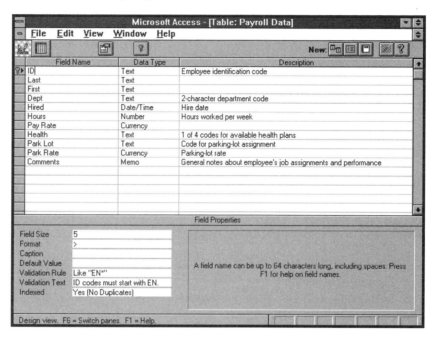

9. In the Pay Rate field for the record with the ID code EN99 (Record 58), type **47.5**, and then press **Tab**. Access opens a dialog box containing the validation text you typed, informing you that a pay rate cannot exceed $45.00 (see Figure 8.11).

10. Click on **OK**, replace 47.5 with **27.5**, and then press **Tab**. Access accepts the new pay rate.

Figure 8.11 **Your validation text in a dialog box**

11. Complete the record with the following values:

Last:	**Osborn**
First:	**Lloyd**
Dept:	**ee**
Hired:	**5/14/93**
Hours:	**40** (default value)
Pay Rate:	**27.5** (press Tab to skip)
Health:	**c**
Park Lot:	**ne**
Park Rate:	**55**
Comments:	(leave blank)

 EXAMINING A MEMO FIELD

Text fields can hold up to 255 alphanumeric characters each. If you need more room than that (for example, to store notes on individual employee performance), you can use a memo field. Memo fields can hold up to 32,000 alphanumeric characters.

Depending on the amount of data stored in a record's memo field, you may not be able to see all of that data in Datasheet view. However, you can easily view and edit the contents of a memo field through the Zoom box. To open the Zoom box for a memo field in a Table window's Datasheet view, place the focus in the desired memo field, and then press Shift+F2. (Forms offer other alternatives for viewing and editing memo fields. You'll learn about working with memo fields on forms in Chapter 9.)

Let's look at a memo field in the Payroll Data table:

1. Press **Ctrl+Home** to return to the top of the table; then scroll to the right and observe the table's rightmost field, Comments. In some of the records, the Comments field contains text, but you can't see all of the text because the column is too narrow.

2. Move the focus to the Comments field for Jane Martin's record (Record 7), and then open the field's Zoom box (press **Shift+F2**).

3. Observe the Zoom box. Its contents exceed the 255-character maximum for text fields (see Figure 8.12).

Figure 8.12   **Using the Zoom box to display the contents of a memo field**

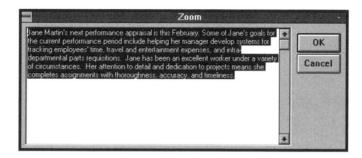

4. Click on **Cancel** to close the Zoom box, and then switch to Design view.

5. Observe the Comments row. Comments is set to the Memo data type.

6. Close the Table window.

WORKING WITH KEYED TABLES

In Chapter 2, you learned that a table's primary key is a field or combination of fields that enables Access to uniquely identify each table record.

In addition, you learned that Access automatically sets a primary-key field's Indexed property to Yes (No Duplicates). This property setting instructs Access to:

- Automatically sort records in a table by values in that field.

- Automatically index records by those values in order to speed data retrieval.

- Prevent you from entering duplicate values in the primary-key field or fields.

In this next section, you'll learn ways to remove, change, and work with primary keys.

REMOVING A PRIMARY KEY

As you learned in Chapter 2, it is relatively easy to set a primary key: In a Table window's Design view, select or place the focus in the row of the field you wish to use for the primary key, and then choose Edit, Set Primary Key or click on the Primary Key button. However, it is not as easy to remove a primary key.

To remove a table's primary key, you would follow these steps:

- Open the Table window in Design view.

- Click on the Properties button or choose View, Table Properties to open the table's property sheet.

- Delete the primary-key field name or names from the property sheet's Primary Key property box.

- Close the property sheet.

Let's remove the primary key from the Suppliers table:

1. Open and examine the Suppliers table. The table's records are in order by telephone number.

2. Switch to Design view and examine the Phone row. A key indicator displays on the row's field selector, indicating that Phone is the table's primary-key field.

3. Click on the **Properties button** (or choose View, Table Properties) to open the table's property sheet.

4. Observe the property sheet. It contains a table description and the name of the table's primary-key field, Phone.

5. Delete **Phone** from the property sheet's Primary Key property box (Figure 8.13 shows Phone partially deleted). Then close the property sheet (click on the **Properties button**; choose **View, Table Properties**; or double-click on the box's **Control menu box**).

6. Observe the Phone row. The row's field selector no longer displays a key indicator, indicating that Phone is no longer the primary-key field.

Figure 8.13   **Removing the Suppliers table's primary key**

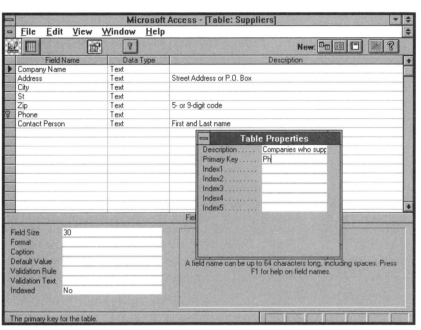

ADDING A COUNTER DATA TYPE PRIMARY-KEY FIELD

Perhaps it is somewhat tedious to remove a table's primary key because Access works much faster and more easily with tables that do have primary keys. Although Access doesn't require you to set a primary key for every table, it does strongly encourage you to do so. In fact, whenever you create a new table without setting a primary key or remove the primary key from an existing table, and then try to save the table design, Access opens a dialog box warning you that you haven't set a primary key and offers to create a primary-key field for you.

When it does, you have three options:

- Click on Yes if you want Access to use the Counter data type to create as a primary key a counter field named ID. (If your table already has a counter field, Access instead sets that counter field as the primary key; if your table already has a noncounter field named ID, Access names its new field ID1.) In counter fields, Access automatically inserts sequential numbers, starting with 1, for all existing and new records. Because sequential numbers will never duplicate, this enables Access to uniquely identify every record.

- Click on No if you want to save the table design without setting a primary key (not recommended).

- Click on Cancel if you want to return to the table design and set a primary key yourself.

When entering data, you cannot enter values into a counter field; instead, Access provides sequential numbers automatically. When entering and viewing data, you may find that values in a counter field look similar to record numbers. However, counter-field values and record numbers may not necessarily be the same for every record. To determine a record's number, move the focus to that record, and then observe the Specific Record Number box.

Try to save the table design without a primary key, have Access create a primary-key field for you, and then see how a counter field works in Datasheet view:

1. Choose **File, Save** to start saving the modified table design. Access opens a dialog box to inform you that the Suppliers table has no primary key and to ask if you want Access to create a primary key for you.

2. Click on **Yes**, and then observe the table design. Access has added a primary-key field, ID, that has the Counter data type, and has set that field's Indexed property to Yes (No Duplicates) (see Figure 8.14).

3. Switch to Datasheet view, and then observe the ID field. Access automatically added consecutive numbers, beginning with 1, to the ID field (see Figure 8.15).

4. Move the focus to the last, blank record's (Record 5) Company Name field, and then type **Electrical Connections**.

5. Save the record (move the focus off the record or choose **File, Save Record**), and then observe your record's ID field. Access automatically added the next consecutive value, 5.

Figure 8.14   **The table design after Access has added a primary-key field**

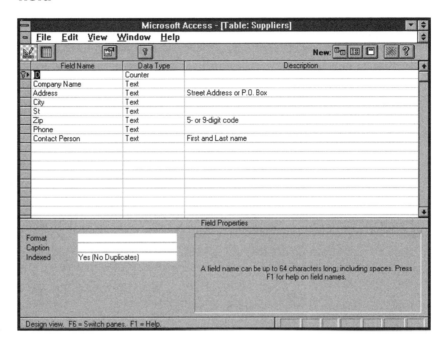

6. Complete the record with the following values:

Address:	**20 Outlet Road**
City:	**Wyoming**
St:	**NY**
Zip:	**14591**
Phone:	**898-2100**
Contact Person:	**John McVay**

CHANGING THE PRIMARY-KEY FIELD

Although you can always use a counter field as a primary-key field, you may prefer to minimize the number of fields in your tables by identifying an existing field or set of fields that will uniquely identify your records.

Figure 8.15   **The ID counter field in Datasheet view**

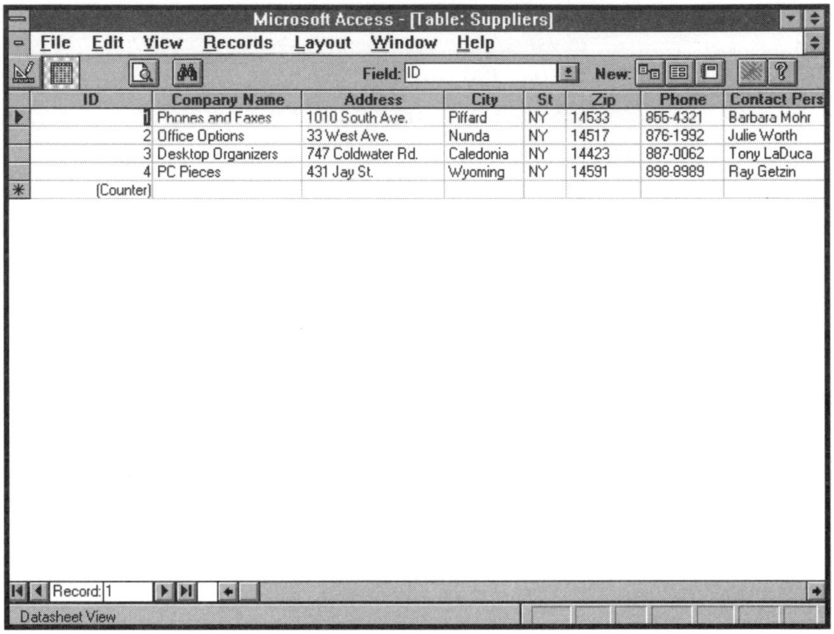

To change a table's primary-key field, select and set the new field or fields as you would if the table did not already have a primary key. When you do, Access automatically reassigns the primary key to the new field or fields and removes the former primary-key assignment. Once you've reassigned a primary key to another existing field, you may want to delete Access' counter field.

Let's change the primary-key field from Access' ID field to the Phone field, and then delete the ID field:

1. Switch to Design view, and then open and observe the table's property sheet (click on the **Properties button** or choose **View, Table Properties**). ID is the primary-key field.

2. In the Table window, move the focus to the Phone row; then click on the **Primary Key button** (or choose Edit, Set Primary Key). Access moves the key indicator from the ID row's field selector to the Phone row's field selector, indicating that Phone is now the primary-key field (see Figure 8.16).

Figure 8.16   **The table design after setting Phone as the primary-key field**

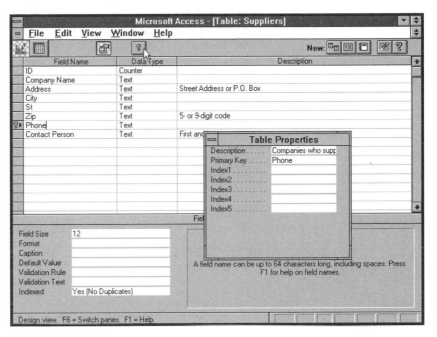

3. Observe the property sheet. It also reflects the primary-key change.

4. Observe the Phone field's Index property. Access has set the property to Yes (No Duplicates).

5. Close the property sheet.

6. Select the ID row (click on the row's field selector), and then press the **Delete** key. Access opens a dialog box to inform you that deleting the ID field will also delete the data contained within the field.

7. Click on **OK** to delete the ID field and its data.

8. Save the table design, and then switch to Datasheet view.

9. Observe the table (see Figure 8.17). Notice that the record you added (Electrical Connections) is no longer displayed at the end of the table, but rather is sorted with the other records by telephone number. Also notice that the ID field is no longer a part of the table.

Figure 8.17   **The Suppliers table in Datasheet view after deleting the ID field**

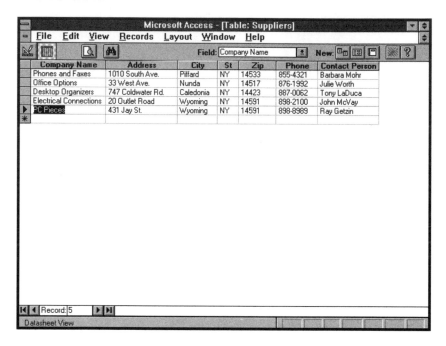

Company Name	Address	City	St	Zip	Phone	Contact Person
Phones and Faxes	1010 South Ave.	Piffard	NY	14533	855-4321	Barbara Mohr
Office Options	33 West Ave.	Nunda	NY	14517	876-1992	Julie Worth
Desktop Organizers	747 Coldwater Rd.	Caledonia	NY	14423	887-0062	Tony LaDuca
Electrical Connections	20 Outlet Road	Wyoming	NY	14591	898-2100	John McVay
PC Pieces	431 Jay St.	Wyoming	NY	14591	898-8989	Ray Getzin

TESTING A DUPLICATE VALUE IN A PRIMARY-KEY FIELD

You've learned that Access sets the primary-key field's Indexed property to Yes (No Duplicates) to prevent duplicate values from being entered in that field.

Now see what happens when you try to enter a duplicate value in a primary-key field:

1. Add the following values to the table's last, blank record (Record 6), and then attempt to save the record:

Company Name:	**Commercial Decorators**
Address:	**440 Washington St.**
City:	**Nunda**
St:	**NY**

Zip:	**14517**
Phone:	**876-1992**
Contact Person:	**Valerie Hernandez**

Access opens a dialog box to inform you that you can't have duplicate values in a primary-key field.

2. Click on **OK**, and then compare the telephone numbers for Office Options (Record 2) and Commercial Decorators (Record 6). The telephone numbers are identical (see Figure 8.18).

Figure 8.18   **The Suppliers table with identical values in its primary-key field**

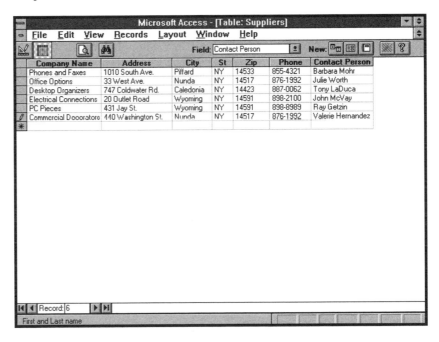

3. Change the telephone number for Commercial Decorators to **876-1002**, and then save the record.

4. Choose **Records, Show All Records**. Access reorders the records according to the primary-key field, Phone. (You saw in Chapter 7 that the Records, Show All Records command refreshes the contents of open windows. To accomplish the same thing, you could have also closed and then reopened the Table window.)

PRACTICE YOUR SKILLS

1. Add the following values to the table's last, blank record (Record 7), and then attempt to save the record:

Company Name:	**Computer Solutions**
Address:	**310 Oxford Street**
City:	**Piffard**
St:	**NY**
Zip:	**14533**
Phone:	**887-0062**
Contact Person:	**Kat Clark**

2. Close Access' dialog box, and then change the Phone field to **855-0062**.

3. Save the record, reorder the records according to the primary-key field, and then compare your screen to the table pictured in Figure 8.19.

4. Close the Table window.

CREATING RELATIONSHIPS BETWEEN TABLES

In Chapter 7, you learned how to create a temporary join between tables in order to run a multiple-table query. This kind of temporary joining, however, only begins to touch on Access' power to bring together data from multiple tables.

You learned in Chapter 1 that Access is a database-management system: a system whose purpose is to collect, retrieve, and present data. Beyond that, Access is a *relational* database-management system: a system whose purpose is to collect, retrieve, and present data from *related tables*.

Figure 8.19   **The Suppliers table after adding a seventh record**

Company Name	Address	City	St	Zip	Phone	Contact Person
Computer Solutions	310 Oxford Street	Piffard	NY	14533	855-0062	Kat Clark
Phones and Faxes	1010 South Ave.	Piffard	NY	14533	855-4321	Barbara Mohr
Commercial Decorators	440 Washington St.	Nunda	NY	14517	876-1002	Valerie Hernandez
Office Options	33 West Ave.	Nunda	NY	14517	876-1992	Julie Worth
Desktop Organizers	747 Coldwater Rd.	Caledonia	NY	14423	887-0062	Tony LaDuca
Electrical Connections	20 Outlet Road	Wyoming	NY	14591	898-2100	John McVay
PC Pieces	431 Jay St.	Wyoming	NY	14591	898-8989	Ray Getzin

The chief advantage (and challenge) of a relational database is that it enables you to store a particular set of data in only one place but to use that data in any number of places. For example, if you store a customer's name in a single customer information table, you can still use that name on mailing labels, in a sales report, on an invoice, and on a customer-telephone list.

But why is storing a particular set of data in one place so advantageous? Consider this: If you stored that customer's name in separate tables for each of the items just described, you would be maintaining four copies of that customer's name. This quadruples your chance of misspelling that customer's name and wastes computer storage space. Worse yet, what happens if that customer's name changes? You would have to find *every* occurrence of that name and change it manually. With the customer's name in only one place, you would only have to change the name once.

The key to creating and maintaining a successful relational database is in carefully designing each table, and then carefully relating those tables to each other so that they can work together seamlessly. Access does much of the work of bringing together data from related tables; your job is to determine the contents of those tables and how those tables should be related.

As you learned in Chapter 2, a well-designed table contains fields and data that are related to one particular subject. For example, employee names belong in an employee-information table, while customer names belong in a customer-information table.

ESTABLISHING TABLE RELATIONSHIPS

You saw in Chapter 7 that to join tables temporarily in a multiple-table query, you need to identify a common, linking field or fields between those tables. The same holds true for joining tables permanently by using the Edit, Relationships command.

In a successful relational database, each table must have a field that it shares in common with at least one other table, and these fields (with some minor exceptions) must share the same data type. (However, the fields do not have to have the same name.) For example, in a customer-information table, you might include a field that stores employee IDs so that you can relate your sales-people data to your customer data; or, an inventory table might contain a field for supplier IDs so that you can relate your product data to your supplier data.

When establishing table relationships, you first need to select a *primary table*, a *related table*, and a common field or fields between those tables. Either table in a table relationship can serve as the primary table or related table, but the common field or fields between the two tables *must* be the primary table's primary key. For example, if an employee-ID field is the primary-key field in an employee-information table, but not in a customer-information table, and you wish to join the tables through the employee-ID field, the employee-information table must be the primary table.

In the example above, the employee-ID field in the customer-information table would be called a *foreign key*. A foreign key is the common field or fields in a relationship's related table.

Once you have established the two tables and their common fields, you need to decide between the two table relationship types that Access offers: one-to-one and one-to-many. In a *one-to-one relationship,* each record in the primary table can relate to only one record in its related table, and the common field or fields between the tables must be each table's primary key. You might use a one-to-one relationship, for example, when you want to store confidential and nonconfidential employee information in separate tables. Each record in those tables would relate to only one record in the other table. In a *one-to-many relationship,* each record in a primary table can relate to any number of records in its related table. You might use a one-to-many relationship, for example, between a supplier-information table and a product-information table because *one* supplier supplies *many* products. For example, the supplier-information table might contain one record for the XYZ company while the product-information table contains ten records for the ten products the XYZ company supplied. In most cases, table relationships will be one-to-many relationships.

To establish a permanent table relationship from the Database window, you would follow these steps:

- Choose Edit, Relationships.

- In the Relationships dialog box, select the primary and related tables.

- If necessary, select a relationship type (Access uses one-to-many as the default).

- If necessary, select the common, linking field or fields in the related table (you can use the Suggest button to ask Access to suggest a field for you). Remember that common fields do not have to share the same field name.

- If desired, check Enforce Referential Integrity. (For more information on enforcing referential integrity, see your Access documentation.)

- Click on Add, and then click on Close.

When you establish a table relationship, you also automatically establish relationships between any queries based on those tables.

Let's establish a one-to-one relationship between the Addresses and Payroll Data tables, which are both employee-information tables:

1. From the Database window, choose **Edit, Relationships** to open the Relationships dialog box.

2. In the Primary Table drop-down list box, select **Addresses**. Access automatically displays the Address table's primary-key field, ID, below the table's name.

3. In the Related Table drop-down list box, select **Payroll Data**.

4. In the Type option box, select **One** to specify a one-to-one relationship between the Addresses and Payroll Data tables.

5. Observe the Select Matching Fields drop-down list box. Access selects the primary-key field, ID, from the Payroll Data table to match the ID field from the Addresses table (see Figure 8.20).

Figure 8.20   **Creating a table relationship**

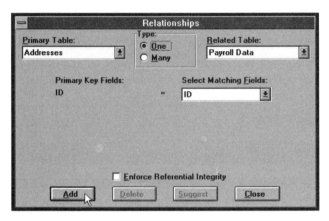

6. Click on **Add** to create the table relationship, and then click on **Close** to close the dialog box.

CREATING A MULTIPLE-TABLE QUERY BASED ON RELATED TABLES

Once you have established a table relationship, Access makes it easier to create multiple-table queries by automatically creating a join line between those tables in the query's design.

Because field names coming from multiple tables might be confusing, you might want to rename one or more fields in your multiple-table queries. For example, if you design a query that combines name fields from both an employee-information table and a customer-information table, you may not be able to distinguish in your dynaset which are employee names and which are customer names. To rename a regular field for a dynaset, precede that name in its QBE-grid Field cell with a new name followed by a colon to separate the two names.

Now create a multiple-table query based on the tables you just joined:

1. From the Database window, create a new query based on the Addresses and Payroll Data tables. (Display the list of query object names, click on **New**, use the Add Table dialog box to add both tables to the query design, and then close the Add Table dialog box.)

2. Observe the join line between the ID fields in the two field lists. Because a relationship already exists between the query's two tables, Access automatically joins the tables in the query (see Figure 8.21).

3. From the Payroll Data field list, add **Last** and then **First** to the QBE grid's first two Field cells.

Figure 8.21   **Automatically joined field lists**

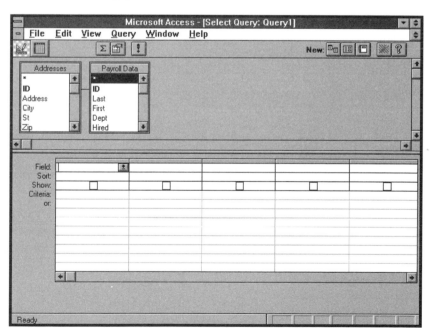

4. From the Addresses field list, add **Phone** to the QBE grid's third Field cell.

5. Select **Ascending** in both the Last and First column's Sort cells.

6. In the Phone Field cell, place the insertion point to the left of the *P* in *Phone,* and then type **Home Phone**: to rename the field for the query's dynaset.

7. Run the query, and then observe the dynaset. It displays values from both tables, and lists them in order by last and then first name. Notice that the Phone field is labeled Home Phone (see Figure 8.22).

Figure 8.22 **The dynaset of the multiple-table query**

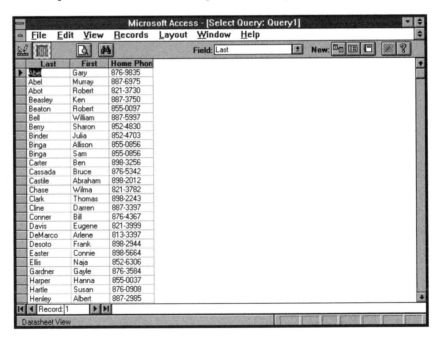

8. Close the Query window without saving the query, and then close the Database window.

The concept of relational databases can seem formidable. Before creating a relational database, therefore, you might consider diagramming table relationships on paper to identify common fields and relationship types *before* you create any of your own tables. Then, be ready to fine-tune your database design as necessary. Your Access documentation provides some examples of relational databases for your study.

Bear in mind that creating and managing a relational database is an evolving process. You may not get your design right from step one, and your database may need to meet new and unexpected challenges, but you should find that Access is flexible and forgiving enough to let your database grow as your knowledge and needs grow.

PRACTICE YOUR SKILLS

In Chapter 7, you learned how to create advanced select queries, as well as parameter, action, and multiple-table queries. In this chapter, you learned how to work with a variety of field properties, how to remove and change primary keys, and how to establish table relationships. The following two activities give you an opportunity to apply some of these techniques.

After each activity step, a chapter reference (in parentheses) informs you where we introduced the relevant technique for that step.

In this activity, you will create a parameter query to produce the dynaset of employees who park in the SW parking lot, as shown in Figure 8.23:

1. Open the practice.mdb database file, and then, if necessary, maximize the Database window (Chapter 1).

2. Open and observe the Parking Lots and Rates table (Chapter 1).

3. From the Table window, create a new query based on the Parking Lots and Rates table (Chapter 7).

4. Add the **Last** field to the QBE grid's first Field cell (Chapter 4).

5. In the QBE grid's second Field cell, enter an expression to concatenate the First and Last fields with a space in between (Chapter 7).

6. Name the concatenated field **Employee Name** (Chapter 7).

7. Add the Park Lot field to the QBE grid's third Field cell (Chapter 4).

8. Specify that the records be sorted in ascending order by the Last field (Chapter 4).

9. Specify that the query not display the Last field in its dynaset (Chapter 7).

10. In the Park Lot field's Criteria cell, set a parameter expression to ask for a parking-lot value (Chapter 7).

11. Run the query, providing **sw** as the value for the Park Lot field's parameter (Chapter 7).

12. Compare your dynaset to the one shown in Figure 8.23 (Chapter 4).

Figure 8.23   **The parameter query's dynaset**

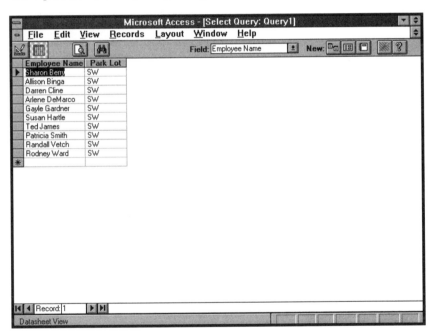

13. Save the query as **My Parameter Parking Lots** (Chapter 4).

14. Close the Query window, leaving the Parking Lots and Rates Table open and active (Chapter 1).

In this activity, you will modify and test some field properties in the Parking Lots and Rates table. You will also remove the table's primary key, let Access create a primary key for you, and then reassign the primary key and delete Access' field.

1. Switch to the Parking Lots and Rates Table window's Design view (Chapter 2).

2. For the Park Lot field, set a default value of **sw** (Chapter 8).

3. For the Park Rate field, set a validation rule that requires a minimum parking rate of $50, and then set some appropriate validation text to accompany the rule (Chapter 8).

4. Save the table design; then switch to Datasheet view (Chapter 2).

5. Move to and observe the default Park Lot value of SW in the table's last, blank record (Chapter 2).

6. In the blank record's Park Rate field, type **45**, and then attempt to save the record (Chapter 2).

7. Close Access' dialog box, and then change the Park Rate value to **55** (Chapter 8).

8. Add the following values to the remainder of the record (Chapter 2):

Last:	**Bonski**
First:	**Igor**
Dept:	**EE**
ID:	**EN88**

9. Return to Design view and remove the table's primary key (Chapter 8).

10. Attempt to save the table design, and then let Access create a primary-key field for you (Chapter 8).

11. Switch to Datasheet view, and then return to the top of the table (Chapter 2).

12. Observe the new primary-key field and compare your screen to Figure 8.24 (Chapter 8).

13. Return to Design view and change the primary key back to ID (Chapter 8).

14. Delete the counter field Access created (Chapter 2).

15. Close the property sheet (Chapter 7).

16. Save the table design, and then close the Table and Database windows (Chapter 2).

Figure 8.24   **The Parking Lots and Rates table after Access has added a primary-key field**

ID1	Park Lot	Park Rate	Last	First	Dept	ID
1	SW	$50.00	James	Ted	MK	EN01
2	NW	$65.00	Harper	Hanna	ES	EN03
3	NW	$55.00	Packer	Penny	MK	EN04
4			Binder	Julia	MS	EN05
5			Sanders	Maria	ES	EN07
6	NW	$62.00	Easter	Connie	EE	EN08
7	SE	$55.50	Martin	Jane	EE	EN10
8	SW	$55.75	Binga	Allison	EE	EN11
9			Conner	Bill	CE	EN12
10	NE	$65.00	Osowski	Dominick	SA	EN13
11	NW	$60.00	Binga	Sam	SS	EN14
12	NE	$62.00	Abel	Murray	CE	EN15
13	NW	$65.00	Abot	Robert	MK	EN16
14	NE	$67.75	Zambito	Joseph	CE	EN17
15	NE	$60.00	McDonald	Peter	EE	EN18
16	SE	$52.00	Chase	Wilma	SS	EN19
17	SW	$55.00	DeMarco	Arlene	ES	EN20
18	NE	$67.75	Desoto	Frank	MS	EN23
19	SE	$52.50	Henley	Albert	ES	EN24
20			Kyler	Dennis	MK	EN26
21	NE	$67.75	Zangari	Nick	EE	EN27
22	SE	$55.00	Jones	Hugh	CE	EN30
23	SW	$50.00	Vetch	Randall	SS	EN32
24	SE	$52.50	Horn	Jason	SS	EN34
25	NW	$60.50	Castile	Abraham	MK	EN36
26	NW	$65.50	Wilson	Judy	MK	EN38

SUMMARY

In this chapter, you learned how to use field properties to enhance the performance of your tables, how to remove and reset a table's primary key, and how to create and use table relationships.

Here's a quick reference guide to the Access features introduced in this chapter:

Desired Result	How to Do It
Use context-sensitive Help	Press **F1**
Modify field properties	Open the Table window containing the field in Design view, move the focus to the field's row, and then use the field's property boxes

Desired Result	How to Do It
Modify a date/time field's display format	Change the field's Format property
Modify a number field's display format	Change the field's Format and/or Decimal Places property
Set a default value for a field	Type the value in the field's Default Value property box
Set a validation rule for a field	Type a value or expression in the field's Validation Rule property box
Set validation text for a field	Type the text in a field's Validation Text property box
Remove a table's primary key	Open the Table window in Design view, click on the **Properties button** (or choose **View, Table Properties**), and then delete the field name or names from the table's Primary Key property box
Change a table's primary key	Open the Table window in Design view, place the focus in the row for the new primary-key field, and then click on the **Primary Key button** (or choose **Edit, Set Primary Key**)
Create a relationship between two tables	From the Database window, choose **Edit, Relationships**, select the primary and related tables, select the relationship type, select the common linking field or fields, click on **Add**, and then click on **Close**

In Chapter 9, you'll learn how to use control properties and various control styles to create enhanced forms. You'll also learn how to use the Main/Subform FormWizard to create two forms that enable you to view data from two tables and/or queries in a single Form window.

IF YOU'RE STOPPING HERE

If you need to break off here, please exit Access. If you want to proceed directly to the next chapter, please do so now.

CHAPTER 9: ENHANCED FORM DESIGN

Editing a Memo
Field and
Enhancing Its
Control

Adding Controls to
Enhance an
Existing Form

Creating a Form
that Contains a
Subform

In Chapter 5, you learned how to use a FormWizard to create a basic single-column form, and how to modify that form's design by deleting, moving, sizing, and aligning controls. In Chapter 6, you learned how to modify controls on a report by changing control properties through the tool bar. In this chapter, you will learn how to enhance the performance and appearance of your forms by modifying and adding control properties through a control's property sheet, and by adding controls to existing forms. You will also learn how to create and use a form that displays data from two related tables and/or queries at the same time.

When you're done working through this chapter, you will know how to:

- Use an enlarged control to view and edit a memo field

- Use a control's property sheet to modify control properties

- Add a control to an existing form

- Add a *calculated control* to calculate values not available through the form's underlying table or query

- Add a *rectangle control* to display a rectangle

- Add a *list box control* to enable you to select values from a list

- Add an *unbound object frame control* to display a *Paintbrush picture*—a graphic that was created and saved through the Windows Paintbrush accessory program

- Use the Main/Subform FormWizard to create a form that displays data from two related tables and/or queries

EDITING A MEMO FIELD AND ENHANCING ITS CONTROL

You learned in Chapter 8 that you can use memo fields to store values up to 32,000 characters long, and that you can use the Zoom box in a table's Datasheet view to view and edit those values more easily.

Forms, however, are more flexible in displaying data than tables; instead of using the Zoom box for lengthy values, you can use an enlarged control to provide a large area for viewing and editing a memo field. By changing control properties, you can also add scroll bars to a control, enabling you to scroll through lengthy values.

 EDITING A MEMO FIELD

You can view and edit a memo field much as you would any other field. An enlarged control on a form, however, makes the task a little easier. If a memo field's bound control (that is, the control that displays the contents of a memo field) still is not large enough to display the entire field, you can use your arrow keys to navigate through the field.

If you do not have both the Access application and the COMPANY Database windows opened and maximized, please open and maximize them now.

Now, let's use a form with an enlarged memo-field control to view and edit a memo field:

1. From the Database window, open the Comments form.

2. Observe the form. It displays five fields and their labels, arranged vertically. The Comments field is very large.

3. Move to Jane Martin's record (Record 7), and then observe the text in the Comments field. Even though the field is large, you still cannot see all of the text.

4. Place the insertion point at the end of the Comments field's visible text, and then press **Down Arrow** to move the insertion point to the end of the text.

5. Press **Spacebar**, and then type **Jane's position is under review by management for possible reclassification.** Notice as you type that the text automatically wraps from one line to the next as necessary (see Figure 9.1).

Figure 9.1   **Editing a memo field**

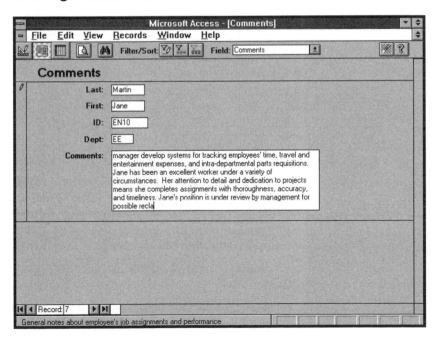

DISPLAYING AND MODIFYING CONTROL PROPERTIES

In Chapter 6, you learned how to modify some control properties—such as font, font size, and alignment—in a Report window's Design view by selecting the control, and then using drop-down list boxes and buttons on the tool bar. Because controls work much the same in both form and report designs, these drop-down list boxes and buttons are also usually available when you select a control in a form's design.

These boxes and buttons, however, enable you to modify only *some* control properties. To view and be able to modify *all* of a control's properties, you must work through a control's property sheet. Like the table property sheet you worked with in Chapter 8, a control's property sheet lists all of the properties that affect the appearance and behavior of a control.

To open a control's property sheet in Design view, select that control, and then click on the Properties button or choose View, Properties. If the property sheet is already open, simply click on the control to display that control's properties. By clicking away from controls, you can also use the property sheet to view properties for each of the form's sections (Form Header, Detail, and Form Footer) and for the form itself. A property sheet's title bar always reflects the type of control or other object for which it is currently displaying properties.

The number of available properties can seem daunting, but as you work with property sheets, remember that Access' context-sensitive Help system is only a keystroke away. To get help on any specific property, move the focus to that property's box in the property sheet, and then press F1.

The control property that you're going to change in this next task is the Scroll Bars property. This property is often useful for lengthy memo fields; by setting the Scroll Bars property to Vertical, you instruct Access to display a vertical scroll bar for that field whenever you are in Form view and the focus is in that field. Scroll bars can make a lengthy field easier to move through.

Let's change the Scroll Bars property for the Comments bound control:

1. Switch to Design view, and then observe the form's sections. The Form Header section contains a control for the form title,

Comments; the Detail section contains five white bound controls and their shaded labels; the Form Footer section is empty.

2. Click on the **Properties button** (or choose **View, Properties**) to open the form's property sheet. If the property sheet is not entitled Form, click to the right of the form's border (past the 5-inch mark on the horizontal ruler) to display the form's properties.

3. Observe the form's Record Source property. It indicates that this form is based on the Payroll Data table (see Figure 9.2).

Figure 9.2   **The Comments form's property sheet**

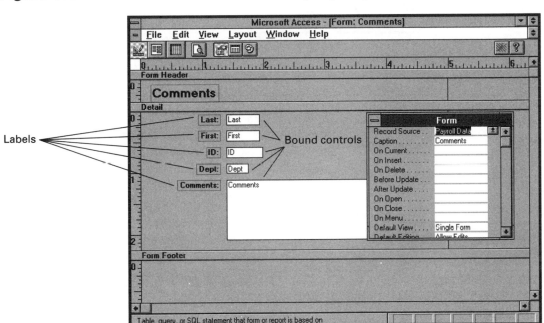

4. Select the **Last label**, and then observe the property sheet. It is now entitled Label, and displays the selected label's properties.

5. Select the **Last bound control**. The property sheet indicates that the Last bound control is a *text box control*. (Text box controls and labels are two *styles* of controls. You'll learn about other control styles later in this chapter.)

6. Select the **Comments bound control**, and then observe the property sheet. The Comments bound control is also a text box control.

7. In the property sheet, if necessary, scroll down and observe the Comments control's Scroll Bars property. The property is set to None.

8. Open the Scroll Bars property box's drop-down list; then select **Vertical** (see Figure 9.3).

Figure 9.3   **Changing the Comments control's Scroll Bars property**

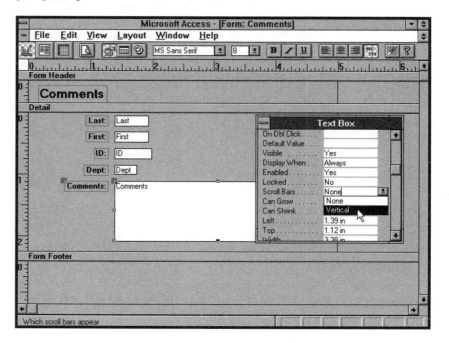

9. Close the property sheet, and then switch to Form view.

10. Observe the Comments field. It does not seem to have changed.

11. Move the focus to the Comments field. Access now displays a vertical scroll bar (see Figure 9.4). Use the scroll bar to scroll through the Comments field.

Figure 9.4   **The Comments field with a vertical scroll bar**

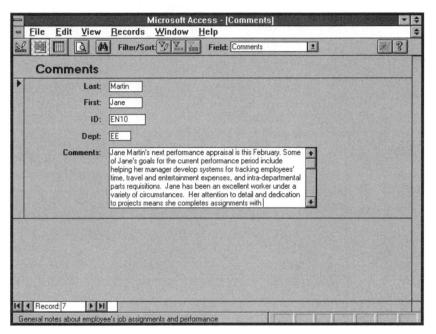

12. Save the form as **My Comments**, and then close the Form window.

ADDING CONTROLS TO ENHANCE AN EXISTING FORM

In Chapter 5, you learned how to use a FormWizard to create a basic form. FormWizards are fast and convenient to use because they ask you key questions about your form design, and then do the detail work of creating the form for you.

If you rely solely on FormWizards, however, you can only create forms that are designed by the FormWizard, rather than by *you*. Also, FormWizards are useful only for creating new forms; they are useless for modifying existing forms. Knowing how to add controls to forms manually will significantly improve your ability to produce forms that work and look the way you want them to.

By knowing how to add controls manually, you can

• Create forms from scratch without using a FormWizard

- Add controls *after* creating a form, rather than starting from scratch as a FormWizard would require you to do

- Create controls to display values that are not available through the form's underlying table or query

- Use various control styles beyond the label and text-box controls you've seen in forms created by FormWizards

 EXAMINING AN ENHANCED FORM

Before you start creating your own enhanced form, take a look at an existing enhanced form that is based on the Form Data query:

1. From the Database window, open the Form Data Query window in Design view.

2. Observe the query's design. The query is based on the Payroll Data table, and Gross Pay is a calculated field that multiplies the Hours and Pay Rate fields. (You may need to scroll to the right to see the Gross Pay field.)

3. Use the Window menu to switch to the Database window.

4. From the Database window, open the Payroll form.

5. Observe the form. The Form Header section contains a company logo, today's date, and a form title. In the form's Detail section, the Gross Pay field and its label are enclosed within a rectangle; department codes and full names are displayed in a list box; and the Monthly Parking Rate field exists only on this form, not in the form's underlying Form Data query (see Figure 9.5).

6. Observe the Dept list box as you click on the **Next Record navigation button** several times. The highlighted department code and name change to reflect the appropriate department for each employee record.

7. Switch to Design view; then observe the Gross Pay and Monthly Parking Rate controls. The Gross Pay control is a bound control based on the Form Data query's Gross Pay calculated field. The Monthly Parking Rate control is a calculated control based on the Form Data query's regular Park Rate field (see Figure 9.6).

Figure 9.5   **The Payroll form in Form view**

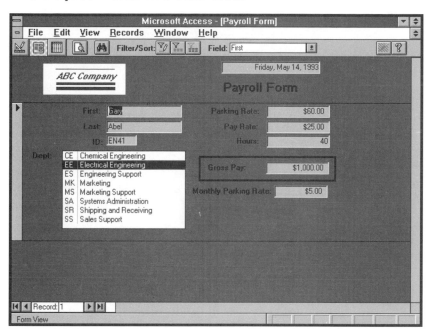

Figure 9.6   **The Payroll form in Design view**

Bound control

Calculated control

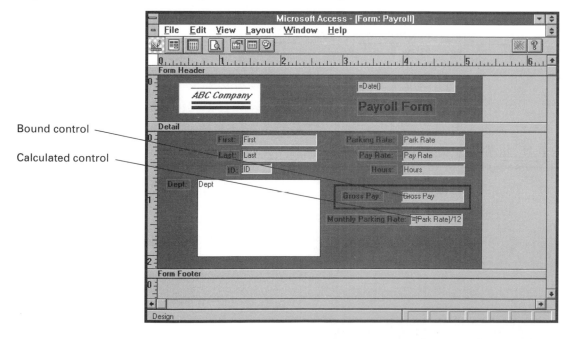

EXAMINING THE TOOLBOX

You've already learned in Chapter 5 that Access provides three control types: bound, unbound, and calculated. For each of these control types, Access also provides a selection of control *styles*. (Note: Your Access documentation makes no distinction between control types and control styles. For the purposes of this book, however, we have defined these two terms separately. A control type determines *what* information a control displays; a control style determines *how* that information is displayed.)

Before this chapter, the only control styles you had seen on forms were text boxes and labels. In Form view, the text-box style of control enables you to view, type, and delete values. The label style of control displays information, but cannot be edited in Form view.

The Payroll form, however, contains some controls with other styles: The company logo is contained within an *unbound object frame control*, the rectangle enclosing the Gross Pay field and its label is a *rectangle control*, and the department codes and names are displayed in a *list box control*. Other available control styles include *combo boxes* (also known as drop-down list boxes), *check boxes*, *option buttons*, *toggle buttons*, and *lines*.

Some of these control styles may seem familiar to you because you have seen similar elements in dialog boxes and throughout Access. In fact, by using various control styles, you can design forms that look and work much like Access' own dialog boxes. For example, rather than having users type in a department code for an employee record, you can design a form that enables users to select a department from a drop-down list (combo) box.

Various control styles enable you to create enhanced forms that are easy to use, promote data consistency, and look better than forms that use only a few control styles.

To add controls to a form manually, you must use the *toolbox*. Not to be confused with the tool *bar*, the toolbox contains specialized tools that enable you to specify the style of control you'd like to add to a form. To display the toolbox, choose View, Toolbox.

Before you start using the toolbox, let's use Access' Help system to learn more about it:

1. From the Payroll form window's Design view, choose **View, Toolbox** to display the toolbox.

2. Click on the toolbox's title bar to activate the toolbox, press **F1** to open the Help window for the toolbox, and then maximize the Help window.

3. Observe the Help window. Each tool on the toolbox is labeled (see Figure 9.7).

Figure 9.7   **The Help window on the toolbox**

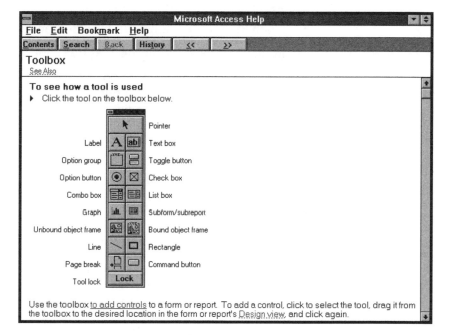

4. In the Help window, click on the **Label tool** to display a description of that tool. Then, read that description.

5. Click on **Back** to return to the toolbox Help window; then click on the **Text box tool** and read the description of that tool.

PRACTICE YOUR SKILLS

1. Click on **Back** to return to the toolbox Help window.

2. Click on the toolbox's other tools and read their descriptions, returning to the toolbox Help window between each description.

3. Close the Help window, and then close the Form window. If Access displays a dialog box asking if you want to save changes, click on **No**.

ADDING A BOUND TEXT BOX CONTROL

To add a bound text box control to a form, you would follow these steps:

- Open the Form window in Design view.

- Open the toolbox, if it's not already open.

- In the toolbox, click on the Text box tool.

- If it is not already open, open the field list by clicking on the Field List button (the sixth button from the left on the toolbar, it displays a three-column list) or by choosing View, Field List. This field list will list all of the regular and calculated fields from the form's underlying table or query.

- Drag the desired field name from the field list to the desired position on the form. By default, Access automatically adds a label with that field's name next to your new text box control.

You can also create a bound text box control without using the field list by clicking on the Text box tool, clicking on the form to create an *unbound* text box control, and then binding the control to a field by setting the control's Control Source property to that field's name. However, using the field list is simpler and enables Access to automatically provide text for the bound control's label.

A more significant advantage of using the field list when adding a bound control is that Access automatically copies the field's properties into the control's properties; this does not happen when you convert an unbound control to a bound control. For example, if you use the field list to add a pay-rate field that is formatted as currency in the form's underlying table or query, Access automatically sets your control's Format property to Currency as well. (All of this happens automatically when you use a FormWizard.)

Let's add the Form Data query's calculated Gross Pay field to a form:

1. From the Database window, open the New Payroll form.

2. Observe the form. Like the Payroll Form, this form is based on the Form Data query. However, this form does not include a

company logo or many of the Payroll Form's bound controls
and labels (see Figure 9.8).

Figure 9.8   **The New Payroll form**

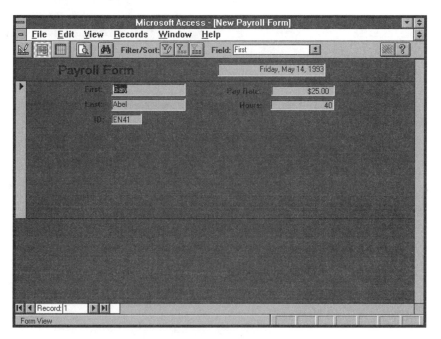

3. Switch to Design view, and then click on the **Field List button**
   (or choose **View, Field List**) to display the list of fields from the
   form's underlying query, Form Data.

4. In the toolbox, click on the **Text box tool**. Your mouse
   pointer should change to crosshairs with the Text-box-tool
   icon attached.

5. Use the pointer to drag **Gross Pay** from the field list to just
   below the Hours bound control. As you drag, notice that the
   mouse pointer changes to a field icon.

6. Release the mouse button. Access places a Gross Pay bound
   text box control and its label below the Hours bound text box
   control and label.

7. Use the Gross Pay label's move handle (the large handle on the label's upper-left corner) to align the label under the Hours label (see Figure 9.9).

8. Save the form as **My New Payroll**.

Figure 9.9   **The New Payroll form after adding and aligning the Gross Pay controls**

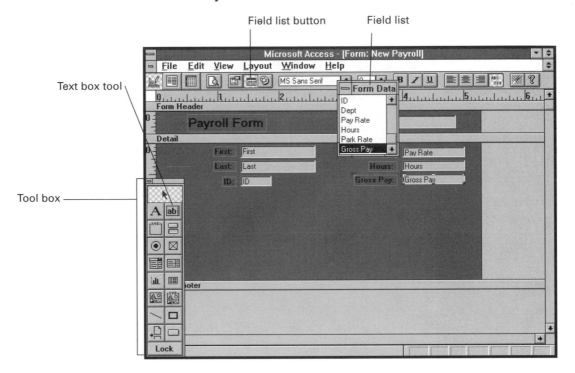

MODIFYING A BOUND CONTROL'S FORMAT PROPERTY

You've learned that if you use the field list when adding a bound control to a form, that control inherits its associated field's properties as control properties. However, Access does not maintain a link between field and control properties. If you change a field property, Access does not automatically change the properties of any existing controls bound to that field. Likewise, if you change a bound control's properties, you do not affect the properties of that control's associated field.

This ability to set control properties independently of field properties provides you with a great deal of freedom in designing forms. For example, suppose you need to design two forms based on the same table: one for top managers, another for line managers. The only difference between the two forms is that top managers can set an employee's pay rate at any level, while line managers cannot assign pay rates of greater than $20 per hour. If you set a validation rule for the pay-rate field in the forms' underlying table, both levels of managers would be bound by the same rule. The solution: Instead of setting the validation rule as a field property in the table, set the validation rule as a control property in the line managers' form, and set no validation rule in the top managers' form.

Another common need for control properties is in handling a query's calculated field. For example, as you've seen throughout this book, whenever you created a calculated gross-pay field by multiplying an hours-worked field and a pay-rate field, Access did not format the gross-pay field as currency. Access does provide a Format function that you can use in a query to control the format of a calculated field. (For more information on the Format function, see your Access documentation.) However, if you plan on using the calculated field on a form anyway, you may find it simpler just to add the calculated field as-is to the form, and then change control properties.

Take a look at how Access displays the Gross Pay control you just added to your form, and then change that display by modifying the control's Format property:

1. Switch to Form view and observe the Gross Pay field. It is not formatted as currency (see Figure 9.10).

2. Use the Window menu to switch to the Form Data Query window.

3. Run the query, and then observe the dynaset. In the query, the Gross Pay field is not formatted as currency either.

4. Use the Window menu to return to the Form window.

5. Switch to Design view, verify that the Gross Pay bound control is still selected, and then open the property sheet for that control.

6. In the Gross Pay bound control's Format property box, select **Currency**.

7. Close the property sheet, and then close the field list.

8. Save the form design, and then switch to Form view.

Figure 9.10   **The unformatted Gross Pay field**

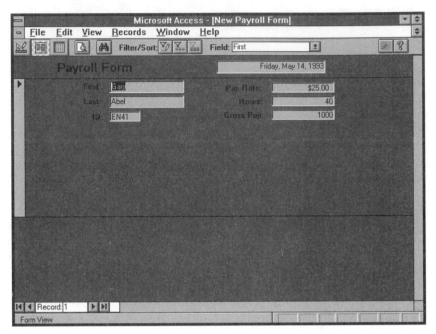

9. Observe the Gross Pay field. Its contents are now formatted as currency (see Figure 9.11).

10. Switch to the Form Data Query window, and then observe the Gross Pay field. Changing the Gross Pay field's Format property in the form did not affect the Gross Pay field here.

ADDING A CALCULATED CONTROL

As you've seen in this and earlier chapters, you can use a query's calculated field to display values on your form that are not stored in any tables. However, to display values on your forms that are neither stored in tables nor calculated through queries, you can use calculated controls.

You have seen calculated controls a number of times already in this book. Access has used them to display the current date, page numbers, and summary information. You can create your own calculated controls for these same purposes. You can also use a calculated control in place of a query's calculated field to calculate values from existing fields in a form's underlying table or query.

Figure 9.11   **The formatted Gross Pay field**

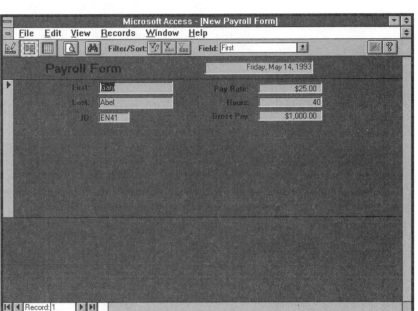

Calculated controls provide you with a great deal of flexibility: They are not limited by the choice of fields from a form's underlying table or query, and you can modify calculated controls directly from a Form window's Design view rather than modifying the design of the form's underlying table or query.

Because calculated fields and calculated controls have similar names and can perform similar functions, it is easy to confuse the two. Keep in mind that you create calculated *fields* in a query and calculated *controls* in a form or report. Also, in a form's design, a calculated field's bound control looks just like a regular field's bound control; a calculated control, on the other hand, displays an expression.

To create a calculated text box control, you would follow these steps:

- Open the Form window in Design view.

- In the toolbox, click on the Text box tool.

- Click on the form where you want to add the control. By default, Access automatically adds a label next to your new control.

- Click in the new unbound text box control, and then type the desired expression to convert the unbound control to a calculated control. Alternatively, you can select the unbound control, open the property sheet (if it isn't already open), and then type the expression in the control's Control Source property box.

You can enter expressions for a calculated text box control just as you would enter expressions for a calculated field in a QBE grid's Field cell. However, calculated-control expressions must begin with an equal sign (=). For example, to create a gross-pay calculated field, you might type [hours]*[pay rate]. For a calculated control, you would type this expression as =[hours]*[pay rate]. As you've already seen in forms and reports, you can also enter expressions such as =Now() and =Page to display the current date and page number.

Because Access cannot determine appropriate text for the labels of calculated and unbound controls as it can for bound controls, you may want to provide your own descriptive text. To change a label's text in Design view, select the label, select the text within the label, and then type your new text over the selected text.

Let's create a calculated text box control to display each employee's monthly parking rate:

1. Observe the Form Data query's dynaset. It does not contain a Monthly Parking Rate field. However, it does contain a Park Rate field for annual parking rates.

2. Close the Query window and return to the Form window.

3. Switch to Design view.

4. In the toolbox, click on the **Text box tool**; then click just below the Gross Pay bound control. Access places a default-size label and text box control beneath the Gross Pay bound control and label.

5. Click in the new text box control; then type **=[park rate]/12** to create a calculated control that calculates a monthly parking rate from the Form Data query's annual Park Rate field (see Figure 9.12).

6. Press **Enter** to select the calculated control, and then open the control's property sheet.

Figure 9.12   **Creating a calculated control**

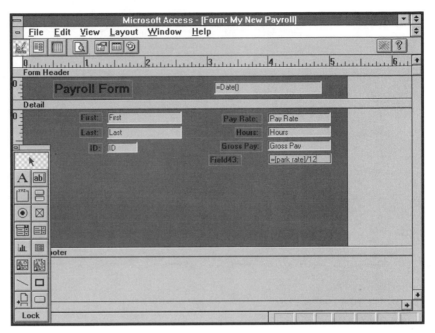

7. Observe the calculated control's Control Source property. It is the same expression you typed directly into the control.

8. Set the calculated control's Format property to **Currency**, and then close the property sheet.

9. Select the calculated control's label, double-click on the label's text to select all of the text except the colon, and then type **Monthly Parking Rate** to provide a more descriptive label for your calculated control. Access automatically expands the label's size to fit the new text.

10. Press **Enter** to select the Monthly Parking Rate label, and then align the label under the Gross Pay label (see Figure 9.13).

11. Save the form; then switch to Form view.

12. Use the form's navigation buttons to view several records. Access calculates the monthly parking rate for each record, and formats the result as currency.

Figure 9.13   **The completed Monthly Parking Rate controls**

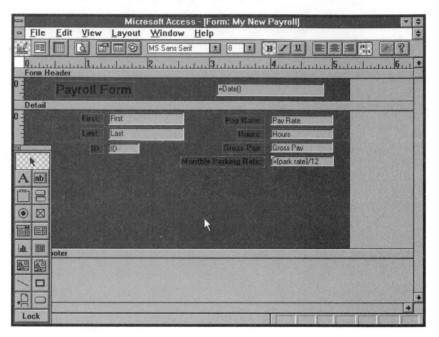

 ADDING A RECTANGLE CONTROL

You can use rectangle controls on your forms as a design feature—for example, to highlight certain controls or to bring related controls together visually.

To add a rectangle control to a form, you would follow these steps:

• Open the Form window in Design view.

• In the toolbox, click on the Rectangle tool.

• Position the mouse pointer on the form where you want one of the rectangle control's corners, drag to the opposite corner, and then release the mouse button.

Because Access creates opaque rectangle controls by default, rectangle controls may hide other controls on your form. To solve this problem, you can make a rectangle control transparent by changing the control's Back Style property to Clear.

Rectangle controls do not display values. Therefore, you cannot create rectangle controls as bound or calculated controls.

Let's draw a rectangle control around the Gross Pay bound control and label to highlight those controls:

1. Switch to Design view.

2. In the toolbox, click on the **Rectangle tool**. Your mouse pointer should change to crosshairs with a Rectangle-tool icon attached.

3. Position the center of the crosshairs just above and to the left of the Gross Pay label, drag to just below and to the right of the Gross Pay bound control, and then release the mouse button. As you drag, Access displays an outline of your rectangle around the two controls (see Figure 9.14). When you release the button, Access inserts an opaque rectangle control that hides the Gross Pay bound control and label.

Figure 9.14   **Adding a rectangle control**

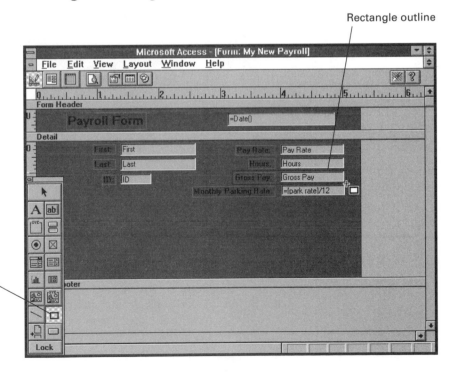

4. Open the rectangle control's property sheet, and then move the property sheet down next to the toolbox so that you can see the entire rectangle control.

5. Change the control's Back Style property from Normal to **Clear**. The Gross Pay bound control and label should now be visible through the rectangle control (see Figure 9.15).

6. Close the property sheet, and then save the form.

Figure 9.15   **The completed rectangle control**

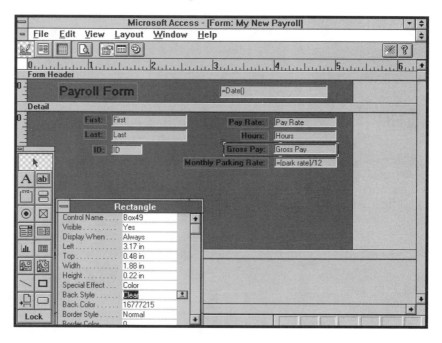

 ## ADDING A LIST BOX CONTROL

Text box controls are a good way to enter a wide variety of values into fields. For example, you would probably want to use text box controls for employee names and pay rates because these values vary widely. For a field such as a department field, however, which should contain one of a very limited set of values, you may instead want to use a list box control. A list box control eliminates the need to remember a list of department codes or names, since it lists them all for you. To set the department field for any employee record, you could then display that record in Form view and simply select the appropriate department.

List box controls can also help to increase data-entry accuracy. For example, if you use short department codes such as EE, you could easily type DE instead of EE. Because a list box control would enable you to choose only from a list of preset options, however, it would eliminate this type of error.

List box controls can also speed data entry. For example, if you use full department names instead of codes, you may find yourself typing Electrical Engineering or Chemical Engineering over and over. With a list box, you simply click.

To create a list box control, you would follow these steps:

- Open the Form window in Design view.

- In the toolbox, click on the List box tool.

- If you want your list box control to be bound to a field, drag that field's name from the field list to the form. If you want an unbound list box control, click on the form. By default, Access adds a label next to your new control.

When you create a list box control, you must supply Access with a list of values for that control. One way to provide a source for list-box values is to specify in the list box control's Row Source Property box the name of a table or query containing those values. In Form view, the list box will then display all of the values contained, by default, in that table or query's *first* field. When you then select that value from the list box while entering records, Access copies that value from the Row Source property's table or query into the form's underlying table or query. For existing records, Access uses the value in the form's underlying table or query to select the matching value in the list box.

To have your list box control list the first *two* fields from the Row Source table or query, set the control's Column Count property to 2. Doing so will split the list box into even halves. To specify custom column widths instead for values that do not fit well into even halves, type those widths, separated by a semicolon, in the control's Column Widths property box.

Let's create a list box control bound to the Dept field that displays values from the Dept Codes and Names table:

1. Click on the **List box tool**.

2. Open the field list (click on the **Field List button** or choose **View, Field List**), and then drag **Dept** from the field list to about half an inch below the ID bound control (use the on-screen rulers for scale). Access places a Dept list box and its label on the form.

3. Close the field list.

4. Align the Dept label under the ID label.

5. Use the list box's sizing handles to enlarge the list box to about 2 inches wide and about 1 ¼ inches high (see Figure 9.16).

Figure 9.16   **The enlarged Dept text box**

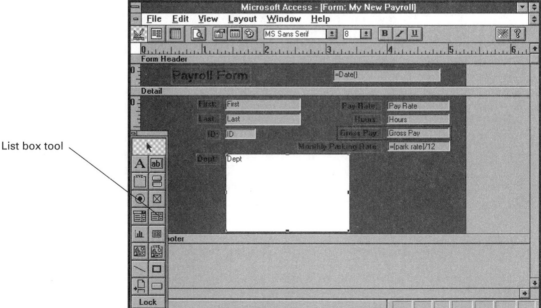

List box tool

6. Use the Window menu to switch to the Database window; then open and observe the Dept Codes and Names table. This table contains the two-letter code and corresponding full name for each department (see Figure 9.17).

Figure 9.17   **The Dept Codes and Names table**

Dept. Code	Department
CE	Chemical Engineering
EE	Electrical Engineering
ES	Engineering Support
MK	Marketing
MS	Marketing Support
SA	Systems Administration
SR	Shipping and Receiving
SS	Sales Support

7. Close the Table window, and then switch back to the Form window.

8. Open the Dept list box's property sheet; then set the Row Source property to **Dept Codes and Names**.

9. Switch to Form view, and then observe the Dept list box. It displays only department codes.

10. Return to Design view, and then change the list box's Column Count property from 1 to **2**.

11. Switch to Form view, and then observe the Dept list box. It now displays department codes *and* names. However, the list box is split evenly in half, providing too much room for the codes and not enough room for the names.

12. Return to Design view, and then type **.25;1.75** in the list box's Column Widths property box.

13. Close the property sheet, switch to Form view, and then observe the Dept list box. The left column is now ¼ of an inch wide and the right column is 1¾ inches wide, providing enough room for both department codes and names (see Figure 9.18). (Your list might display scroll bars.)

14. Save the form.

ADDING A PAINTBRUSH PICTURE

Microsoft Windows enables you to bring objects produced in one Windows application into another. For example, if you draw a picture using the Windows Paintbrush accessory program, you can add that picture to your form in Access. (For more information about the Paintbrush program, see your Microsoft Windows documentation.)

Figure 9.18   **The completed Dept list box**

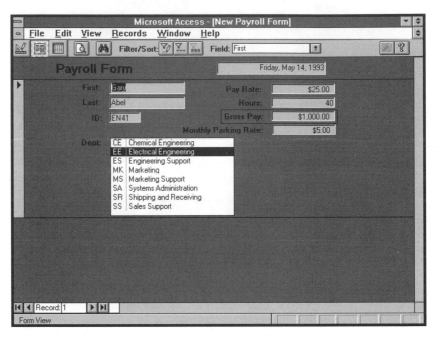

One way to add a saved object such as a Paintbrush picture to an Access form is through an unbound object frame control. To add to a form an unbound object frame control containing a saved Paintbrush picture, you would follow these steps:

- Open the Form window in Design view.

- In the toolbox, click on the Unbound object frame tool.

- On the form, use the mouse as you would for a Rectangle control to drag a size and location for the control. Access automatically opens the Insert Object dialog box so you can specify an object type. The contents of the dialog box's Object Type list box will vary depending on what Windows applications you have installed on your computer.

- Select Paintbrush Picture, and then click on File. Access opens the Insert Object from File dialog box so you can specify the file containing the Paintbrush picture.

- Double-click on the file name. Access then displays the Paintbrush picture in your new control.

When you add large controls to a form, a form's section may not be large enough to hold the new control. To increase the size of a form's section, place the mouse pointer on the bottom edge of the section until the pointer changes to a cross with a vertical, two-headed arrow; then drag down.

Let's add a Paintbrush picture of the company logo to the Form Header section of your form:

1. Switch to Design view, and then observe the Form Header section. It contains little room to add a company logo.

2. Position your mouse pointer on the bottom edge of the Form Header section until the pointer changes to a cross with a vertical, two-headed arrow.

3. Use the pointer to drag down the bottom edge of the Form Header section until the section is about ¾ of an inch high (see Figure 9.19).

Figure 9.19   **Enlarging the Form Header section**

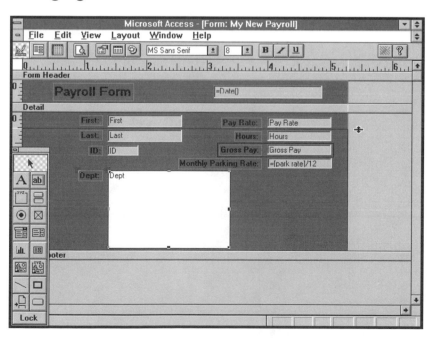

4. Drag the **Payroll Form** label to a location under the date control.

5. In the toolbox, click on the **Unbound object frame tool**, and then use the pointer to drag an outline about ½ inch high and 1 ¼ inches wide in the Form Header section's upper-left corner. Access opens the Insert Object dialog box so you can specify an object type.

6. In the Object Type list box, select **Paintbrush Picture**; then click on **File**. Access opens the Insert Object from File dialog box.

7. In the File Name list box, double-click on **abc.bmp** to insert the logo contained in the abc.bmp file into the unbound object frame you created. (If abc.bmp does not display in the File Name list box, use the Drives drop-down list box and/or the Directories list box to move to the drive and directory where you installed the company.mdb database file.)

8. Observe the company logo. If it does not fit well within the unbound object frame, use the frame's sizing handles to adjust the frame (see Figure 9.20).

Figure 9.20   **The company logo after sizing its control**

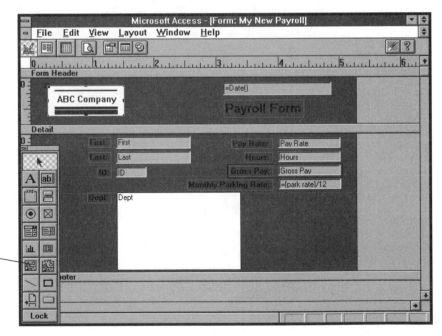

Unbound object frame tool

9. Close the toolbox, and then switch to Form view. The company logo displays in the Form Header section.

10. Save the form, and then close the Form window.

CREATING A FORM THAT CONTAINS A SUBFORM

If you have a one-to-many relationship between tables or queries, you can use a *main form* and a *subform* within a single Form window to view both sides of that relationship. (See Chapter 8 for an explanation of one-to-many relationships.) For example, if you have a one-to-many relationship between a department-information table and an equipment-inventory table, you can use a main form to select a department (the "one" side), and then view that department's equipment inventory in the subform (the "many" side).

To display two forms within a single Form window, Access uses a *subform control* on a main form. You can think of a subform control as an intelligent window through which you can view subform data. It's intelligent because, as you move from record to record in the main form, Access automatically applies a filter to the subform so that the subform only displays records relevant to the main form's current record. For example, when you move to the Chemical Engineering department's record in the main form, the equipment-inventory subform displays only the Chemical Engineering department's equipment.

 EXAMINING A FORM WITH A SUBFORM

When Access displays a main form and subform within a single Form window, it provides two sets of record navigation buttons to enable you to scroll through both forms independently. The main form's navigation buttons are at the bottom of the Form window, and the subform's navigation buttons are at the bottom of the subform itself.

Let's look at an existing form that contains a subform:

1. From the Database window, open and observe the Dept Equipment Purchased form.

2. Observe the Form window. It displays two forms: a larger main form, which contains the form title, Department field, and Department label; and a smaller subform, which contains

the department's equipment inventory with serial numbers and purchase dates (see Figure 9.21).

Figure 9.21   **The Dept Equipment Purchased form in Form view**

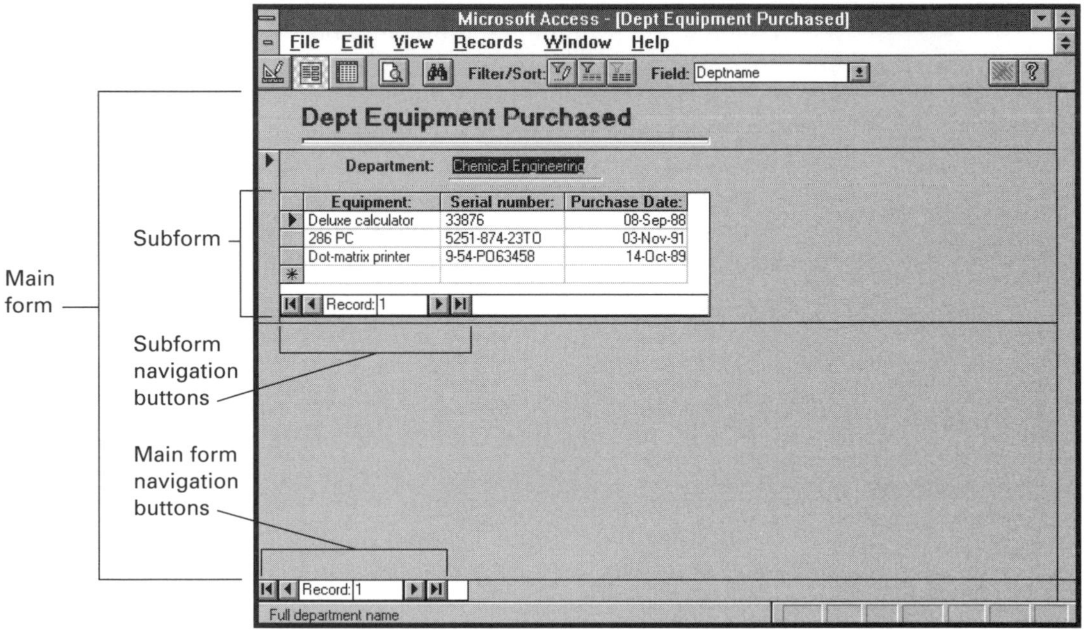

3. Observe the two sets of record navigation buttons. Access displays the main form's navigation buttons at the bottom of the Form window; the subform's navigation buttons are directly beneath the equipment list.

4. Observe the Form window as you click on the main form's **Next Record navigation button** several times. As the department name changes, the data in the subform also changes to display each department's equipment inventory.

5. Switch to Design view, and then observe the form design. You can now see more clearly the distinction between the shaded main form and the white Equipment subform control contained within it (see Figure 9.22).

6. Close the Form window.

Figure 9.22   **The Dept Equipment Purchased form in Design view**

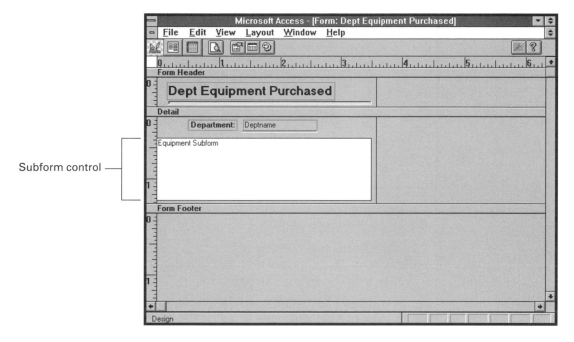

Subform control

 SELECTING THE DATA SOURCES FOR THE MAIN FORM AND THE SUBFORM

The toolbox contains a Subform/subreport tool that enables you to add subform controls to a main form's design. However, if you want to create from scratch a main form and subform based on related table or queries, you can instead use the Main/Subform FormWizard. This FormWizard, like other FormWizards, asks you questions about your forms, and then creates them for you. The Main/Subform FormWizard handles the details of placing the appropriate controls on the forms and establishing the link between the two forms it creates.

Let's use the Main/Subform FormWizard to create a main form and subform to take advantage of the one-to-many relationship between the Dept Codes and Names table and the Equipment table:

1. From the Database window, open and examine the Equipment table. It contains information about each department's equipment inventory (see Figure 9.23).

Figure 9.23   **The Equipment table**

DeptCode	Equipment	Serial number	Purchase Date	Warranty	Wty duration
SS	Calculator with tape	15845239	17-Mar-92	No	0
CE	Deluxe calculator	33876	08-Sep-88	No	0
ES	PC	4235-234-98	24-Jul-89	Yes	2
EE	Pencil sharpener	4380	27-Feb-92	No	0
MK	Portable PC	5123-354-42RK	01-Feb-92	Yes	1
CE	286 PC	5251-874-23TO	03-Nov-91	Yes	2
EE	Deluxe calculator	54-1325-0	12-Aug-89	No	0
EE	286 PC	5643-243-48DE	03-Nov-91	Yes	2
SA	External modem	5MD-30758	18-Jul-92	Yes	1
MS	386 PC	823\22308	01-Feb-92	Yes	1
MS	Answering machine	87346-AT24	24-Apr-91	Yes	1
MS	Mini calculator	88-1534-0	18-Jul-86	No	0
ES	Faxfast	8JA4133707	30-Apr-90	Yes	3
CE	Dot-matrix printer	9-54-PO63458	14-Oct-89	Yes	1
SA	386 PC	968\45082	18-Jul-92	Yes	1
SS	Laser printer	ABA-62906	03-Nov-91	Yes	2
MS	Fax machine	TO/444/14N6	01-May-92	Yes	2
*					

2. Close the Table window.

3. In the Database window, display the list of form object names, and then click on **New** to start creating a new form. Access opens the New Form dialog box.

4. In the Select a Table/Query drop-down list box, select **Dept Codes and Names** as the data source for the main form, and then click on **FormWizards**.

5. In the Microsoft Access dialog box, select **Main/Subform**, and then click on **OK** to start the Main/Subform FormWizard.

6. In the Microsoft Access FormWizard dialog box, select **Equipment** as the data source for the subform, and then click on **Next** to advance to the next dialog box.

COMPLETING THE MAIN FORM AND SUBFORM

When the Main/Subform FormWizard completes your two forms, it's a good idea to check the subform control's Link Master Fields and Link Child Fields properties. These two control properties determine the link between the two forms' underlying tables or queries. The Link Master Fields property specifies the linking field from the main form's underlying table or queries while the Link Child Fields property specifies the linking field from the subform's underlying table or query. If these property boxes are blank, the FormWizard has not successfully linked the two forms, and your main and subform most likely will not operate together correctly. In that case, you will need to establish the correct linking fields yourself. (For more information on how table relationships affect main forms and sub-forms, see your Access documentation.)

Complete your main form and subform now, examine the subform control's Link Master Fields and Link Child Fields properties, and then try out your new main form and subform in Form view:

1. Observe the Microsoft Access FormWizard dialog box. It enables you to specify which fields from the Dept Codes and Names table to include on the main form.

2. Move **Deptname** to the Fields On Main Form list box; then click on **Next** to advance to the next dialog box.

3. Observe the dialog box. It enables you to specify which fields from the Equipment table to include on the subform.

4. Move **Equipment**, **Serial Number**, and **Purchase Date**, respectively, to the Fields On Subform list box, and then click on **Next** to advance to the next dialog box.

5. Select the **Chiseled** form look, and then click on **Next** to advance to the next dialog box.

6. In the Form Title text box, type **Dept Equipment Purchased**, and then click on **Design**. Access opens a dialog box to inform you that you must save your subform before the Main/Sub-form FormWizard can create the main form.

7. Click on **OK**. Access opens the Save As dialog box so you can name and save your subform. In the Form Name text box, type **My Equipment Subform**, and then click on **OK**. The Main/Subform FormWizard creates the main form and opens its new Form window in Design view.

8. If necessary, maximize the Form window.

9. Observe the Form window. It contains a main form and a subform.

10. Open and observe the My Equipment subform control's property sheet. The Link Child Fields property is set to the subform table's DeptCode field, and the Link Master Fields property is set to the main form table's Deptcode field, indicating that the Main/Subform FormWizard has successfully linked the main form and subform (see Figure 9.24).

11. Close the property sheet; then switch to Form view (see Figure 9.25).

Figure 9.24   **Verifying that Access has successfully linked the main form and subform**

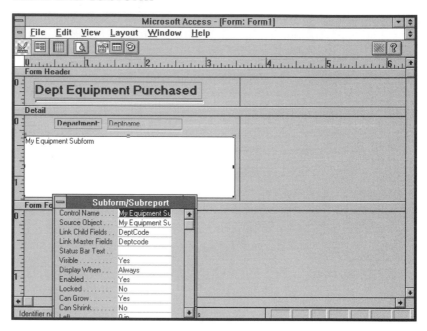

Figure 9.25   **The new form in Form view**

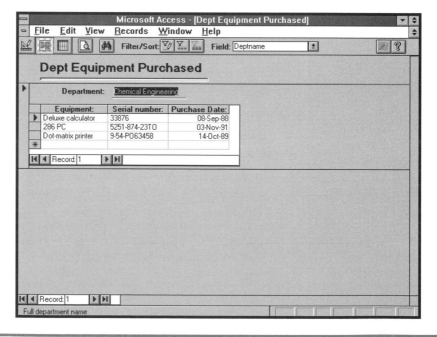

12. Click on the main form's **Next Record navigation button** several times. Like the Form window you saw earlier, as this window displays each department's name in the main form, it displays that department's equipment inventory in the subform.

13. Save the main form as **My Dept Equipment**, and then close the Form window.

14. Observe the Database window. It displays the two forms you just created: My Dept Equipment and My Equipment Subform.

SUMMARY

In this chapter, you learned how to use control properties and various control styles to enhance the look and performance of your forms. You also learned how to use the Main/Subform FormWizard to create two forms that work together in a single Form window.

Here's a quick reference guide to the Access features introduced in this chapter:

Desired Result	How to Do It
Display a control's properties	Open the window of the form containing the control in Design view, select the control, and then click on the **Properties button** (or choose **View, Properties**) to open the control's property sheet
Modify a control's properties	Change values in the control's property sheet
Display the toolbox	In a Form window's Design view, choose **View, Toolbox**
Display the field list	In a Form window's Design view, click on the **Field List button** (or choose **View, Field List**)
Add a bound text box control to a form	In a Form window's Design view, click on the toolbox's **Text box tool**, and then drag the desired field name from the field list to the form

Desired Result	How to Do It
Create a calculated text box control on a form	In a Form window's Design view, click on the toolbox's **Text box control**, click on the form to add an unbound control, click in the unbound control, and then type a calculation expression
Modify a label's text	In a Form window's Design view, select the label, and then replace the label's text
Add a rectangle control to a form	In a Form window's Design view, click on the toolbox's **Rectangle tool**, and then drag a rectangle on the form
Make a rectangle control clear	Change the control's Back Style property to **Clear**
Add a bound list box control to a form	In a Form window's Design view, click on the toolbox's **List box tool**, and then drag the desired field name from the field list to the form
Supply values for a list box control	Specify a table or query in the control's Row Source property box
Add a saved Paintbrush picture to a form	In a Form window's Design view, click on the **Unbound object frame tool**, on the form drag the desired size and position of the picture, select **Paintbrush Picture** in the Insert Object dialog box, click on **File**, and then double-click on the name of the file containing the Paintbrush picture in the Insert Object From dialog box
Start the Main/Subform FormWizard	In the Database window, display the list of form object names, click on **New**, select the main form's table or query, click on **FormWizards**, select **Main/Subform**, and then click on **OK**

In the next chapter, you'll learn how to use macros and command buttons to open and synchronize forms automatically.

IF YOU'RE STOPPING HERE

If you need to break off here, please exit Access. If you want to proceed directly to the next chapter, please do so now.

CHAPTER 10: USING MACROS WITH FORMS

Creating a Macro to Open a Form Window

Creating a Command Button to Run a Macro

Synchronizing Forms

Controlling the Form Window Placement

Macros are database objects that you can use to automate Access. For example, if you need to run a query and then print a report every time you open a certain database, you can create a macro to perform those tasks for you automatically.

Macros list a series of steps, called *actions*. A single macro action, for example, can print a report. When you run a macro, Access uses it as a to-do list to perform that macro's actions in the order in which they are listed. The advantages of using macros over running the actions manually are twofold: Macros automate repetitive tasks and they help ensure that those tasks are performed consistently and completely each time.

You can use macros in an almost unlimited number of ways to automate and customize Access. In this chapter, you'll discover the very basics of macros by learning how to create and use a simple macro that opens one Form window from within another Form window.

When you're done working through this chapter, you will know how to:

- Use a *command button* to run a macro from a Form window
- Create a macro to open a Form window
- Add a command button control to a form
- Use a macro to synchronize two forms
- Use a macro to control the placement of a Form window

CREATING A MACRO TO OPEN A FORM WINDOW

Through macro actions, macros can perform many of the steps you would perform manually while working with a database. Among other things, macro actions can

- Open a window
- Close a window
- Find a record
- Apply a filter
- Print an object
- Run a query

Access supplies over 40 macro actions; the two macro actions you'll learn about in this chapter are the *OpenForm action*, which opens a Form window, and the *MoveSize action*, which controls the placement and position of a window. (You'll learn how to get information about other macro actions later in this chapter.)

In Chapter 9, you learned how to use a main form and subform to view data from two forms in a single Form window. If you'd prefer, however, you can use a macro to view data from two forms in separate Form windows. For example, if you regularly use a form to enter and review employee records, you might want to open a second Form window from within that form in order to see the name of the current employee's manager.

Using a macro to view data in two separate Form windows provides two advantages over using a main form and subform. First, because the Form windows are separate, you can move through records in either form independently. Second, using the preceding example, because Access does not need to determine and display the correct manager record for each and every employee record, you can scroll through employee records more quickly, viewing manager names only as needed.

Throughout this book, we have instructed you to maximize all Database and, when necessary, object windows. By maximizing windows, you reduce screen clutter and increase the available amount of window space for each object. At times, however, it's beneficial *not* to maximize windows—for example, when you want to view data in two Form windows at once. As you continue through this chapter, you'll learn some other advantages of working with non-maximized windows.

To restore a maximized Database or object window, click on the window's Maximize/Restore button, located at the right end of the menu bar. When you restore one Database or object window in Access, Access restores all Database and object windows. When you maximize a Database or object window, Access maximizes all Database and object windows.

RUNNING A MACRO WITH A FORM'S COMMAND BUTTON

Access provides many ways to run macros, both from Database and object windows. One way of running a macro from a Form window is by using a command button that is bound to the macro. (You'll learn how to create your own command button control later in this chapter.)

If you do not have both the Access application and the COMPANY Database windows opened and maximized, please open and maximize them now.

Let's work with a form that contains a command button that opens a second Form window:

1. From the Database window, open the Payroll Managers form.

2. Observe the form. It contains a command button entitled Manager.

3. Observe the current record. It is the record for Gary Abel (Record 1), who works in the Electrical Engineering department.

4. Click on the Form window's **Maximize/Restore button** (at the right end of the menu bar) to restore the Form window to its

previous size so that it no longer completely fills the Access application window.

5. Click on the **Manager command button**. The Dept Managers Form window opens to display the manager for the Electrical Engineering department (see Figure 10.1).

Figure 10.1 **Viewing both the Payroll Managers and Dept Managers Form windows**

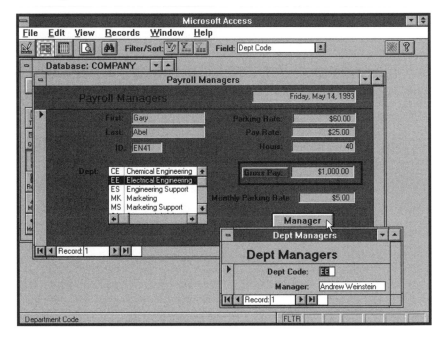

6. In the Payroll Managers Form window, click on the **Next Record navigation button**. The form now displays the record for Murray Abel (Record 2), who works in the Chemical Engineering department.

7. Click on the **Manager command button**. The Dept Managers form now displays the manager for the Chemical Engineering department.

8. Close the Dept Managers Form window.

EXAMINING A MACRO'S DESIGN

To determine the name of the macro that a command button runs when clicked, you can examine the command button control's On Push property. You can view the properties of a command button control as you would any other control on a form: Switch to the Form window's Design view, select the control, and then open the control's property sheet.

Once you have determined the name of the macro, you can examine its design by opening the macro's window in Design view. To open a Macro window in Design view, you would follow these steps:

- From the Database window, click on the Macro object button to display the list of macro object names.

- Select the desired macro object name.

- Click on Design.

You learned earlier that a macro lists macro actions: a series of steps to be performed. A Macro window in Design view lists these actions in the order in which they should be performed. As in the Design views of Table and Query windows, Access divides the Design view of a Macro window into an upper and a lower pane. The upper pane contains *Action cells* for specifying macro actions and *Comment cells* for your (optional) comments about those actions. The lower pane contains *argument boxes* that enable you to specify *arguments* for each macro action. Arguments are similar to field and control properties: They determine the behavior of each action.

Let's examine the Manager command button control's On Push property to determine the macro that the command button runs, and then examine the design of that macro:

1. Maximize the Payroll Managers Form window, and then switch to the window's Design view.

2. Select the **Manager command button control**, and then open the control's property sheet.

3. Observe the control's On Push property. It is set to Managers, which is a macro (see Figure 10.2).

4. Close the property sheet, and then close the Form window. If Access asks you if you want to save changes, click on **No**.

Figure 10.2   **Viewing the Manager command button control's properties**

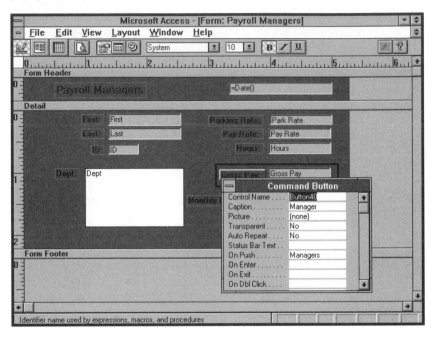

5. In the Database window, click on the **Macro object button** to display the list of macro object names. This database contains only one macro: Managers.

6. Click on **Design** to open the Managers Macro window in Design view.

7. Observe the Macro window. Access divides this window into an upper and lower pane (see Figure 10.3).

8. Observe the upper pane. Two actions comprise the Managers macro: The OpenForm action opens the Dept Managers Form window, and the MoveSize action controls the placement of that window.

9. Observe the lower pane. Because the focus is in the Open-Form Action cell, the lower pane displays arguments for that action.

10. Close the Macro window.

Figure 10.3   **The Managers Macro window in Design view**

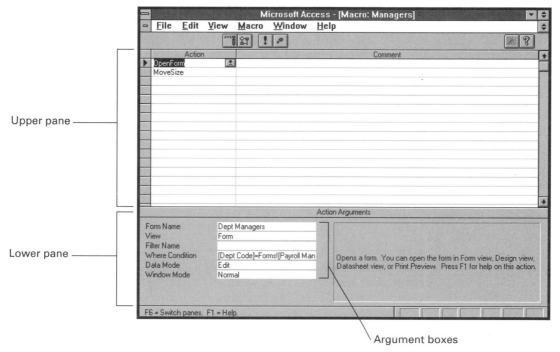

Upper pane

Lower pane

Argument boxes

CREATING AND RUNNING A MACRO

Now that you've seen a macro in action and in design, you are ready to create and run your own macro. By the end of this chapter, your macro will perform the same tasks that the existing Managers macro performs: It will open the Dept Managers Form window, display the current employee's manager in that window, and move the window to the lower-right corner of your screen.

The first step in creating a new macro is opening a new Macro window. To open a new Macro window from the Database window, click on the Macro object button to display the list of macro object names, and then click on New.

Once you have opened a new Macro window, you can begin building the macro by specifying actions in the macro's Action cells. Like many cells you've seen throughout Access, each of a macro's Action cells displays a drop-down list arrow that enables you to open and select from a drop-down list of macro actions. (For information on macro actions not covered in this book, press F1 when the focus is in an Action cell.)

Once you've selected an action, Access will display that action's relevant argument boxes in the Macro window's lower pane. For example, if you want your macro to open a form, you would select OpenForm from the appropriate Action cell's drop-down list, and then set the desired action arguments (such as the Form Name argument, which specifies which form the OpenForm action should open).

When you don't maximize your Database and object windows, Access provides other alternatives for adding actions to macros. For example, if you want your macro to open a particular form, you can drag that form's object name from the Database window directly to an Action cell in your Macro window. When you do, Access selects the OpenForm action, and specifies that form's name automatically in the action's Form Name argument box.

To use this shortcut, you need to be able to view both the form object name in the Database window and the appropriate Action cell in the Macro window. One way to neatly arrange and view multiple windows (maximized or not) contained within the Access application window is by choosing Window, Tile. When you do, Access arranges all of the open windows in a tiled fashion so that the windows do not overlap each other. If you still cannot see the appropriate parts of each window, you can use the scroll bars to scroll the appropriate area into view.

The Windows, Cascade command offers another way to arrange open windows neatly. When you choose Windows, Cascade, Access arranges all open windows in an overlapping fashion, keeping each window's title bar visible.

Once you've added an action to a macro, you can test the macro from the Macro window by clicking on the Run button (the same button you used in Chapter 7 to run action queries; it displays an exclamation point) or by choosing Macro, Run.

Let's create a new macro and use the dragging method just described to instruct that macro to open the Dept Managers Form window:

1. In the Database window, click on **New** to open a new Macro window.

2. In the first Action cell, click on the **drop-down list arrow** to display a list of macro actions.

3. From the list, choose **OpenForm**, and then observe the lower pane. Access automatically supplies default values for the View, Data Mode, and Window Mode arguments. However, it does not supply a value for the Form Name argument (see Figure 10.4).

Figure 10.4   **Default argument values for the OpenForm action**

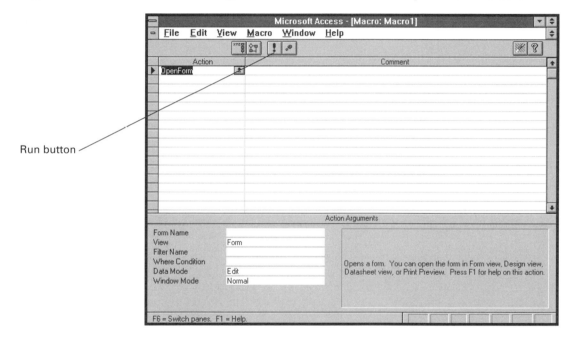

Run button

4. Press **Delete** (or choose Edit, Delete) to delete the OpenForm action.

5. Choose **Window, Tile**. Access arranges the Database and Macro windows side by side (tiled).

6. In the Database window, click on the **Form object button** to display the list of form object names.

7. Drag the **Dept Managers form object name** from the Database window to the first Action cell in the Macro window. When you release the mouse button, Access adds the OpenForm action to the Action cell, and automatically sets the action's Form Name argument to Dept Managers (see Figure 10.5).

Figure 10.5   **The macro design after dragging the Dept Managers form object name to the Macro window**

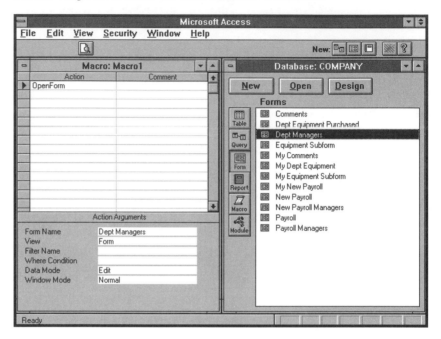

8. Click anywhere in the Macro window to activate the window (or choose the window's name from the Window menu), and then save the macro as **My Managers**.

9. Click on the **Run button** (or choose Macro, Run) to run the macro. (The Run button is shown in Figure 10.4) Access opens the Dept Managers Form window (see Figure 10.6).

10. Close the Form window and the Macro window.

CREATING A COMMAND BUTTON TO RUN A MACRO

As you learned earlier in this chapter, once you have created and saved a macro, you can use a command button on a form to run that macro.

Using the techniques you learned in Chapter 9, you could manually add a command button control to a form by opening the Form window in Design view, opening the form's toolbox, clicking on the toolbox's Command button tool, clicking on the form to add an unbound command button control, and then setting the appropriate control properties to bind that control to the macro and provide the appropriate text for the face of the button. (For example, the command button you used earlier was entitled Manager because it ran a macro to display the current employee's manager.)

Figure 10.6   **Opening the Dept Managers Form window by running the My Managers macro**

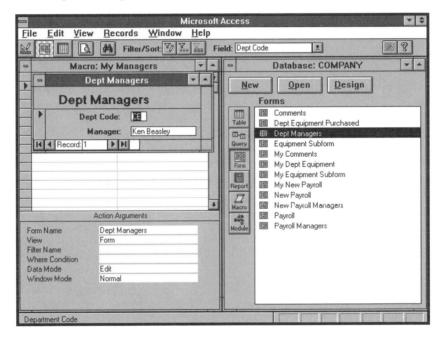

Another alternative, however, is to drag the macro's object name from the Database window to the location on the form design where you want to place the command button control. When you do, Access automatically creates a command button control, binds that control to the macro for you, and displays the name of the macro on the control's face. For macros with long names, Access sometimes displays only part of the macro's name; if this creates a problem, you can enlarge the control or select and edit the control's text.

As you can see, dragging between open windows provides a convenient way to link database objects together.

ADDING A COMMAND BUTTON CONTROL TO A FORM

Let's use the dragging method described earlier to add to a form a command button that will run the My Managers macro:

1. From the Database window, open the New Payroll Managers Form window in Design view. This form is similar to the My New Payroll form you created in Chapter 9.

2. Tile the Form and Database windows (choose **Window, Tile**).

3. In the Form window, scroll to the right until the space below the Monthly Parking Rate controls is visible.

4. In the Database window, display the list of macro object names, and then drag the **My Managers macro object name** from the Database window to the space on the form below the Monthly Parking Rate controls. Access creates a command button control entitled My (see Figure 10.7).

Figure 10.7   **Adding a command button control to the New Payroll Managers form**

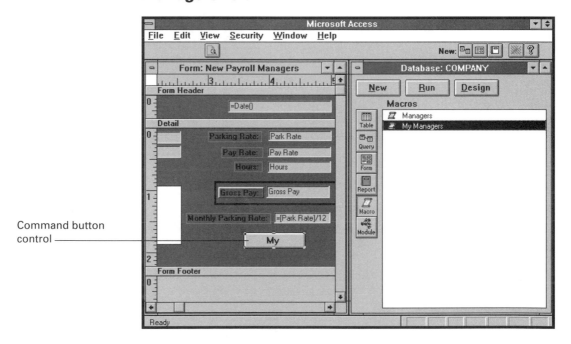

5. Click once on the new control to display the entire macro name, My Managers, and then delete **My** to change the control's text to Managers.

6. Press **Enter** to select the command button control; then open the control's property sheet and observe the control's properties. Access has automatically set the On Push property to My Managers.

7. Close the property sheet, and then save the form as **My Payroll Managers**.

TESTING THE COMMAND BUTTON

Now let's test your new command button and see how it works:

1. Choose **Window, Cascade** to layer the Form window over the Database window (see Figure 10.8).

Figure 10.8   **Cascaded windows**

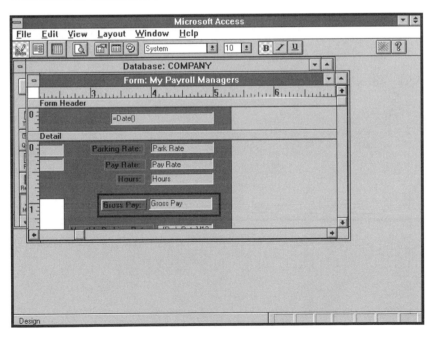

2. Switch the Form window to Form view, and then observe the form. The form displays the record for Gary Abel (Record 1), who works in the Electrical Engineering department.

3. Click on the **Managers command button**. The My Managers macro opens the Dept Managers Form window (see Figure 10.9).

Figure 10.9   **Opening the Dept Managers Form window with the Managers command button**

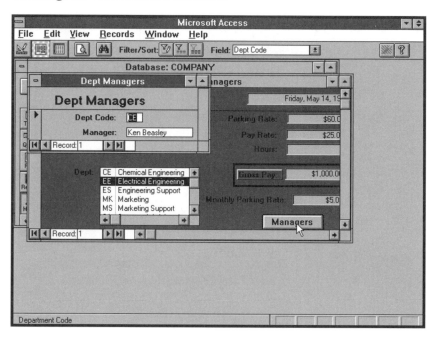

4. Observe the Dept Managers form. The Dept Code control on the Dept Managers form (CE) does not match the Dept control on the My Payroll Managers form (EE).

5. In the Dept Managers Form window, click on the **Next Record navigation button**. The Dept Managers form now displays the correct manager.

6. In the My Payroll Managers Form window, click on the **Next Record navigation button** to display the record for Murray Abel (Record 2), who works in the Chemical Engineering department.

7. Click on the **Managers command button**, and then observe the Dept Managers form. The form does not automatically move to the record for the Chemical Engineering department manager.

8. Close the Department Managers Form window.

SYNCHRONIZING FORMS

As you can see from the last task, using a macro from one Form window to open a second Form window does not guarantee that the second Form window will display the record or records relevant to the record in the first Form window.

When you used the Main/Subform FormWizard to create a main form and subform in Chapter 9, the FormWizard automatically *synchronized* the two forms so that the records in the subform were always relevant to the record in the main form. To accomplish the same thing using a macro and two Form windows, you need to use the OpenForm action's Where Condition argument in the macro's design.

 ### SETTING THE WHERE CONDITION ARGUMENT

To synchronize two Form windows using the OpenForm action's Where Condition argument, you write an expression in the Where Condition argument box that equates a control on one form with a control on a second form (much as you would use two fields to create a relationship between two tables). This argument then behaves like a filter on the Form window that the action opens; the second Form window will display only those records that are relevant to the current record in the first Form window.

For example, suppose you want the My Managers macro, run from the My Payroll Managers Form window, to open the Dept Managers Form window and display the department manager for the employee currently displayed in the My Payroll Managers Form window. To do so, you would set a Where Condition expression in the macro's design to equate the My Payroll Managers form's Dept Code control with the Dept Managers form's Dept control.

A Where Condition expression has two parts separated by an equal sign (=). On the right side of the equal sign, you specify the linking control that is on the form that controls the synchronization—that is, the form from which you run the macro. Using the previous example, that would be the Dept control on the My Payroll Managers form because the My Payroll Managers form contains the macro's command button. On the left side of the equal sign, you specify the linking control on the form that the macro's OpenForm action opens. In this example, that would be the Dept Code control on the Dept Managers form. In the simplest of terms, then, your Where Condition expression would be

```
[Dept Code]=[Dept]
```

Because the macro's OpenForm action opens the Dept Managers form, Access assumes that the left side of this expression refers to the Dept Code control on that form. From this expression, however, Access cannot determine which form contains the Dept control. Therefore, you need to be more specific about the Dept control by using the following syntax

```
Forms![formname]![controlname]
```

Your Where Condition argument would therefore be

```
[Dept Code]=Forms![My Payroll Managers]![Dept]
```

Let's use this expression in the My Managers macro to synchronize the two forms:

1. Activate the Database window, and then open the My Managers Macro window in Design view.

2. In the OpenForm action's Where Condition argument box, type **[Dept Code]=Forms![My Payroll Managers]![Dept]** to link the Dept Code control on the Dept Managers form to the Dept control on the My Payroll Managers form (see Figure 10.10).

3. Save the revised macro, and then close the Macro window.

4. Activate the My Payroll Managers Form window, and then move to the record for Gary Abel (Record 1), who works in the Electrical Engineering department.

5. Click on the **Managers command button**. The Dept Managers form opens and automatically displays the record for the Electrical Engineering department manager (see Figure 10.11).

6. In the My Payroll Managers Form window, move to the record for Murray Abel (Record 2), who works in the Chemical Engineering department.

Figure 10.10 **Entering a Where Condition expression to synchronize two forms**

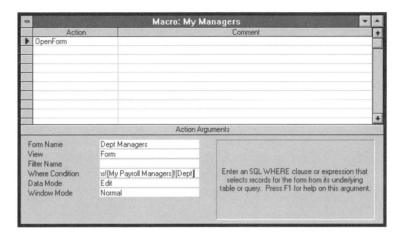

Figure 10.11 **Synchronized forms**

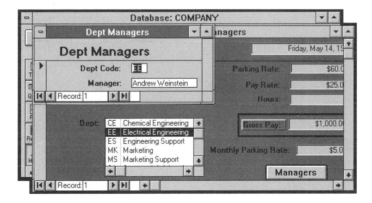

7. Click on the **Managers command button**. The Dept Managers form now displays the record for the Chemical Engineering department manager.

PRACTICE YOUR SKILLS

1. Navigate through several records in the My Payroll Managers Form window, using the Managers command button on each record to test your macro.

2. In the My Payroll Managers Form window, return to Gary Abel's record (Record 1), and then display the manager for Gary Abel's department. Your screen should once again match Figure 10.11.

CONTROLLING THE FORM WINDOW PLACEMENT

When you use a macro's OpenForm action to open one Form window from another, Access by default places the new Form window over the upper-left corner of the existing Form window. This can be inconvenient if the new window blocks important controls on the existing window; each time you run the macro, you may need to move the new window manually to uncover those controls in the existing window.

When you ran the Managers macro earlier in this chapter, the macro automatically placed the Dept Managers Form window in the lower-right corner of the screen so that the window did not block controls in the Payroll Managers Form window. It accomplished this through the MoveSize action, which enables a macro to control both the placement and size of any window it opens.

The MoveSize action has four arguments:

- The Right argument controls the horizontal position of the new window measured from the existing window's left edge.

- The Down argument controls the vertical position of the new window measured from the existing window's top edge.

- The Width argument controls the new window's width.

- The Height argument control's the new window's height.

If you leave any of these arguments blank, Access uses defaults to determine the new window's position and size. Because the Dept Managers Form window is already a good size, you can leave the Width and Height arguments blank. However, set the Right and Down arguments so that the Dept Managers Form window no longer blocks the My Payroll Managers Form window:

1. Observe the Dept Managers Form window. It blocks Gary Abel's name and ID code controls.

2. Switch to the Database window, and then open the My Managers Macro window in Design view.

3. In the second Action cell, select **MoveSize,** and then observe the action's argument boxes. The MoveSize action enables you to specify the position and size of the Form window that the OpenForm action opens.

4. In the Right argument box, type **3.25** to specify that the macro position the Dept Managers Form window 3 ¼ inches to the right of the My Payroll Managers Form window's left border.

5. In the Down argument box, type **2.75** to specify that the macro position the Dept Managers Form window 2 ¾ inches down from the My Payroll Managers Form window's top border (see Figure 10.12).

Figure 10.12   Setting arguments for the MoveSize action

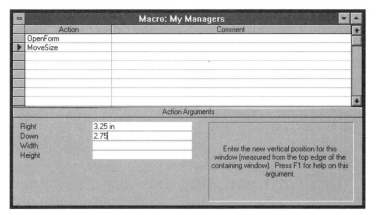

6. Save the revised macro, and then close the Macro window.

7. Activate the My Payroll Managers Form window, and then click on the form's **Managers command button**. The macro opens the Dept Managers Form window in the lower-right corner of the screen so that it does not block any control on the My Payroll Manager's form (see Figure 10.13).

8. Close both Form windows, and then close the Database window.

Figure 10.13   **Opening the Dept Managers Form window in a new position**

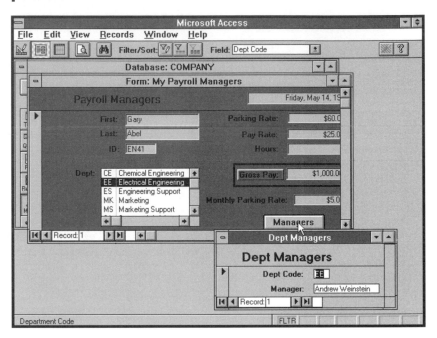

PRACTICE YOUR SKILLS

In Chapter 9, you learned how to use control properties and various control styles to enhance the look and performance of your forms, and how to use the Main/Subform FormWizard to create two forms that work together in a single Form window. In this chapter, you learned how to create and use a macro to open, synchronize, and control the position of one Form window from within another Form window. The following two activities give you an opportunity to apply some of these techniques.

After each activity step, a chapter reference (in parentheses) informs you where we introduced the relevant technique for that step.

In this activity, you will add to a form a list box that displays health-company options:

1. Open the practice.mdb database file, and then, if necessary, maximize the Database window (Chapter 1).

2. Open and examine the Health Plan form, and then switch the Form window to Design view (Chapter 5).

3. Open and use the toolbox and field list to place below the form's First controls a list box control bound to the Health field. Then close the toolbox and field list (Chapter 9).

4. Enlarge the Health list box control to about 2 inches wide (Chapter 5).

5. Change the Health label's text to **Health Company** (Chapter 9).

6. Switch to the Database window, and then open and examine the Health Codes and Names table (Chapter 7).

7. Close the Table window, and then return to the Health Plan Form window (Chapter 7).

8. Use the property sheet to change the Health list box control's Row Source property to **Health Codes and Names** (Chapter 9).

9. Specify two columns for the list box control, and then set the control's column widths to **.25** and **1.75** inches (Chapter 9).

10. Close the property sheet, and then save the form as **My Health Plan** (Chapter 9).

11. Switch to Form view, and then compare your form to the one pictured in Figure 10.14 (Chapter 5).

12. Close the Form window (Chapter 1).

In the next activity, you will create a macro and command button control to open one Form window from within another, synchronize the forms, and position the new Form window:

1. Open and examine both the Vendor Contacts and Equipment forms (Chapter 1).

2. Save the Equipment form as **My Equipment**, and then close both Form windows (Chapter 2).

3. Open a new Macro window, and then tile the Database and Macro windows (Chapter 10).

4. Drag the **Vendor Contacts form object name** from the Database window to the macro's first Action cell (Chapter 10).

Figure 10.14   **The completed My Health Plan form**

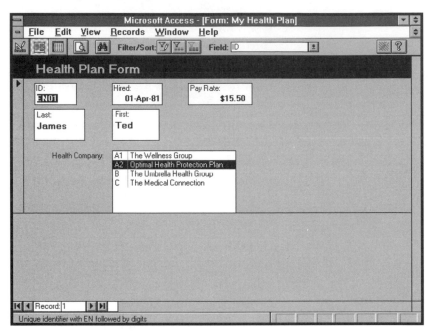

5. In the OpenForm action's Where Condition argument box, type an expression that equates the Code control on the Vendor Contacts form with the Vendor Code control on the My Equipment form (Chapter 10).

6. Save the macro as **My Vendor**, and then close the Macro window (Chapter 10).

7. Open the My Equipment Form window in Design view, and then tile the Form and Database windows (Chapter 10).

8. By dragging the **My Vendor macro object name** from the Database window, add a My Vendor command button control directly under the My Equipment form's Vendor Code controls (Chapter 10).

9. Change the My Vendor command button's text to **Vendor**.

10. Save your form design changes, and then cascade the Form and Database windows (Chapter 10).

11. Switch the Form window to Form view, and then test the command button (Chapter 10).

12. Close the Vendor Contacts Form window, and then open the My Vendor Macro window in Design view.

13. Add the **MoveSize** action to the macro's second Action cell, set the action's Right argument to **3** and its Down argument to **1.5**, save the macro, and then close the Macro window (Chapter 10).

14. Activate the My Equipment Form window, click on the **Vendor command button**, and then compare your screen to Figure 10.15 (Chapter 10).

15. Close both Form windows and the Database window (Chapter 1).

Figure 10.15   **The Form windows after completing and running the My Vendor macro**

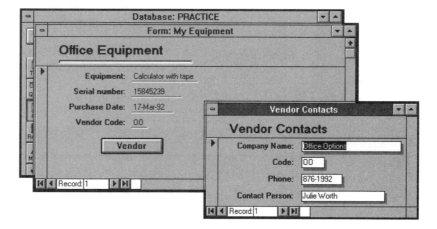

SUMMARY

In this chapter, you learned how to use a command button from within one Form window to run a macro that opens a second Form window. You also learned how to create your own macro by setting macro actions and arguments for those actions, and how to add a command button to a form that enables you to run the macro.

Here's a quick reference guide to the Access features introduced in this chapter:

Desired Result	How to Do It
View a macro's design	In the Database window, select the macro object name, and then click on **Design**
Open a new Macro window	In the Database window, display the list of macro object names, and then click on **New**
Design a macro	Set macro actions in the Macro window's Action cells, and then set arguments for each action as necessary
Add the OpenForm action to a macro	Use an Action cell's drop-down list to select the OpenForm action, and then set the action's Form Name argument to a form name; or, drag the form object name from the Database window to an Action cell in the Macro window
Tile open windows	Choose **Window, Tile**
Run a macro	From the Macro window, click on the **Run button** or choose **Macro, Run**; from a Form window with a command button, click on the command button; from the Database window, select the macro object name, and then click on **Run**
Add a command button control to a form	In the Form window's Design view, click on the toolbox's **Command button tool**, click on the form where you want to place the control, and then set the control's On Push property to a macro name; or, drag the macro object name from the Database window to the Form window
Change a command button control's text	In the Form window's Design view, select the command button control, select the existing text, and then type new text
Cascade open windows	Choose **Window, Cascade**

Desired Result	How to Do It
Synchronize two forms	In the design of the macro that opens one of the forms, set the OpenForm action's Where Condition argument to an expression that equates the two forms' common controls
Use a macro to control window placement	In the design of the macro that opens the window, add the **MoveSize** action, and then set the action's Right and Down arguments

In Chapter 11, you'll learn how to enhance a report by creating calculated controls, by changing the report's page layout, and by adding a line control to separate visually the groups within that report. You'll also learn how to use the Mailing Label ReportWizard to create a mailing-labels report based on a table, and then change that report's design in order to base that report on a query.

IF YOU'RE STOPPING HERE

If you need to break off here, please exit Access. If you want to proceed directly to the next chapter, please do so now.

CHAPTER 11: ENHANCED REPORT DESIGN

Adding Controls to a Report

Changing a Report's Page Layout

Creating Mailing-Label Reports

In Chapter 6, you learned how to use a ReportWizard to create reports, and how to modify a report's design by using the tool bar to change some control properties. In Chapter 9, you learned how to use the property sheet to modify control properties in a form, and how to use the toolbox to add controls to a form. In this chapter, you are going to combine these skills with new skills to modify and enhance an existing report's design, and to create two mailing-label reports.

When you're done working through this chapter, you will know how to:

- Add a line control to a report
- Add calculated controls to a report
- Change a report's page layout
- Use the Mailing Labels ReportWizard to create a mailing-label report
- Change a report's record source

ADDING CONTROLS TO A REPORT

Most of the techniques you learned in Chapter 9 for adding controls to forms also apply to adding controls to reports. However, a report's different sections are more varied and critical to a report design than a form's sections are to a form design. Therefore, it's important to understand clearly how a report design's different sections affect controls contained in those sections before you start adding controls to a report.

As you learned in Chapter 6, each report usually has at least five sections: a Report Header section, which contains controls that print at the beginning of the report; a Page Header section, which contains controls that print at the beginning of each page; a Detail section, which contains controls that print once for each record in the report's underlying table or query; a Page Footer section, which contains controls that print at the bottom of each page; and a Report Footer section, which contains controls that print at the end of the report. A grouped report's design will also include a group header and group footer section for each of the report's grouping levels.

As you can see, some sections, such as the Report Header and Report Footer sections, use controls only once, while other sections, such as the Detail section, use controls over and over. Therefore, *where* you place a new control on a report will determine how often that report will use the control. For a calculated control that uses field values in its calculations, the placement of a control is particularly critical, not only for how often the control prints, but for what field values the control uses. For example, a calculated control in a Detail section uses field values from one record at a time, a calculated control in a group header or footer section uses field values from every record in that group, and a calculated control in a Report Footer section uses field values from every record in that report.

In this chapter, you'll add both unbound and calculated controls to different report sections to see how placement affects a control's use and behavior.

ADDING A LINE CONTROL TO A REPORT

In Chapter 9, you learned how to add a rectangle control to a form. You also learned that a rectangle control is always an unbound control because it cannot display data but is instead used for its visual effect.

Access also offers a *line control* that operates like the rectangle control but displays straight lines instead of rectangles. Your line control can be vertical, horizontal, or slanted at any angle. Because it can be difficult to drag a perfectly horizontal or vertical line control, you can use the Shift key while adding a line control to force the control to be perfectly horizontal or vertical.

To add a horizontal line control to a form, you would follow these general steps:

- Open the Report window in Design view.
- Open the toolbox, if it isn't already open.
- Press and hold down the Shift key.
- In the toolbox, click on the Line tool.
- Position the mouse pointer on the report where you want the line control to begin, press and hold down the mouse button, and then drag horizontally to where you want the line to end.
- Release the mouse button, and then release the Shift key.

As you have learned, where you place the line control determines where and how often that control will print. In this task, you will add a line control at the bottom of a group footer section so that the line prints once at the end of each group.

If you do not have both the Access application and the COMPANY Database windows opened and maximized, please open and maximize them now.

Follow these steps to preview a report with two line controls that each print once for each page, and then add a third line control that prints once for each group:

1. From the Database window, preview and then observe the Pay Rates and Hours report. Lines display above and below the column headings on the top of each page (see Figure 11.1).

Figure 11.1   **Previewing the Pay Rates and Hours report**

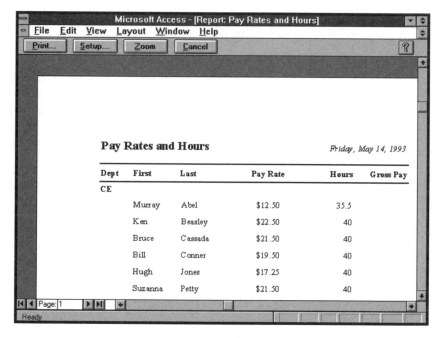

2. Close the Report window; then, from the Database window, reopen the Pay Rates and Hours Report window in Design view.

3. Observe the Page Header section. It contains two line controls above and below the column-heading controls.

4. If the toolbox is not open, open it (choose **View, Toolbox**), and then drag it to the right edge of the Report window.

5. Press and hold down the **Shift** key, and then click on the **Line tool** in the tool bar. Your mouse pointer should change to crosshairs with the Line-control icon attached.

6. While still holding down the Shift key, place the mouse pointer near the lower-left corner of the Dept Footer section, press and hold down the mouse button, drag horizontally to the 5-inch mark on the horizontal ruler (see Figure 11.2), release the mouse button, and then release the Shift key. Access adds a perfectly horizontal line control to the report.

Figure 11.2   **Adding a line control**

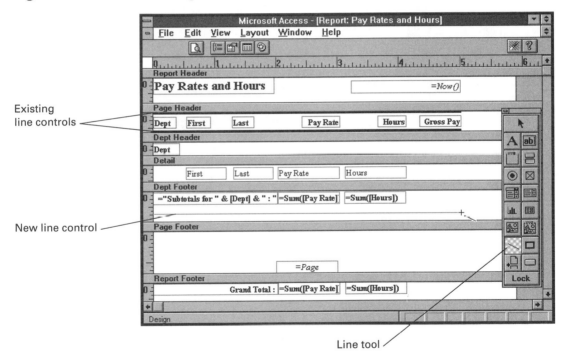

7. Preview and then observe the report. It now includes lines to separate each department group (see Figure 11.3).

8. Save the report as **My Pay Rates and Hours**.

Figure 11.3   **Lines separating departmental groups**

Microsoft Access - [Report: Pay Rates and Hours]				
File	Edit	View	Layout	Window	Help

Print... Setup... Zoom Cancel

Linda	Tobin	$20.00	40
	Sub totals for SA :	$139.50	280
SS				
Robert	Beaton	$12.50	35
Sam	Binga	$13.30	35.5
Wilma	Chase	$15.50	40
Darren	Cline	$7.50	20
Naja	Ellis	$13.50	40
Susan	Hartle	$17.50	25
Jason	Horn	$13.50	40
Edward	Pierce	$12.50	40
Randall	Vetch	$14.00	25
	Sub totals for SS :	$119.80	300.5

Page: 3

Ready

ADDING A CONTROL TO PERFORM A HORIZONTAL CALCULATION

In Chapter 4, you learned that you can use queries to perform both horizontal calculations (that is, calculations that use field values within a single record) and vertical calculations (that is, calculations that use field values from a group of records).

In Chapter 9, you created calculated controls that performed horizontal calculations on forms. In reports, however, you can use calculated controls to perform both horizontal and calculated controls. The placement of calculated controls determines whether the control can perform a horizontal or vertical calculation. To have a calculated control perform a horizontal calculation, place it in the Detail section.

For the most part, you can use calculated controls that perform horizontal calculations in the place of a control bound to a query's calculated field. As you learned in Chapter 9, calculated controls save you the trouble of opening the design of an underlying query, creating a calculated field there, and then creating a control bound to that calculated field.

To add to a report a calculated text box control that performs a horizontal calculation, you would follow these steps:

- In a Report window's Design view, add an unbound text box control and label to the Detail section and then, if desired, delete the unbound control's label.

- Select the unbound control; then click to place the insertion point in the control.

- Type a calculation expression that includes field names. Because this is a calculated control, remember to begin the expression with an equal sign. For example, an expression that multiplies the Pay Rate field by the Hours field is =[Pay Rate]*[Hours].

- If you like, change the control's properties and position so that it displays its values appropriately and understandably. For example, if the control is to display dollar amounts, set the control's Format property to Currency.

Because the current report's underlying Report Data query does not have a gross-pay field, create a calculated field that calculates each employee's gross pay:

1. Observe the previewed report's Gross Pay column. It does not display gross-pay values.

2. Cancel the preview, and then observe the Detail section. It does not include a gross-pay control.

3. Open and observe the field list. The report's underlying Report Data query does not contain a gross-pay field.

4. Close the field list.

5. To the right of the Detail section's Hours bound control, add an unbound text control and label. (Click on the toolbox's **Text box tool**, and then click in the Detail section.)

6. Select and delete your unbound control's label, and then select your unbound control.

7. Click to place the insertion point inside the selected control, and then type **=[pay rate]*[hours]** to convert your unbound control to a calculated control that will display each employee's gross pay.

8. Press **Enter** to select the control, and then open and observe the control's property sheet. The control's Control Source

property is set to the same expression you typed directly into the control.

9. Set the Format property to **Currency,** and then close the property sheet.

10. Align your control's right edge with the horizontal ruler's 5-inch mark, and then use the control's lower-left sizing handle to size the control to about ¾-inch wide so that it no longer overlaps the Hours bound control.

11. Preview and then observe your report. Your new calculated control displays the gross pay for each employee (see Figure 11.4).

12. Cancel the preview.

Figure 11.4   **The report displaying each employee's gross pay**

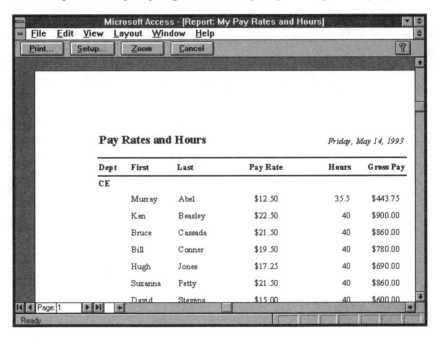

ADDING A CONTROL TO PERFORM A VERTICAL CALCULATION

To create a calculated control that performs a vertical calculation, place that control in the Report Header or Footer section, or in a group header or footer section. A calculated control in a Report Header or Footer section will use fields from every record in the report; a calculated control in a group header or footer section will use only the fields from records in that group. For example, the calculated control =Avg([Pay Rate]) averages Pay Rate fields. In a Report Header or Footer section, it would average the Pay Rate fields of every record in the report; the same control in a group header or footer section would average the Pay Rate fields for each group separately.

Because calculated controls that perform vertical calculations provide summary, or *aggregate,* information, they use aggregate functions such as the Sum function, which totals values, and the Avg function, which averages values. (For a review of aggregate functions, see Chapter 4.)

In Chapter 6, ReportWizards automatically created calculated controls with aggregate functions. In this chapter, you'll create these controls manually. To use an aggregate function in a calculated control, use the syntax =*function*(*argument*). For example, to use the Sum function to total the Hours field, use the expression =Sum([Hours]).

Besides using single fields, you can use expressions as a function's argument—for example, =Sum([Hours]*1.07) or =Avg([Hours]*[Pay Rate]).

Use the Sum function in a calculated control to total your entire report's gross-pay costs:

1. Observe the =Sum([Pay Rate]) and =Sum([Hours]) calculated controls in the Dept Footer section. They perform vertical calculations to total each department's Pay Rate and Hours fields.

2. Observe the =Sum([Pay Rate]) and =Sum([Hours]) calculated controls in the Report Footer section. They perform vertical calculations to total every Pay Rate and Hours field in the report.

3. Add an unbound text box and label directly to the right of the Report Footer section's =Sum([Hours]) calculated control.

4. Delete the new unbound control's label, and then select the unbound control.

5. Click in the unbound control, and then type **=sum([pay rate]* [hours])** to convert your unbound control into a calculated control that totals the overall gross-pay costs for every employee in the report.

6. Press **Enter** to select your calculated control. Then open the control's property sheet, set the control's Format property to **Currency**, and close the property sheet.

7. On the tool bar, click on the **Bold button** to boldface your calculated control's text.

8. Align your control's right edge with the horizontal ruler's 5-inch mark, and then use the control's lower-left sizing handle to size the control to about ¾-inch wide so that it no longer overlaps the =Sum([Hours]) calculated control.

9. Preview your report and then scroll to and observe the end of the report. Your newest calculated control has calculated the report's gross-pay total (see Figure 11.5).

10. Cancel the preview.

Figure 11.5   **The end of the report displaying a gross-pay total**

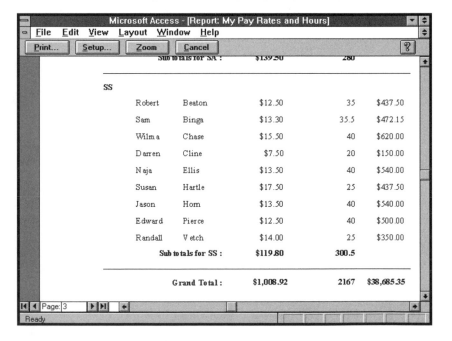

PRACTICE YOUR SKILLS

1. Directly to the right of the Dept Footer section's =Sum([Hours]) calculated control, add an unbound text box control and label.

2. Close the toolbox, and then delete the unbound control's label.

3. Convert the new unbound control into a control that calculates each department's gross-pay total.

4. Select the control, use the property sheet to set the control's Format property to **Currency,** and then close the property sheet.

5. Boldface the control's text.

6. Align the control's right edge with the horizontal ruler's 5-inch mark, and then size the control so that it no longer overlaps the =Sum([Hours]) calculated control.

7. Preview and scroll through the report to observe each department's gross-pay subtotals.

8. Return to the top of the report, and then compare your screen to Figure 11.6.

9. Save the report.

CHANGING A REPORT'S PAGE LAYOUT

You can control the page layout of a report (or any object that you can preview, for that matter) through the Print Setup dialog box. A report's *page layout* affects the position of the report's data on paper. Page layout settings include margins, page orientation, and paper size.

To open the Print Setup dialog box from a previewed report's window, click on the Setup button or choose File, Print Setup. To open the Print Setup dialog box from a Report window in Design view, choose File, Print Setup. Once you have opened the Print Setup dialog box, you can view additional page-layout settings by clicking on the dialog box's More button to expand the dialog box.

If you use the Print Setup dialog box from a previewed report's window, you will see the effect of those changes when you click on OK to close the dialog box.

Figure 11.6   **The report displaying gross-pay subtotals**

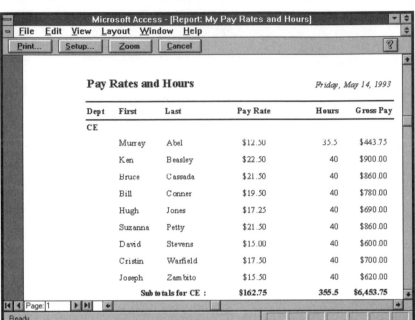

Use the Print Setup dialog box to improve your report's page layout:

1. From the previewed report's window, click on **Zoom**, and then observe the report's page layout. Most of the report is on the left side of the page.

2. Click on **Setup** (or choose **File, Print Setup**) to open the Print Setup dialog box, and then observe the dialog box. By default, Access sets all report margins to 1 inch.

3. Change the value in the Margins Left text box to **1.75** to increase the report's left margin (see Figure 11.7), and then click on **OK**. (Remember from Chapter 1 that because the current printer is the Windows default printer, your Print Setup dialog box may differ slightly from the one shown in Figure 11.7.)

4. Observe the previewed report. The report now is more centered on the page (see Figure 11.8).

5. Save the report, and then close the Report window.

Figure 11.7   **Changing the report's left margin**

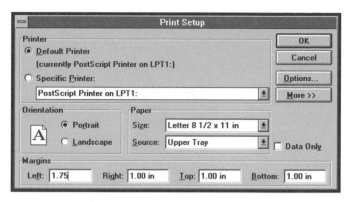

Figure 11.8   **The previewed report after changing its page layout**

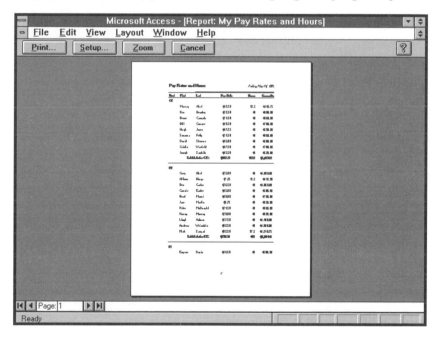

CREATING MAILING-LABEL REPORTS

You can use the Mailing Labels ReportWizard to create reports that are designed for printing mailing labels. Like other ReportWizards, the Mailing Labels ReportWizard asks you a series of questions, and then creates a report for you.

In Chapter 7, you learned how to use the tool bar's New Query button to create a new query based on the active or currently selected table or query. For example, to create a new query based on the Suppliers table, you could create a query based on that table simply by clicking on the New Query button from the Suppliers Table window. To create new reports, you can instead use the third button from the right on the tool bar, the New Report button, which displays the same icon as the Database window's Report object button.

(The New Form button, which is not used in this book, helps create new forms much as the New Query and New Report buttons help create new queries and reports. It is the fourth button from the left on the tool bar, and displays the same icon as the Database window's Form object button.)

To start the Mailing Labels ReportWizard using the New Report button, you would follow these steps:

- Open the window for the table or query upon which you wish to base your report; or, in the Database window, select the desired table or query object name.

- Click on the New Report button. Access opens the New Report dialog box and automatically selects the active or currently selected table or query as the report's data source.

- Click on ReportWizards.

- In the Microsoft Access dialog box, select Mailing Label, and then click on OK.

 DESIGNING MAILING LABELS

Once started, the Mailing Labels ReportWizard asks you these three questions:

- How do you want each mailing label to appear?

- How do you want your mailing labels sorted?

- What size mailing labels are you using?

So you can determine how each mailing label will appear, the Mailing Labels ReportWizard provides a dialog box that asks you to build a sample label. To build the label, you use a combination of *punctuation buttons* and available field names. To add a field name to the sample label, select the field name in the Available Fields list box and then click on >, or double-click on the field name. To add to a label a punctuation mark such as a line break, space, or comma, click on the appropriate punctuation button.

Once you complete the label's design and move to the next dialog box, select a sort order by moving the appropriate field or fields from the Available Fields list box to the Sort Order list box.

Finally, so you can specify the size of the mailing labels you will use to print your report, the Mailing Labels ReportWizard provides an extensive list of label sizes according to their Avery product numbers. If you are not using Avery brand labels, check your labels for an Avery equivalency number or use the measurements that the ReportWizard lists alongside each Avery product number.

Use the New Report button and Mailing Labels ReportWizard to create a mailing-label report based on the Suppliers table:

1. From the Database window, open and then observe the Suppliers table. It contains seven records with all of the fields necessary for mailing labels: Company Name, Address, City, St, and Zip.

2. From the Table window, click on the **New Report button** to start creating a new report.

3. Observe the New Report dialog box. Because you used the New Report button from the Suppliers Table window, Access automatically selected Suppliers as the report's data source (see Figure 11.9).

4. Click on **ReportWizards**.

5. In the Microsoft Access dialog box, select **Mailing Label**, and then click on **OK** to start the Mailing Labels ReportWizard.

6. Observe the Microsoft Access ReportWizard dialog box. In the center is an Available Fields list box. Below that is a set of punctuation buttons. To the right is a Label Appearance list box for building your sample label.

7. Double-click on **Company Name** in the Available Fields list box to add Company Name to the Label Appearance list box.

Figure 11.9   **Creating a new report with the New Report button**

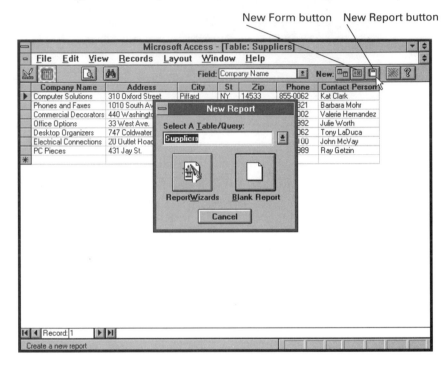

8. Click on the **Enter punctuation button** to add a new line to the Label Appearance list box (see Figure 11.10).

9. Add **Address** to the Label Appearance list box, click on the **Enter punctuation button** to add a third line to the Label Appearance list box, and then add **City** to the Label Appearance list box.

10. Click on the **Comma punctuation button**, and then click on the **Space punctuation button** to add a comma and space after City in the Label Appearance list box.

11. Add **St** to the Label Appearance list box, click twice on the **Space punctuation button**, and then add **Zip** to the Label Appearance list box to complete the sample label appearance (see Figure 11.11).

12. Click on **Next** to advance to the next Microsoft Access ReportWizard dialog box.

Figure 11.10 **Adding a new line to the Label Appearance list box**

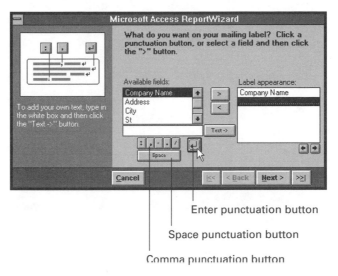

Enter punctuation button

Space punctuation button

Comma punctuation button

Figure 11.11 **The completed sample label appearance**

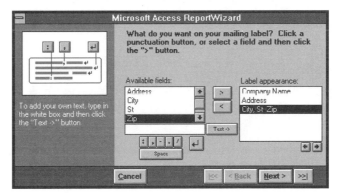

13. Move **Zip** from the Available Fields list box to the Sort Order list box to specify that your labels be sorted by zip code, and then click on **Next** to advance to the next Microsoft Access ReportWizard dialog box.

14. Observe the dialog box's list box. It lists a variety of label sizes according to their Avery product number, and displays the label dimensions and number of columns for each size.

15. Scroll down in the list box, select Avery Number **5160** (see Figure 11.12), and then click on **Next** to advance to the next Microsoft Access ReportWizard dialog box.

Figure 11.12 **Selecting a label size**

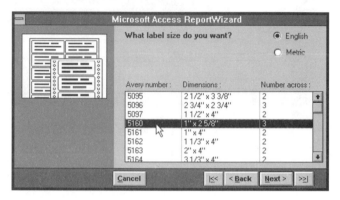

16. Click on **Print Preview** to complete and then preview your mailing-label report.

EXAMINING A MAILING-LABEL REPORT AND ITS DESIGN

No matter how many columns of labels there are in your mailing-label report, the Mailing Labels ReportWizard uses a single set of controls. To specify that the report should use the single set of controls for more than one column of labels, the Mailing Labels ReportWizard sets the value in the Print Setup dialog box's Items Across text box to a number greater than 1. For example, to specify three columns of labels, the ReportWizard sets the Items Across text box to 3.

To view the Items Across text box, open the Print Setup dialog box, and then click on More.

Take a look at the mailing-label report you just created, and then observe its design and settings in the Print Setup dialog box:

1. If necessary, maximize the Report window, and then click on **Zoom** to view the report's full page.

2. Observe your report. It contains three columns of labels. Because the Suppliers table contains only seven records, the report contains only seven labels (see Figure 11.13).

Figure 11.13  **Previewing the mailing-label report**

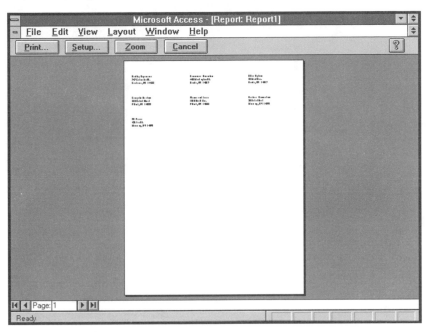

3. Click on **Zoom** again to return to a close-up view, and then observe the visible labels. They are sorted by zip code.

4. Click on **Cancel** to switch to Design view, and then observe the report's design. The report's Detail section contains controls for a single label.

5. Choose **File, Print Setup** to open the Print Setup dialog box, click on **More** to expand the dialog box, and then observe the Items Across text box. It is set to 3, instructing your report to create three columns of labels from a single set of controls (see Figure 11.14).

6. Click on **Cancel** to close the dialog box, and then save your report as **My Supplier Labels**.

Figure 11.14   **Examining the Items Across text box**

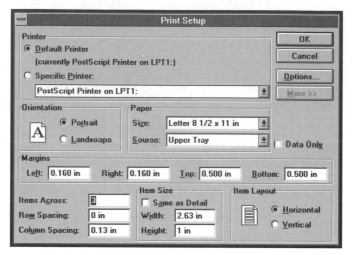

 CHANGING A REPORT'S RECORD SOURCE

If you need to generate mailing labels from more than one table or query, you could use the Mailing Labels ReportWizard to create from scratch a new mailing-label report for each table or query. However, if your mailing-label designs are similar, you may find it easier to create and save a single mailing-label report, change that existing report's design so that it uses data from a different table or query, and then save the new report design with a different name.

To change a report's design so that it uses data from a different table or query, use the property sheet to change the report's Record Source property.

Because field names often vary among tables and queries, you may also need to change some of the control names in the report design and/or some of the field names in the new table or query design to ensure that the Record Source property change will succeed. For example, if you create a mailing-label report based on a query with a field named Add for address information, and then switch the report's Record Source property to a query that uses a field named Address instead, you will need either to change the name of the Add control in the report or the name of the Address field in the query.

Because query designs are more flexible than table designs, it's better to change a report's record source to a query rather than to a table. In a query, it's easier to rename and create fields as necessary for your mailing-label report.

Change your new mailing-label report's Record Source property from the Suppliers table to a query, and then change the design of the query and of the report to make the property change a success:

1. Use the Window menu to switch to the Database window.

2. From the Database window, run the Home Addresses query, and then observe the query's dynaset. Most of its fields have the same names as the fields you used from the Suppliers table for your mailing-labels report (refer back to Figure 11.9). However, this dynaset has separate First and Last fields; your mailing-labels report uses a single Company Name field.

3. Switch to Design view, and then select and delete the QBE grid's **First column**.

4. In the Last Field cell, delete **Last**, and then type **Employee Name:[first]&" "&[last]** to create an Employee Name field that concatenates the First and Last fields.

5. Run the query, and then observe the dynaset. It now contains a single Employee Name field for employee names (see Figure 11.15).

6. Save the query as **My Home Addresses**, close the Query window, and then switch back to the Report window.

7. Open and observe the report's property sheet. The Record Source property is set to the Suppliers table.

8. Change the Record Source property to **My Home Addresses**, and then close the property sheet.

9. Observe the =[Company Name] control. It does not match the Home Addresses query's Employee Name field.

10. In the =[Company Name] control, replace Company with **Employee**. The control should now read =[Employee Name] (see Figure 11.16).

11. Preview and then observe your mailing-label report. The labels now contain data from the My Home Addresses query (see Figure 11.17).

12. Save your report as **My Home Address Labels**, and then exit Access.

Figure 11.15 The modified query's dynaset

Employee Name	Address	City	St	Zip
Ted James	34 Fields Street	Walworth	NY	14568
Hanna Harper	82 East Avenue	Adams Basin	NY	14410
Penny Packer	450 N. Madison St.	Holley	NY	14470
Julia Binder	10 Cory Drive	Hulberton	NY	14473
Maria Sanders	12 East Avenue	Leicester	NY	14481
Connie Easter	21 Stonecreek Rd.	Shortsville	NY	14548
Jane Martin	50 Smart Drive	Knowlesville	NY	14479
Allison Binga	50 Dallas Street	South Byron	NY	14557
Bill Conner	32 Ash Lane	Perkinsville	NY	14529
Dominick Osowski	23 Lakeside Ave.	Pultneyville	NY	14538
Sam Binga	50 Dallas Street	South Byron	NY	14557
Murray Abel	127 Ford Avenue	Lakeville	NY	14480
Robert Abot	99 Stonecreek Rd.	Gorham	NY	14461
Joseph Zambito	81 Pleasing Lane	Rose	NY	14542
Peter McDonald	8165 Main Street	Oaks Corners	NY	14518
Wilma Chase	52 Pempleton Dr.	Wyoming	NY	14591
Arlene DeMarco	34 Sable Ave.	Gorham	NY	14461
Frank Desoto	P.O. Box 7234	Wayland	NY	14572
Albert Henley	12 Divine Drive	Holley	NY	14470
Dennis Kyler	273 Fireside Dr.	Dresden	NY	14441
Nick Zangari	34 Park Street	Retsof	NY	14539
Hugh Jones	466 Fairhaven St.	Leicester	NY	14481
Randall Vetch	45 Central Blvd.	Hall	NY	14463
Jason Horn	453 Lakeshore Dr.	Pultneyville	NY	14538
Abraham Castile	67 Fargo Road	Ionia	NY	14475
Judy Wilson	532 Union Street	Waterport	NY	14571

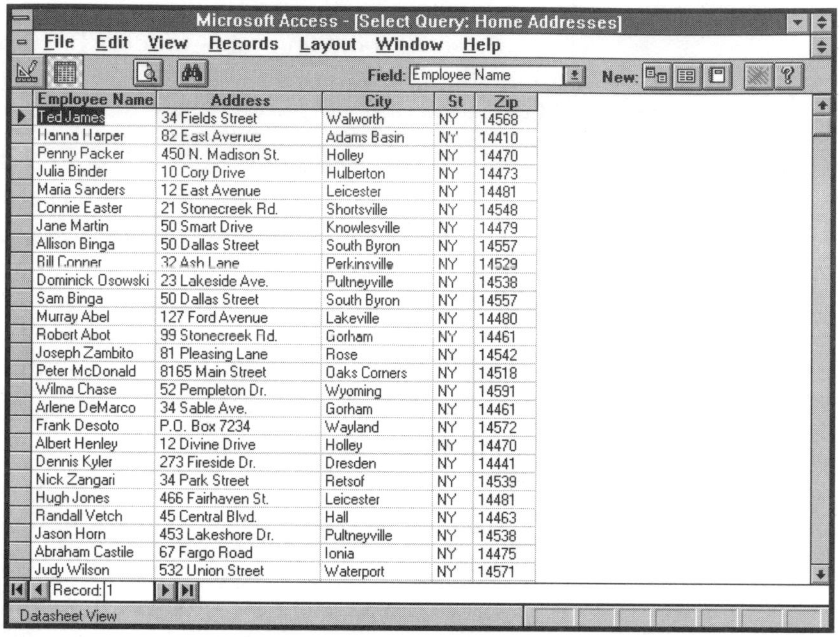

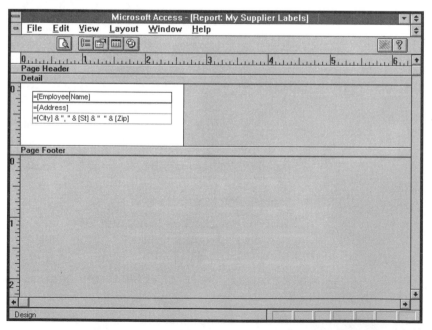

Figure 11.16 Changing a control name

Figure 11.17   **Previewing the modified report**

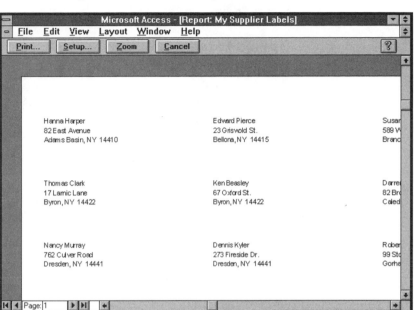

SUMMARY

In this chapter, you learned how to enhance reports by adding line controls and calculated controls, and by changing the report's page layout. You also learned how to use the Mailing Labels ReportWizard to create a mailing-label report, and how to change that report's record source.

Congratulations! Having finished this chapter, you have completed your foundation of Access skills. You are now prepared to take all that you've learned and apply it to your own databases. Remember, in order to keep and master the skills that you've acquired, you must now supply the most important ingredient: *practice*. Good luck!

Here's a quick reference guide to the Access features introduced in this chapter:

Desired Result	How to Do It
Add a horizontal line control to a report	In the report's design, press and hold down the **Shift** key, click on the toolbox's **Line tool**, position the mouse pointer where you want one end of the control, press and hold down the mouse button, drag horizontally to the opposite end of the line control, release the mouse button, and then release the Shift key
Cause a calculated control to perform a horizontal calculation	Place the control in a report's Detail section
Cause a calculated control to perform a vertical calculation	Place the control in a report's Report Header, Report Footer, group header, or group footer section
Create a calculated control that uses an aggregate function	In an unbound text box control, type an expression using the =*function*(*argument*) syntax
Open a report's Print Setup dialog box	From the previewed report, click on the **Setup** button, or choose **File, Print Setup**; from a Report window in Design view, choose **File, Print Setup**
Change a report's page layout	Change settings in the report's Print Setup dialog box
Use the New Report button to start the Mailing Labels ReportWizard	Open the table or query upon which you wish to base the report, or in the Database window select the desired table or query object name, click on the **New Report button**, click on **ReportWizards**, select **Mailing Label**, and then click on **OK**
Design a mailing label	In the Mailing Labels ReportWizard's appropriate dialog box, double-click on field names and click on punctuation buttons

Desired Result	How to Do It
Change a report's record source	Change the report's Record Source property and then, if necessary, change control names in the report and/or the field names in the report's new table or query

Following this chapter are three appendices: Appendix A, "Installation," walks you through Access 1.0 installation. Appendix B, "Tool Bar and Shortcut Key Reference," labels the various tool bar buttons and drop-down list boxes, and lists many keyboard shortcuts available in Access and Windows. Appendix C, "Creating a Database," discusses creating your own database from scratch, and importing existing data into that database.

APPENDIX A: INSTALLATION

Preparing Your
Computer for
Access
Installation

Installing
Access on
Your Computer

This appendix contains instructions for installing Access on your computer.

Because Access is such a customizable program, you can change its screen setup and overall appearance by simply running and using Access. For this reason, we at PC Learning Labs have written this book on the assumption that you have just installed Access and have not yet run the program. If you *have* already installed and used Access, you may want to delete all of the Access files from your computer and then reinstall Access to guarantee that your version of Access will run as described in this book. If you use Access on a network or other shared computer system, check first with your network system administrator. In any case, be sure to back up important files before deleting them!

PREPARING YOUR COMPUTER FOR ACCESS INSTALLATION

There are two requirements that must be met before you begin to install Access. First, DOS version 3.1 or higher and Windows version 3.0 or higher must be installed on your computer. If they are not, please install them now. (For help, see your DOS and Windows documentation.) Second, there must be enough free space on your hard disk to hold the Access files.

Perform the following steps to meet this second requirement:

1. You need to have your computer on and running in DOS. If Windows is running, choose **File, Exit** (or **File, Exit Windows**) from the Program Manager window to exit to DOS.

2. Type **c:** (or, if you intend to install Access on another hard drive, type the letter of this drive followed by a colon), and then press **Enter** to make your hard drive the current drive.

3. Type **dir**, and then press **Enter**. DOS lists the files contained in the current directory and, at the very end of this list, reports the number of free hard-disk bytes.

4. Observe this last number. You need at least 13 megabytes (approximately 14,000,000 bytes) of free hard-disk space to install Access.

5. If the number of free hard-disk bytes is 14,000,000 or over, skip the rest of this activity. If the number is under 14,000,000, delete enough files from your hard disk to free the space required for the Access installation. Be sure to back up any files that you want to save before deleting them!

6. Type **dir**, and then press **Enter**. DOS should now report at least 14,000,000 free hard-disk bytes. If it does not, return to step 5.

INSTALLING ACCESS 1.0 ON YOUR COMPUTER

Now that you've met the two requirements above, you can begin the actual Access installation. If you are reinstalling Access from installation disks that have already been used, some of the following steps may work differently or be unnecessary:

1. Type **win**, and then press **Enter** to start Windows.

2. Insert the Access installation disk labeled "Disk 1 - Setup" in the appropriately sized disk drive.

3. If necessary, activate the **Program Manager window.** (If Program Manager is running as an icon, double-click on the icon to open it into a window. If Program Manager is running in a window, click on the title bar of the window to activate it.)

4. From the Program Manager, choose **File, Run...** to open a dialog box entitled Run. (Chapter 1 discusses dialog boxes.)

5. Type **a:setup** in the box if the Setup disk is in drive A or **b:setup** if the disk is in drive B, and then click on **OK** to begin the Access setup program.

6. After a moment, the setup program opens a User Information dialog box to ask for your name and your company's name. Type your name in the Name box, press **Tab** to move to the Company box, type your company's name, and then click on **Continue**.

7. The setup program opens a second User Information dialog box to ask you to confirm the information you just typed. If the information is correct, click on **Yes** and skip to the next step. If the information is incorrect, click on **No** to return to the first User Information dialog box. Then, correct the information, click on **Continue** again, and click on **Yes**.

8. After a moment, the setup program opens a Specify Directory dialog box to ask you to specify a directory and hard drive for installing the Access files. By default, the setup program suggests C:\ACCESS. To accept this default drive and directory, just click on **Continue**. If you need to install Access on a hard drive other than C or in a directory other than ACCESS, type

the appropriate hard-drive letter and directory and then click on **Continue**.

9. The setup program opens an Installation Options dialog box showing three installation options: 1. Complete installation, 2. Custom installation, and 3. Minimum installation. Click on the button to the left of **1. Complete installation**.

10. The setup program may open a Multiuser Installation dialog box to ask you whether you would like to join a *workgroup* to enable you to share Access database files with other computer users. To complete the activities in this book, you do not need to join a workgroup, so you can click on **No**. If you work on a computer network and *would* like to join an existing workgroup for your own purposes, consult your Access documentation and check with your network system administrator before clicking on Yes.

11. If you clicked on No, or if the Multiuser Installation dialog box never opened, the setup program begins copying files from the Setup disk to your hard drive. Follow the on-screen instructions to insert and copy files from subsequent installation disks as necessary. As it installs Access, the setup program displays information about each disk's progress, as well as general information about the Access program.

12. After the setup program is finished with the sixth installation disk, it opens a box to ask if you want to update your computer's AUTOEXEC.BAT file with SHARE.EXE, a DOS utility that expands your computer's and Access' capabilities. (AUTO-EXEC.BAT is a special file that determines activities for your computer to perform automatically whenever you start the computer.) For the purposes of this book, you can select any option and then click on **Continue**. If you are unsure of the correct option to choose, use the default option: **Modify AUTO-EXEC.BAT and save the original as AUTOEXEC.BAK**.

13. If you chose to modify AUTOEXEC.BAT, the setup program opens a Microsoft Access Setup dialog box to inform you that the AUTOEXEC.BAT file was successfully modified. Click on **OK** to close the dialog box.

14. The setup program may then open a Microsoft Access dialog box to inform you that the FILES setting in your computer's CONFIG.SYS file is less than 50. (CONFIG.SYS is a companion file to AUTOEXEC.BAT; it, too, determines activities for your

computer to perform automatically whenever you start the computer.) For the purposes of this book, you do not need to change the FILES setting. Click on **OK** to close the dialog box.

15. If you chose to modify the AUTOEXEC.BAT file in step 12, the setup program opens a Reboot dialog box to inform you that you need to reboot (restart) your computer before running Access in order for the changes you made to AUTOEXEC.BAT to take effect. For the purposes of this book, rebooting is unnecessary; instead, click on **Exit to Windows**. The setup program then returns you to Program Manager and displays a new window entitled Microsoft Access, which contains a number of Access icons.

Do not start Access at this point; you will learn how to start Access in Chapter 1.

APPENDIX B: TOOL BAR AND SHORTCUT KEY REFERENCE

The Access Tool Bar

Access Shortcut Keys

This appendix illustrates and labels the various buttons and boxes that display on the Access tool bar and lists a number of shortcut keys available in Access.

THE ACCESS TOOL BAR

As you work through this book, the buttons and boxes on the tool bar change according to the task at hand. Tables B.1 and B.2 individually label the buttons and boxes that display on the tool bar. Note that some of these buttons and boxes apply to tasks not covered in this book.

For detailed information on these tool bar buttons and boxes, search Access Help for "tool bars."

Table B.1   **Tool Bar Buttons**

Button	Name
	Align-Left button
	Align-Right button
	Apply Filter/Sort button
	Bold button
	Breakpoint button
	Center button
	Conditions button
	Datasheet View button
	Design View button
	Edit Filter/Sort button
	Field List button
	Find button
	Form View button
	General Alignment button
	Help button

Table B.1   **Tool Bar Buttons (Continued)**

Button	Name
	Italic button
	Macro Names button
	New Form button
	New Query button
	New Report button
	Next Procedure button
	Palette button
	Previous Procedure button
	Primary Key button
	Print Preview button
	Procedure Step button
	Properties button
	Reinitialize button
	Run button
	Show All Records button
	Single Step button
	Sorting and Grouping button
	Totals button
	Underline button
	Undo button

Table B.2 **Tool Bar Boxes**

Box	Name
Field: Last	Field box
Arial	Font box
8	Font-size box
Procedure: (declarations)	Procedure box

ACCESS SHORTCUT KEYS

In Access, virtually any action that can be performed with the mouse can also be performed with the keyboard using shortcut keys. Choose the method—mouse or keyboard—that works best for you.

For Access actions covered in this book, Tables B.3, B.4, and B.5 describe their corresponding shortcut keys. For information on shortcut keys not covered in this appendix, search Access Help for "keys."

Table B.3 **Navigation and Selection Shortcut Keys**

Shortcut Key	Action
F2	Switch the focus between the insertion point and a selection
F5	Move to and select the Specific Record Number box
F6	Move the focus between the upper and lower panes of multiple-pane windows
Home	If the focus is an insertion point, move to the beginning of a field or line; if an entire field is selected, move to the first field in the current record
Ctrl+Home	If the focus is an insertion point in a multiple-line field, move to the beginning of the field; if a record is selected, move to the first field in the first record

Table B.3   **Navigation and Selection Shortcut Keys (Continued)**

Shortcut Key	Action
End	If the focus is an insertion point, move to the end of the field or line; if an entire field is selected, move to the last field in the current record
Ctrl+End	If the focus is an insertion point in a multiple-line field, move to the end of the current field; if a record is selected, move to the last field in the last record
Up Arrow	If the focus is an insertion point in a multiple-line field, move to the previous line; if a record is selected, move to the current field in the previous record
Down Arrow	If the focus is an insertion point in a multiple-line field, move to the next line; if a record is selected, move to the current field in the next record
Left Arrow	If the focus is an insertion point, move one character to the left; if an entire field is selected, move to the previous field
Right Arrow	If the focus is an insertion point, move one character to the right; if an entire field is selected, move one field to the right
Tab	Move to the next field in a record
Shift+Tab	Move to the previous field in a record
Shift+Spacebar	Select or deselect the current record
Ctrl+Spacebar	Select or deselect the current column

Table B.4   **Editing and Data Entry Shortcut Keys**

Shortcut Key	Action
Backspace	Delete the selection or the character to the left of the insertion point
Delete	Delete the selection or the character to the right of the insertion point
Ctrl+X	Cut the selection (same as Edit, Cut)
Ctrl+C	Copy the selection (same as Edit, Copy)
Ctrl+V	Paste the copied or cut selection (same as Edit, Paste)
Ctrl+Z	Undo typing
Esc	Undo changes to the current field or record
Shift+F2	Open the Zoom box
Ctrl+" or Ctrl+'	Copy the value from the same field in the previous record
Ctrl+-	Delete the current record
Shift+Enter	Save the current record

Table B.5   **Miscellaneous Shortcut Keys**

Shortcut Key	Action
F1	Open context-sensitive Help
Ctrl+F4	Close the active window
Alt+F4	Exit Access or close a dialog box
Ctrl+F6	Move between open windows
F11 or Alt+F1	Activate the Database window

Table B.5   **Miscellaneous Shortcut Keys (Continued)**

Shortcut Key	Action
F12 or Alt+F2	Open the Save As dialog box
Shift+F12 or Alt+Shift+F2	Save the current object

APPENDIX C: CREATING A DATABASE

Creating a New
Database File

Importing Data

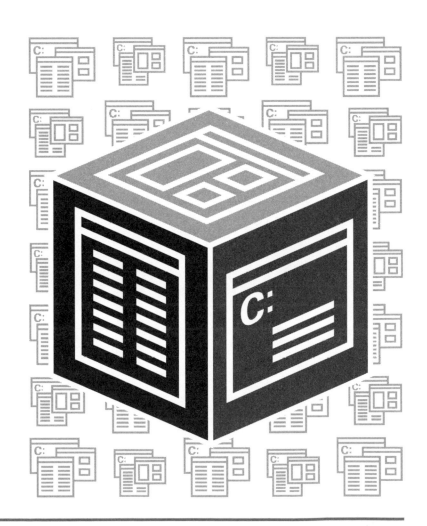

This appendix explains how to create a database file from scratch and describes ways to bring existing data into a database.

CREATING A NEW DATABASE FILE

Throughout this book, you have used Access database files that we supplied on the Data Disk. Now that you've nearly finished the book, you are ready to create your own database file.

To create a new Access database file:

- Choose File, New Database from the Access start-up window or any Database window. Access opens the New Database dialog box.

- In the File Name text box, type a name for your new database file. Database file names can be from one to eight characters long and cannot include spaces and many special characters, including periods, asterisks, and question marks. You do not need to end your database file name with .MDB; Access will add .MDB automatically.

- Use the Drives drop-down list box and the Directories list box to specify the appropriate location to store your new database file.

- Click on OK. After a moment, Access will display a new, empty Database window bearing the name you provided in the New Database dialog box.

Once you have created a new database file, you are ready to use any of the techniques you learned in this book to create new objects. Normally, you will create a number of tables, add data to those tables, and then build forms, queries, and reports based on that data.

IMPORTING DATA

If you have data stored in another Access database file or in a database file created by an application other than Access, you may be able to import that data into your new database file.

Access enables you to import data that is stored in the following formats:

- Microsoft Access
- Paradox
- dBASE III and IV
- Btrieve

- Microsoft SQL Server
- Text
- Microsoft Excel
- Lotus 1-2-3
- FoxPro

You usually can import any type of object from other Access databases. However, when you import from files created by applications other than Access, you usually can import only tables or table data.

Bear in mind that when you import Access objects such as queries, forms, and reports, you may also need to import the tables and/or queries upon which those objects are based. Otherwise, when you try to use your imported object, Access will report an error when the imported object cannot find the table or query upon which it is based.

Two ways to import data from one Access database to another are through the File, Import command and through the Edit, Copy, Edit, Cut, and Edit, Paste commands. See your Access documentation for other ways to move data into and out of Access databases.

IMPORTING THROUGH FILE, IMPORT

To import an object from one Access database to another using the File, Import command:

- Open the Database window for the database into which you want to import an object.
- Choose File, Import to open the Import dialog box.
- Select Microsoft Access, and then click on OK to open the Select Microsoft Access Database dialog box.
- Select the drive and directory where the database containing the object is stored, select the appropriate database file name, and then click on OK to open the Import Objects dialog box.
- Select the appropriate object type and object name.
- If you choose to import a table, you can also choose whether to import both the table design and the data stored in it, or just the table design itself.

- Click on Import. If the import is successful, Access opens a Microsoft Access dialog box to tell you that.

- Click on OK to close the Microsoft Access dialog box, and then click on Close to close the Import Objects dialog box. Your imported object's name will then display in the Database window when you select the appropriate object button.

If the name of the object you import matches the name of an existing object, Access may rename the imported object. For example, if you import a table named Employees into a database that already includes an Employees table, Access might name the imported table Employees1.

Using the File, Import command, you can also import tables from Paradox, dBASE III and IV, Btrieve, Microsoft SQL Server, and FoxPro, and you can create tables by importing data stored in text, Microsoft Excel, and Lotus 1-2-3 files.

Once you've used the File, Import command to import an object from one Access database to another, you may want to delete the table from its original database.

To delete an Access database object:

- Open the Database window for the database that contains the object you wish to delete.

- Select the name of the object you wish to delete.

- Press the Delete key or choose Edit, Delete. Access opens a Microsoft Access dialog box to ask you to confirm the deletion.

- Click on OK.

To remove an object from an Access database, you can also use the Edit, Cut command described below.

IMPORTING THROUGH EDIT COMMANDS

To import an object from one Access database to another using the Edit, Copy, Edit, Cut, and Edit, Paste commands:

- Open the Database window for the database that contains the object you wish to import.

- Select the appropriate object name.

- Choose Edit, Copy or Edit, Cut. The Edit, Copy command leaves the original object intact; the Edit, Cut command removes the object from the current database. (Note that unlike using the Edit, Delete command described earlier, when you use the Edit, Cut command, Access does not ask you for confirmation. Therefore, you should be very careful when using the Edit, Cut command.)

- Close the current Database window, and then open the Database window for the database into which you wish to import the object.

- Choose Edit, Paste. Access will open a dialog box to ask you for an object name. If you are pasting a table, the dialog box also enables you to choose to import just the table's design, to import the entire table, or to append the table's data to an existing table.

- Type an object name, choose a paste option if applicable, and then click on OK. Unless you choose to append data, your imported object's name will then display in the Database window when you select the appropriate object button.

INDEX

■ TO RECEIVE 5¼-INCH DISK(S)

The Ziff-Davis Press software contained on the $3^1/2$-inch disk included with this book is also available in $5^1/4$-inch format. If you would like to receive the software in the $5^1/4$-inch format, please return the $3^1/2$-inch disk with your name and address to:

Disk Exchange
Ziff-Davis Press
5903 Christie Avenue
Emeryville, CA 94608